HUME ON CAUSATION

'This is a sophisticated and sustained discussion of Hume on causal reasoning and the idea of necessary connection. . . . The various issues and authors are always handled with skill, and the main interpretations of Hume's meaning are treated intelligently and fairly.'
Stephen Buckle, Australian Catholic University

Hume is traditionally credited with inventing the 'regularity theory' of causation, according to which the causal relation between two events consists merely in the fact that events of the first kind are always followed by events of the second kind.

Hume is also traditionally credited with two other, hugely influential positions: the view that the world appears to us as a world of unconnected events, and inductive scepticism: the view that the 'problem of induction', the problem of providing a justification for inference from observed to unobserved regularities, is insoluble.

Hume on Causation is the first major work dedicated to Hume's views on causation in over fifteen years, and it argues that Hume does not subscribe to any of these three views. It places Hume's interest in causation within the context of his theory of the mind and his theory of causal reasoning, arguing that Hume's conception of causation derives from his conception of the nature of the inference from causes to effects.

Helen Beebee argues that Hume's interest in inductive reasoning is an interest in the psychological process involved in inferring effects from causes, and not in the epistemological 'problem of induction' as traditionally conceived. She also motivates and develops a projectivist interpretation of Hume's theory of causation, according to which our causal talk is an expression of our inferential habits, and argues that for Hume the projection of those habits affects not only how we conceive of the world, but also how we see it.

Helen Beebee is Professor of Philosophy at the University of Birmingham.

HUME ON CAUSATION

Helen Beebee

Routledge
Taylor & Francis Group

LONDON AND NEW YORK

First published 2006
by Routledge
2 Park Square, Milton Park, Abingdon, Oxon OX14 4RN

Simultaneously published in the USA and Canada
by Routledge
270 Madison Ave, New York, NY 10016

Routledge is an imprint of the Taylor & Francis Group, an informa business

© 2006 Helen Beebee

Typeset in Baskerville by
Taylor & Francis Books
Printed and bound in Great Britain by
TJ International Ltd, Padstow, Cornwall

British Library Cataloguing in Publication Data
A catalogue record for this book is available from the British Library

Library of Congress Cataloging-in-Publication Data
Beebee, Helen.
Hume on causation / by Helen Beebee.
p. cm.
Includes bibliographical references.
ISBN 0-415-24339-4 (hardback: alk. paper) 1. Hume, David, 1711-1776.
2. Causation. I. Title.
B1499.C38B44 2006
122.092——dc22
2005032017

ISBN10: 0–415–24339–4   ISBN13: 978–0–415–24339–1 (hbk)
ISBN10: 0–203–96660–0   ISBN13: 978–0–203–96660–0 (ebk)

CONTENTS

CONTENTS

ACKNOWLEDGEMENTS

I am very grateful to the Arts and Humanities Research Council, whose Research Leave Scheme funded a semester's sabbatical, and to what is now the School of Social Sciences at the University of Manchester, whose Research Support Fund did likewise.

I presented early versions of the material on causal experience and the projectivist interpretation in various places: the Australian National University, Trinity College Dublin, University College Dublin, the Metaphysics of Science Research Group meeting in Athens in 2003, Huw Price's Causal Republicanism conference in Sydney the same year, the University of Stirling, and probably some other places I now can't remember. Thanks to all the audiences for their useful questions and comments, and to the British Academy for funding the Metaphysics of Science Research Group workshops with an International Networks grant. Thanks also to various people whose conversations and email exchanges have helped me work through some central issues: to Peter Kail, Simon Blackburn and Don Garrett, and, again, doubtless many others I have now forgotten about.

I am hugely grateful to Steve Buckle for many discussions over email and in person, and for detailed comments on an earlier draft of the book, which led to large numbers of corrections and improvements; also for his boundless enthusiasm for Hume. Steve's detailed and helpful responses to torrents of often horribly naïve questions turned out to be at least partly responsible for the existence of this book, as opposed to the single chapter on Hume in the entirely different book I was originally going to write. I am also very grateful to Tony Bruce and Sonja van Leeuwen at Routledge for endless patience, flexibility and good humour; to my former colleagues at Manchester, whom I shall greatly miss, for their encouragement and support; and to Matthew Elton. And, finally, to Gavin Brown, who helped me in uncountably many ways to get the book written.

A NOTE ON REFERENCES

Throughout this book, references to Hume's major philosophical works – the *Treatise of Human Nature, An Enquiry Concerning Human Understanding* and *An Enquiry Concerning the Principles of Morals* – take the form of *T* or *E* followed by a page number. The page numbers correspond to the following editions:

T   *A Treatise of Human Nature* (1739–40), edited by L.A. Selby-Bigge, 2nd edition, revised and edited by P.H. Nidditch, Oxford: Oxford University Press (1978).

E   *Enquiries Concerning Human Understanding and the Principles of Morals* (1748/51), edited in one volume by L.A. Selby-Bigge, 3rd edition, revised and edited by P.H. Nidditch, Oxford: Oxford University Press (1975).

Page references *T* 645–*T* 662 refer to the *Abstract* of the *Treatise*, from the original 1740 edition. Page reference *E* 2 refers to the *Advertisement*, which first appeared in the posthumous edition of Hume's *Collected Essays* (including both *Enquiries*) published in 1777. Page references *E* 5–*E* 165 refer to the first *Enquiry*, and *E* 169–*E* 363 to the second *Enquiry*. The expression 'the *Enquiry*' always refers to the first *Enquiry*.

Some readers may be more familiar with the more recent Oxford University Press editions of the *Treatise* and the first *Enquiry* – *David Hume: A Treatise of Human Nature*, edited by David Fate Norton and Mary J. Norton (2000), and *David Hume: An Enquiry Concerning Human Understanding*, edited by Tom L. Beauchamp (1999). In order to make finding relevant passages of the texts slightly easier, Tables 1 and 2 show the page numbers for the beginning of the sections of the first book of the *Treatise* and of the first *Enquiry* in both the Selby-Bigge–Nidditch (SBN) editions and the Norton and Norton (N&N) and Beauchamp (B) editions.

Table 1 A Treatise of Human Nature: Book I (Of the Understanding)

Continued on next page

		SBN	*N&N*
Part IV	*Of the sceptical and other systems of philosophy*		
I	Of scepticism with regard to reason	180	121
II	Of scepticism with regard to the senses	187	125
III	Of the ancient philosophy	219	144
IV	Of the modern philosophy	225	148
V	Of the immateriality of the soul	232	152
VI	Of personal identity	251	164
VII	Conclusion of this book	263	171
	Abstract	645	403

Table 2 An Enquiry Concerning Human Understanding

		SBN	*B*
	Advertisement	2	83
§1	Of the different species of philosophy	5	87
§2	Of the origin of ideas	17	96
§3	Of the association of ideas	23	101
§4	Sceptical doubts concerning the operations of the understanding	25	108
§5	Sceptical solution of these doubts	40	119
§6	Of probability	56	131
§7	Of the idea of necessary connexion	60	134
§8	Of liberty and necessity	80	148
§9	Of the reason of animals	104	165
§10	Of miracles	109	169
§11	Of a particular providence and of a future state	132	187
§12	Of the academical or sceptical philosophy	149	199

1

INTRODUCTION

If (but not only if) you don't know much about Hume, the chances are that you will believe that Hume held the following views:

Thesis 1 All events seem entirely loose and separate.
Thesis 2 All events *are*, ultimately, entirely loose and separate.
Thesis 3 Causation is a matter of temporal priority, contiguity, and constant conjunction.
Thesis 4 Inference from the observed to the unobserved is completely unjustified.

You may also have some beliefs about the nature of Hume's basic arguments for the four theses, as follows. His argument for Thesis 1 has something to do with the fact that on first observing, say, the white billiard ball making contact with the black (event *a*) one cannot predict that the black will move (event *b*); and it also has something to do with the (allegedly) obvious phenomenological fact that, no matter how hard you look, all you will *really* see is *a* happening and then *b* happening: you don't see any third thing that somehow joins *a* and *b* together. Hume's argument for Thesis 2 is a broadly empiricist argument: since sensory experience delivers no 'impression' of necessary connection 'in the objects', we have no reason to believe in, or perhaps cannot so much as form an idea of, mind-independent necessary connections. Hence – given that causal claims ('the contact of the white caused the black to move') are often true, or at least we generally believe them to be true – we need a concept of causation that does not appeal to mysterious necessary connections. The theory of causation that Hume thinks will do the trick is given by Thesis 3: Hume is, to borrow an expression of David Armstrong's, a naïve regularity theorist about causation. And the argument for Thesis 4 is that any attempt to justify inductive inference – inference from the observed to the unobserved – is circular and hence begs the question against the inductive sceptic.

The view that Hume holds these four theses does, of course, have some basis in what Hume says. He says, for example: 'All events seem entirely loose and separate' (*E* 74), which sounds a lot like Thesis 1. He says: 'Necessity . . . is

1

nothing but an internal impression of the mind' (*T* 165), which seems to entail Thesis 2. He also says: 'We may define a CAUSE to be "An object precedent and contiguous to another, and where all the objects resembling the former are plac'd in like relations of precedency and contiguity to those objects, that resemble the latter"' (*T* 170; Thesis 3). And he says that it is 'impossible to satisfy ourselves by our reason, why we shou'd extend [past] experience beyond those particular instances, which have fallen under our observation' (*T* 91; Thesis 4). But there are considerations that tell against taking these and other similar snippets of the text to be neat summaries of Hume's overall view. It is debatable whether Hume subscribes to any of the four theses, let alone all of them; in fact, I shall argue in the course of this book that he does not subscribe to any of them.

1.1 Hume's targets

Edward Craig (1987) tells a compelling historical story according to which, at the time of Hume's writing, philosophy was in the grip of the doctrine that man is made in God's image: the 'Image of God' doctrine. Of course, man is lacking in God's perfection, since man is finite, fallible and of limited powers. Still, our minds and God's are the same *kinds* of thing, in the sense that the qualities of our minds that are self-evidently good – reason and virtue, for example – are imperfect versions of the qualities possessed by God.

The epistemological upshot of the Image of God doctrine – what Craig calls the 'Insight Ideal' – is the thesis that the human mind can in principle have access to true beliefs in a way that is analogous to the way in which God can; for that is part of what it is for man to be made in God's image. A philosopher in the grip of the Image of God doctrine will thus naturally want to give an account of how we know what we take ourselves to know that is consistent with that doctrine.

The obvious place to start is with *a priori* knowledge: with knowledge of mathematics and logic. It is in this area that man appears to come closest to resembling God, for it is here that our knowledge seems certain or infallible, and that is clearly something we have in common with God. But what about knowledge of the external world? Well, God is not merely a passive knower *about* the world. He is also its creator. And, being infinitely wise, he made it the way it is not on a whim, but with good – the best – reason. Given the Insight Ideal, we thus arrive naturally at the thought that the universe is so constructed that it is, in principle, intelligible. God would not have endowed us with cognitive powers that are unsuited to the job of gaining knowledge about the world; hence 'nothing would be more natural . . . than to hope and expect that the universe was in principle intellectually transparent, even though quantitative considerations put complete insight beyond human grasp' (Craig 1987: 38).

So we have, on the one hand, the thought that human understanding is at its most perfect when employing *a priori* reasoning; and, on the other, the thought that nature itself is so constructed as to make it an appropriate object of human understanding. Putting the two together leads naturally to some substantive metaphysical and epistemological claims about the nature of the world, and, in particular, about the nature of causation.

The metaphysical claim is that nature itself operates in a way that is analogous to *a priori* reasoning. The way nature operates is, of course, via causation: the processes we see unfolding around us are *causal* processes, with earlier stages linked to later ones by causal relations. The metaphysical upshot of the Image of God doctrine, as far as causation is concerned, is thus the view that causal relations are, as it were, the worldly correlates of *a priori* inference: causes necessitate their effects, or guarantee that those effects occur, in a way that is somehow analogous to, or perhaps even identical with, the way that premises of an argument necessitate or guarantee the truth of their conclusions.[1]

Central to this conception of causation is the thought that, just like the premises and conclusion of a valid argument, causes and effects are not logically distinct. It is largely thanks to Hume that most contemporary discussions of causation take the logical distinctness of causes and effects for granted, and then seek to uncover the nature of the relation that binds them together. For someone in the grip of the Image of God doctrine, however, this would have seemed an odd way to proceed. That one proposition entails another is determined solely by the contents of the two propositions: given what they assert, there is no further question concerning the nature of the entailment relation that binds them together. Similarly, by analogy, for causation: the effect must, in some sense, be 'contained in' the cause, so if only we could somehow penetrate into the essence of the cause, we would see that the effect could not fail to come about.

What about the epistemological upshot of the Image of God doctrine, as applied to causation? There are two broad philosophical directions in which the Insight Ideal had been taken by Hume's predecessors: one by the rationalist tradition and one by the scholastic tradition. Philosophers of the rationalist tradition – Descartes, for instance – held that causation operates according to principles that are knowable *a priori*. And by invoking those principles, *a priori* reasoning can in principle take us beyond the immediate evidence of our senses to deliver knowledge about aspects of the world that are not available to the senses (because, for example, they are in principle unobservable, or because they happen in the past or future).

One such principle is the principle that causes must contain at least as much 'reality' as their effects – a principle which Descartes claims to be 'manifest by the natural light', that is, by the light of reason (Descartes 1641: 28). For example, when presented with a hot potato, I can infer, via the *a priori* principle that there must be at least as much reality (in this case, heat) in the cause as in the effect, that the potato's heat must have been caused by something that was at least as hot as the potato is – something that is not itself present to my senses. Granted that the first belief, that there is a hot potato present, is certain, or to the extent that that belief is justified, the second will be certain or justified too, since

3

it is entailed by the first together with an *a priori* principle. Reason thus, in favourable circumstances, yields substantive knowledge about the external world.

This principle in turn serves to shore up the Image of God doctrine by acting as a premise in standard arguments for the existence of God. Descartes uses it in his 'trademark argument' in the Third Meditation, arguing that only an infinite being could cause us to form the *idea* of an infinite being. And a corollary of the principle is that nothing can come from nothing – a premise in the Cosmological Argument for the existence of an unmoved mover.

Such allegedly *a priori* principles make perfectly good sense given the metaphysical picture just described, since they are simply material-world analogues of *a priori* principles concerning entailment. The first principle, that causes must contain as much reality as their effects, is related to the thought that the conclusion of a valid argument must be 'contained' in the premises: for a valid argument, as well as the temperature of a hot potato, you only get out what you put in. And the second principle, that nothing can come from nothing, is related to the fact that only necessary truths do not depend on – that is, are not contingent upon – other truths. Hence, according to the material-world analogue, only a necessary being – a being not contingent upon anything else – could be the first cause.

The other tradition that Hume has squarely in his sights is the scholastic tradition, whose roots lie in Aristotelian empiricism. As Stephen Buckle notes, Hume's opposition to the scholastic tradition is overlooked when Hume is forced into the standard 'rationalists vs. empiricists' dispute; but Buckle argues that scholasticism is in fact a much more important target for Hume, at least in the first *Enquiry*.[2] That Hume's aim is not confined to rationalism can be seen from the fact that he so clearly intends to refute the view that we can, by means of sensory experience, penetrate into the essence of causes in such a way as to deliver certain knowledge of effects. This view is not one that Hume's rationalist predecessors held; for Descartes, for instance, we cannot discover the essences of objects by attending to sensory experience. On the contrary: one grasps the true nature of material objects by 'purely mental scrutiny' (Descartes 1641: 21). So insofar as Hume is concerned to refute the view that sensory experience can penetrate into the essences of objects, his target appears to be not rationalism but – as Buckle puts it – 'the Stoic view that knowledge arises through "cognitive impressions": that is, that there are some sense perceptions that are the basis of true judgements about the nature of things' (Buckle 2001: 41).

The Insight Ideal is in the background of the scholastic tradition just as it is in the background of the rationalist tradition, since the view that effects can be inferred *a priori* from causes remains. The traditions differ on the issue of how knowledge of essences arises – from sensation or from 'purely mental scrutiny' – but they agree that, given such knowledge, inference from causes and effects is *a priori*: once we know the essence of the cause, we can know with certainty, and without the need to consult prior experience, what its effects will be.

Hume's overall project, in both the *Treatise* and the *Enquiry*, can be seen as that of showing that the Insight Ideal is completely untenable; but he does not advertise it in quite such confrontational terms. In the Introduction to the *Treatise*, Hume clearly states his intention to provide a 'science of man' by 'the application of experimental philosophy to moral subjects' (*T* xvi), the 'experimental philosophy' having provided such improvements in the understanding of the physical world in the hands of Newton. We must proceed, Hume says, by means of 'careful and exact experiments, and the observation of those particular effects, which result from [the mind's] different circumstances and situations' (*T* xvii); such 'experiments' being our only route to 'any notion' of the mind's 'powers and qualities' (*ibid.*). Hume's declared agenda is thus one that, from our perspective, in some ways has more in common with empirical psychology than with analytical philosophy, except for the fact that, by and large, his only experimental subject is himself. He is interested in providing an account of the workings of the human mind – for example in how we come to acquire knowledge and how we come to infer effects from causes – and in doing so by deploying a broadly scientific method.

It is not hard to see how such an agenda immediately sets Hume in opposition to the Insight Ideal; an empirical investigation into how the mind actually works is likely to deliver the result that it does not work in a way that is remotely analogous to the way in which God's mind is supposed to work. And this is just what Hume's investigation delivers. In particular, it delivers the result that neither *a priori* reasoning nor sensory experience just by themselves, nor the combination of the two, can deliver any substantive knowledge about the causal structure of the world at all. We cannot penetrate into the essences of objects in such a way as to reveal anything analogous to an entailment relation between causes and effects: nothing at all in our experience reveals the world to have the quasi-logical structure suggested by the Image of God doctrine. Rather, our sensory impressions can reveal no more than a succession of events which, insofar as they are represented by those impressions, are 'entirely loose and separate' (*E* 74). Nor are there any causal principles knowable *a priori*: 'If we reason *a priori*, anything may appear able to produce anything' (*E* 164). According to the theory of our access to the world with which Hume replaces the Insight Ideal, the fundamental source of our empirical beliefs is something more animal than divine, namely custom or habit. When we reason from causes to effects, we have much more in common with a dog which expects its walk when it sees its lead being fetched than we do with the mind of God.

1.2 Three concerns: genetic, epistemological and semantic

Hume can be seen as having three distinct but related overall concerns. The first concern is genetic: a concern with the origins or sources of the items that populate the mind – impressions, ideas, beliefs, knowledge – and with the mechanisms by means of which those items interact with one another. Especially relevant to the case of causation are the questions 'what is the mental mechanism by which we infer effects from causes?' and 'what is the source of the idea of necessary connection?' It is this genetic concern that Hume points to when he tells us that his task is to pursue a 'science of man'. The second concern is epistemological: a concern with what can and cannot be known with certainty, with what, if anything, justifies causal claims and claims about the future, and with the epistemic status of belief in the external world. The third concern is semantic: what do we mean when we say that one thing caused another, or that the external world exists? That Hume has all three concerns is undeniable; what is a good deal more controversial is the question of which concern or concerns are most central to his philosophical project.

Many commentators, who have seen Hume as a kind of embryonic positivist, have, at least implicitly, placed a great deal of emphasis on Hume's semantic concern, and taken his greatest lasting contribution to philosophy to be what is often called his 'meaning-empiricism': roughly, the thesis that any expression whose content cannot be traced to the deliverances of experience is meaningless. But care is needed with this conception of what Hume is up to. His famous recommendation, at the end of the *Enquiry*, that we 'commit to the flames' any book that contains neither 'abstract reasoning concerning quantity and number' nor 'experimental reasoning concerning matter of fact and existence', 'for it can contain nothing but sophistry and illusion' (*E* 165), expresses his view that we should not be tempted to engage in abstruse metaphysical speculation nor attempt to demonstrate by *a priori* arguments that, for example, the external world exists or was created by God. But it is entirely possible that Hume takes this dim view of speculative metaphysics without holding that the whole enterprise is literally meaningless. We could instead credit him with the view that the ultimate nature of reality is unknowable, thus rendering attempts at speculative metaphysics pointless rather than incoherent. And we can hold that Hume's claim that every simple idea has its source in an impression – his Copy Principle – is a genetic rather than a semantic claim: a claim about the origin of ideas rather than their content.

Another place where issues surrounding the relative importance of Hume's different concerns come to the fore is his famous discussion of what has come to be known as 'the problem of induction': the problem of showing that inferences from the observed to the unobserved are justified. The problem of induction is, of course, an epistemological problem; but it is less clear that *Hume*'s problem is an epistemological one. He certainly denies that *a priori* reasoning is a source of substantive knowledge of the external world, and hence holds that there is no certain knowledge to be had when it comes to 'matters of fact and existence'. But he is usually taken to be arguing for a much more radical epistemological conclusion: the conclusion that no belief whatsoever about what is currently unavailable to the senses or to memory is ever justified – that, epistemically speaking, any belief about the unobserved is as good as any other.

It is easy to see why one might be tempted to cast Hume in this light. After all, he holds that 'reasoning' from observed causes to as-yet-unobserved effects is a matter of mere habit or custom, and it is hard to see how mere habit or custom can endow a belief with justification. However, Hume himself shows little or no inclination towards endorsing the irrationalist view that no beliefs about the unobserved can be justified. He knows that he has no response to the sceptic who claims to doubt that the external world exists, or that the sun will rise tomorrow, in the sense that he cannot *demonstrate* that the external world really does exist or that the sun really will rise tomorrow; that, after all, is a consequence of his rejection of the Insight Ideal. Nonetheless, he clearly holds that such doubt cannot, as a matter of brute psychological fact, be sustained. We cannot stop ourselves from believing in the external world or inferring effects from causes, and, even if we could, it would be very bad news indeed if we actually did stop: 'all human life must perish, were [the Pyrrhonian sceptic's] principles universally and steadily to prevail. All discourse, all action would immediately cease; and men remain in a total lethargy, till the necessities of nature, unsatisfied, put an end to their miserable existence' (*E* 160).

Hume's interest in induction – or, better, in 'causal reasoning', since for Hume the inference in question is, at least in the first instance, reasoning from causes and effects, and not from observed to unobserved regularities – is, of course, at least partly epistemological. He is concerned to show that causal reasoning is not a product of any special faculty of reason, and so does not generate certain knowledge about the world, because his destruction of the Insight Ideal requires him to show this. But the overall focus of his discussion is on the source, and not the justification, of beliefs about the unobserved. The question is always 'how do we get to *have* these beliefs?' and not 'are these beliefs we find ourselves with justified or not?' The negative answer to the former, genetic question – such beliefs do not come about as a result of *a priori* reasoning – provides Hume with his response to the upholders of the Insight Ideal. But if Hume's positive answer – once we have experienced a constant conjunction of *C*s and *E*s, we will come to expect an *E* to occur on observing a *C* out of sheer habit – is taken at face value, as a genetic answer to a genetic question, it is at best undetermined what he takes its epistemological consequences to be.

I say 'at best' because Hume's discussion of causation itself, as opposed to causal reasoning, provides clear evidence that Hume is no irrationalist when it comes to causal reasoning. Causation and induction are often treated, both in twentieth-century analytic philosophy and in discussion of Hume, as distinct topics. But for Hume, causation and inference from the observed to the unobserved are inseparable: we come to believe that *C*s are causes of *E*s just *because* we instinctively infer *E*s from *C*s. Failure to take this connection seriously leads to very peculiar interpretative consequences. In particular, the dominant view of Hume is that he is both an inductive sceptic and a naïve regularity theorist about causation: he holds that one object or event, *c*, causes another, *e*, if and only if *c* is prior to and spatio-temporally contiguous with *e* and events like *c* (the *C*s) are constantly conjoined with events like *e* (the *E*s). If Hume really does hold both of these views, then he must, trivially, be a sceptic about causation: if we are never justified in believing that *C*s are constantly conjoined with *E*s, then no causal claim is ever justified. But Hume nowhere expresses scepticism about causation: whatever he thinks it *takes* for one event to cause another, he undeniably holds that things *do* cause other things.

One of the assumptions of this book is that Hume's interest in the epistemological and the semantic is largely negative. He is interested in demolishing the Insight Ideal and in arguing that the idea of necessary connection cannot adequately represent (or perhaps represent at all) any mind-independent relation between causes and effects. He is far less interested in offering positive accounts. In the case of causal reasoning, I shall argue, Hume is not an inductive sceptic; he actually presupposes, and certainly never seriously doubts, that causal reasoning is a 'just' form of reasoning. On the semantic side, Hume's lack of interest in what the content of causal claims is, as opposed to what it isn't, goes some of the way towards explaining why the interpretative controversy surrounding that issue is so difficult to resolve.

It might be thought that in dividing Hume's concerns into the genetic, the epistemological and the semantic I have ignored the one concern that ought to be at the forefront in a discussion of Hume on causation, namely metaphysics. So where does Hume stand on the metaphysics of causation? Well, the fact that the *Treatise* and the *Enquiry* are announced as examinations into 'human understanding' and 'human nature' respectively, should immediately make us wonder whether Hume is really very interested in metaphysics – in how the world is, as opposed to what we believe about it and why we believe what we do. Nor does he *need* to be terribly interested in the metaphysics of causation. We have an irresistible habit of, for example, predicting that the black ball will move on observing the white ball make contact with it, and the corresponding habit of calling the first event the cause and the second the effect. When we do so, we are not penetrating into the 'essence' of the cause in such a way as to license inference *a priori* that the effect will occur. We are just acting on habit. Metaphysical speculation into the nature or existence of any alleged connection between cause and effect is to be avoided, since neither *a priori* reasoning nor experience can be employed to produce intelligible results. What more needs to be said?

1.3 The interpretative options

Whether or not more *needs* to be said, Hume does say more, and what he says can be interpreted as committing him to a particular view about the metaphysics of causation. However, *which* view about the metaphysics of causation he thereby commits himself to has been a matter of intense interpretative debate.

We have seen that the Image of God doctrine has both epistemological and metaphysical consequences. The metaphysical consequence is that the world has a causal structure that is analogous to the logical structure of a valid argument: the essence of an object or event guarantees that a particular effect will follow, just as the content of a true proposition guarantees that some other proposition is also true. And the epistemological consequence – the Insight Ideal – is that those essences are 'intelligible': we can in principle grasp their nature, or at least know *a priori* some principles which place constraints on the kinds of event that can be causally related. That Hume rejects the Insight Ideal is beyond dispute; but this leaves the metaphysical question wide open, since it does not follow from this, just by itself, that there *are* no necessary connections in nature. All that Hume's rejection of the Insight Ideal establishes is the epistemological thesis that if there are such things neither their existence nor their nature can be established by sensory experience or by *a priori* reasoning. Indeed, Hume sometimes – occasionally in the *Treatise*, but pervasively in the *Enquiry* – seems to take it for granted that there *are* necessary connections or 'secret powers' in nature: that there is something that lies behind the regularities upon which the 'regular course and succession of objects totally depends' (*E* 55).

However, Hume also holds that the idea of necessary connection is a component of our ordinary idea of causation. In keeping with his theory of ideas, according to which every simple idea must have its source in an impression, he famously identifies the impression-source of the idea of necessary connection as the 'feeling' we get when we infer effects from causes. When I confidently predict that the black ball will move on observing the white ball make contact with it, this 'transition' in the mind, from the impression of the cause to the belief that the effect will follow, somehow gives rise to the impression of necessary connection.

Given all this, what are the interpretative options? Well, let's start by seeing what happens if we hold Hume to the meaning-empiricist line on the metaphysical upshot of the Image of God doctrine. If we hold him to the doctrine that the impression-source of an idea provides its meaning, and put it together with the thesis that the impression-source of the idea of necessary connection is the 'feeling' we get when we infer effects from causes, we appear to rule out the possibility of our even being able to *contemplate* the possibility that there are real necessary connections in nature. We have no idea that corresponds to the expression 'real necessary connection in nature', since the alleged idea does not have its source in any sensory impression. Rather, when we say or think that one event is necessarily connected to another, and hence that the first caused the second, what we really turn out to mean by that claim must have something to do with the transition of the mind from the observation of the first event to the expectation that the second event will follow, and nothing to do with any alleged real connection between the two events.

There are two broad directions in which one can take this line of thought. The first takes Hume towards a naïve regularity theory of causation. Our ordinary concept of causation is a mess: we take ourselves to be referring to real, mind-independent necessary connections, but it turns out that we are really referring to something inside the mind: the 'transition' from one idea to another. So clearly what's needed is conceptual revision: we need a concept of causation that is purged of any purported reference to experience-transcending metaphysical hocus pocus. This is roughly what the traditional interpretation (as I shall call it) says Hume is doing.[3]

Thus characterized, Hume is sometimes taken to be *denying* that there are mind-independent necessary connections in nature. But, given the meaning-empiricist starting point of the traditional interpretation, Hume *qua* naïve regularity theorist is better seen as holding that, since there is no legitimate idea that corresponds to the expression 'necessary connection in nature', any claim about the existence or non-existence of such a thing either lacks in meaning or, at best, attaches an arbitrary name to an unspecified unknowable feature of the world, which may or may not exist and to which our causal talk is utterly oblivious.

The other direction in which one might take the above line of thought is towards a projectivist interpretation. According to the projectivist interpretation, Hume takes our causal claims to involve the 'projection' of the idea of necessary connection on to a world that is – at least as it is revealed to us in sensation – a world of brute regularities. Projectivism about causation works in more or less the same way as projectivism in ethics: when I say that an action is wrong, according to projectivism I am responding to 'natural' features of the world. I am not ascribing what J.L. Mackie (1977) calls a 'queer' moral property to the action; nor am I simply asserting that the action in question has some natural property or properties (that it caused someone to experience pain or to be deprived of their wallet, for example). Rather, I am expressing an ethical attitude: an attitude of disapproval. Similarly, according to a projectivist conception of causation, when we say that *c* caused *e* we do not simply assert that priority, contiguity and constant conjunction obtain (contrary to what the naïve regularity theory claims); neither do we assert that there is a real, mind-independent connection between *c* and *e*. Rather, the claim that *c* caused *e* expresses our natural tendency or habit of thought to infer *E*s from *C*s.

Alternatively, as we saw earlier, one might dispute the claim that Hume is a meaning-empiricist, and hold instead that, according to him, there *are* 'secret powers' in nature – powers whose nature is not revealed in experience. Moreover, it is these secret powers to which our causal talk refers. This is the route taken by the sceptical realist interpretation. According to this interpretation, while there is no *graspable* necessary connection between causes and effects, Hume nonetheless accepts that causes and effects are really, mind-independently connected in some way. However the *nature* of that connection lies beyond our cognitive grip.

The different interpretations thus attribute radically different views to Hume. To some commentators' eyes, Hume argues persuasively that there is no more to the world than a regular succession of events; to others, Hume takes the existence of something lying behind the regularities to be so obvious that it does not even occur to him to question it. To some commentators' eyes, Hume holds that necessity is quite literally a figment of the imagination, while to others he holds that necessity is a thoroughly mind-independent feature of the world. Given that Hume's writing is so often regarded as a model of clarity, the fact that it is at least *prima facie* consistent with such radically different positions on the metaphysics of causation might in itself make one wonder just how central to his thought the metaphysics of causation really is.

1.4 Overview of the book

In line with the thought that interpretative issues concerning the metaphysics of causation have less importance for an understanding of Hume's overall project than one might suppose, I set them aside, by and large, in Chapters 2, 3 and 4. These chapters address Hume's discussions of relations and *a priori* reasoning (Chapter 2), causal reasoning (Chapter 3) and the idea of necessary connection (Chapter 4) – this being the order in which Hume himself takes these topics.

Chapter 2 introduces Hume's basic picture of the mind: the objects with which it is populated – impressions and ideas – and the principles by which ideas are 'associated' together. It also introduces and explains Hume's distinction between 'natural' and 'philosophical' relations. I then turn to Hume's account of 'demonstration': reasoning concerning relations between ideas, which generates *a priori* knowledge. I describe and defend David Owen's interpretation of Hume's account of demonstration, which, I argue, coheres very well with the thought that Hume's primary interest is in the *genesis* of knowledge: how, starting just with ideas and the relations between them, is knowledge generated?

In Chapter 3, I turn to Hume's account of causal reasoning: reasoning from causes to effects. Again, a central claim is that Hume's primary interest here is genetic. Hume holds that beliefs about what is not currently present to the senses or memory are a result of inferring effects from causes or vice versa; and so an account of the process by which that inference takes place provides an account of the genesis of belief. A common way to read Hume's discussion of causal reasoning is as an argument to the effect that inductive inference can never be justified, since any attempt at justification turns out to be circular: it presupposes precisely what it is supposed to show. I argue that, for Hume, the circularity he identifies undermines the possibility of certain kinds of *explanation* of how it is we infer effects from causes.

Hume's positive account of causal reasoning, just by itself – the claim that the inference is a matter of brute habit or custom – leaves open the epistemic status of beliefs acquired as a result of that inference. I argue that Hume does not subscribe to the view that no such beliefs are ever justified. Nor does he subscribe to the view that, since causal reasoning is an unavoidable part of the human condition, questions of justification are simply off the agenda. Rather, he holds, in effect, that causal reasoning is justified because it is reliable: it tracks the regularities in nature. Of course, this is not a good response to the inductive sceptic, who will want to know what grounds we have for thinking that there are any regularities in nature for causal reasoning to track. But scepticism, in this sense, is not a position which Hume shows any interest in rebutting.

In Chapter 4, I turn to Hume's discussion of the idea of necessary connection, focussing on his claim that the source of that idea is the 'transition' in the mind from the impression of the cause to the belief that the effect will occur, and on his famous two definitions of causation. I argue that Hume holds not that 'all events seem entirely loose and separate' (*E* 74), but only that they so seem 'in single instances of the operation of bodies' (*E* 73). In other words, once we have acquired the habit of inferring *E*s from *C*s, we not only come to *judge* that *C*s are causes of *E*s; the *C*s and *E*s no longer *seem* entirely loose and separate. On the two definitions, I argue that the 'definitions' really only describe how we come to make causal judgements; they do not tell us anything at all about the content of those judgements. In other words, the two definitions say nothing at all about the meaning of 'cause'.

In Chapters 5–7, I turn, finally, to the interpretative disputes surrounding Hume's views on causation. In Chapter 5, I discuss what I shall call 'the traditional interpretation'. The name in fact encompasses a variety of different interpretative positions which share a common core in that they all attribute to Hume two central claims: first, that it is illegitimate or incoherent to apply the idea of necessary connection to external events; and, second, that causation 'in the objects' – that is, those features of the world which determine the truth of causal claims – amounts to temporal priority, contiguity and constant conjunction. I argue that the traditional interpretation survives a criticism often levelled at it by defenders of the sceptical realist interpretation. The criticism is that the traditional interpretation commits Hume to a claim that we should not attribute to him, namely the claim that there is no more to nature than mere regularity; the response is simply that Hume can safely remain agnostic about the existence of anything underlying nature's regularities, while still maintaining that our causal talk fails to connect with any such thing. However, I also argue that, in the end, the traditional interpretation is untenable. An important part of the reason is that there is really no serious evidence at all that Hume subscribes to either of the core claims identified above; indeed, there is plenty of evidence that he rejects both of them.

In Chapter 6, I develop a projectivist interpretation: an interpretation that has not, to my knowledge, been articulated or defended in any great detail elsewhere, but which has been suggested by Simon Blackburn in various places. I fill in some of the blanks, and argue that the projectivist interpretation not only avoids the problems that beset the traditional interpretation; it also has some basis in what Hume actually says, particularly given some close parallels between what he say about morals and what he says about causation.

In Chapter 7, I discuss the sceptical realist interpretation. As with the traditional interpretation, 'the sceptical realist interpretation' turns out to encompass a variety of interpretative positions that agree on a common core. In this case, the common core consists of the attribution of the following two central views to Hume: first, that causation is a mind-independent relation that consists in more than mere regularity (hence 'realist'); and, second, that the nature of the 'something more' to which our causal thought and talk refers cannot be known or conceived (hence 'sceptical').

I argue against some claims that have been made on behalf of sceptical realism – in particular Galen Strawson's claim that Hume is a subjectivist about necessity despite being a sceptical realist about causation and Craig's suggestion that Hume may have been persuaded by a philosophical argument to believe that there is something that underlies or sustains nature's regularities – and I also argue that the textual case for the sceptical realist interpretation is not decisive. However, I ultimately remain neutral between the projectivist and sceptical realist interpretations. Or, rather, it seems to me that, in the end, the Hume of the *Treatise* sounds like a projectivist and the Hume of the *Enquiry* sounds like a sceptical realist.

This raises the issue of which of the *Treatise* and the *Enquiry* we should take more seriously as a clear expression of Hume's view – or whether we should regard the two works as actually expressing different views. It is generally, though not universally, thought that Hume intended the *Enquiries* to be a dumbed-down and therefore more popular version of the *Treatise*. Certainly this would explain the omission from the first *Enquiry* of some of the more abstruse material in the *Treatise*, which was unlikely to be of interest to 'the *habitués* of coffee-houses' (*E*, Editor's introduction, xii), and the inclusion of the more enticing discussions of the existence of God and the possibility of miracles.

However, Hume himself claims that the *Enquiries* correct 'some negligences in his former reasoning' and desires that the *Enquiries* 'alone be regarded as containing his philosophical sentiments and principles' (*E* 2). This raises the possibility that there are differences between the views espoused in the *Treatise* and in the first *Enquiry*, and – if there are indeed such differences – that we should regard Hume's considered philosophical views to be those contained in the *Enquiry* rather than the *Treatise*.

Unfortunately, I cannot see a way of decisively resolving this issue. However, there is a clear sense in which the issue does not need to be resolved if what is most central to Hume's thought, and hence what is most important for an adequate understanding of his overall project, leaves the issue undecided. If Hume's overarching ambition is to demolish the Insight Ideal by providing a science of man that shows the Insight Ideal to be untenable, then it does not matter, as far as that ambition is concerned, whether he is really a projectivist or a sceptical realist about causation. Each interpretation is fully consistent with the claim that, at bottom, it is our natural, animal instinct, and not a God-like power of rational insight, that is responsible for our beliefs about the world; and each interpretation is also fully consistent with the claim that the ultimate nature of reality lies beyond our cognitive reach.

2

A PRIORI REASONING AND THE GENESIS OF KNOWLEDGE

Before we can begin to think about Hume's views on causation, we need to focus on some preliminary issues. As we saw in Chapter 1, Hume describes his project as the 'science of man', and to that end, at the beginning of the *Treatise* and the *Enquiry*, he begins to develop his theory of how the mind works. Central to that theory is the notion of a 'relation' between ideas; and by far the most important relation between ideas for Hume, at least as far as the beliefs that enable us to go about our daily lives and to conduct experimental investigations are concerned, is causation, since '[b]y means of that relation alone we can go beyond the evidence of our memory and senses' (*E* 26). Hume's account of how it is that we 'reason' from causes to effects and vice versa cannot, however, be understood in isolation from his account of other kinds of reasoning, in particular his account of *a priori* reasoning – the kind of reasoning that delivers knowledge that 4>2, for example, or that the angles of a triangle add up to 180°. Nor can his views on causation be understood in isolation from his distinction between 'natural' and 'philosophical' relations – a distinction that is crucial for understanding his much-discussed 'two definitions' of causation. These important building blocks of Hume's science of man are the main focus of this chapter, and his account of 'reasoning' from causes to effects is the main focus of Chapter 3.

I begin, in §2.1, by providing a brief summary of Hume's theory of the mind: his views about what 'objects' the mind is populated with, and how those objects interact with one another. In §2.2, I examine Hume's theory of intuition and demonstration. I focus on David Owen's interpretation (1999: ch. 5), according to which intuition and demonstration are a matter of comparison of ideas under relations (e.g. numerical relations, like *greater than*, and qualitative relations like *darker than*). This interpretation differs in important ways from the standard interpretation, according to which demonstration, for Hume, is a matter of deductively valid inference from necessarily true premises.

In §2.3, I argue that Owen's account coheres extremely well with Hume's genetic interest – his interest in providing a science of man. Conceived as concerned primarily with genetic issues, Hume's interest in intuition and demonstration stems from the need to provide an account of how a particular species of belief, namely knowledge, arises, and Owen's interpretation, unlike the standard interpretation, delivers just that: an account of how we can start out with mere ideas and end up with items of knowledge.

In §2.4, however, I argue (*pace* Owen) that there is an important distinction – between comparison of ideas under relations on the one hand and deductive inference on the other – that is implicit in Hume's conception of *a priori* reasoning. When we compare ideas under relations, we compare *distinct* ideas, but when we validly infer a conclusion from premises, the premises and conclusion are not distinct. This difference, I shall later argue, is important for understanding both Hume's discussion of causal reasoning and his distinction between causation conceived as a philosophical relation and causation conceived as a natural relation.

Finally, in §2.5, I describe how Hume's interest in causation stems, in the first instance, from the need to provide an explanation of how we come to have another species of belief: belief about 'matters of fact'.

2.1 Impressions, ideas and relations

In Book I of the *Treatise*, Hume sets out to investigate how the mind works and to trace the epistemological consequences of his view. His theory of the mind is given much shorter shrift in the *Enquiry*, and some parts of it are left out completely. However, there is no evidence that he intended to abandon any substantive part of that theory as presented in the *Treatise*.

Hume regards the mind as populated by mental 'objects', which are of one basic kind, namely 'perceptions'. Perceptions divide into two categories: impressions and ideas. For Hume, as for his empiricist predecessors, all ideas are derived from impressions – impressions either of sensation (heat, colour, taste and so on) or of reflection (such as anger or pleasure). Ideas differ from impressions not in nature but merely in 'vivacity': simple ideas (my ideas of redness and roundness, for example) are 'faint images' of simple impressions (*T* 1); and complex ideas (my ideas of Paris and unicorns) are either faint images of complex impressions (as with my idea of Paris) or are built up from their component simple ideas (as with my idea of a unicorn), which in turn are faint images of simple impressions.

Ideas can be brought before the mind according to 'principles of attraction', as when the idea of a picture of The Queen brings to mind (that is, 'attracts') the idea of The Queen herself; and degrees of 'vivacity' can be transmitted from one idea to another, or from an impression to an idea. Hume thus clearly starts out with a picture of the mind as a kind of natural, quasi-Newtonian system. As he says, there is 'a kind of ATTRACTION, which in the mental world will be found to have as extraordinary effects as in the natural, and to show itself in as many and as various forms' (*T* 12–13). Of course, ideas – unlike billiard balls or planets – are mental rather than physical. The principles underlying their interaction are therefore not to be described in terms of force, mass or motion; rather, the principles work, by and large, according to their *content*.

To say that ideas, on Hume's view, are mental rather than physical, and that the principles according to which they behave are not to be described in physical terms, is not to say that Hume takes either the mind or mental objects to be immaterial. He later argues that there are no good arguments for the immateriality of the soul (*T*, Book I, Part IV, §V), and at *T* 60–1 he speculates that the principles of attraction have a physical basis: it would 'have been easy to have made an imaginary dissection of the brain, and have shewn, why upon our conception of any idea, the animal spirits run into all the contiguous traces, and rouze up the other ideas, that are related to it' (*T* 60). But – scientist of the mind that he is – Hume cannot generally appeal to such speculative suggestions. His theory of the mind must be grounded in correlations between observable phenomena; that is, between ideas *qua* bearers of content. In other words, the relevant principles must be psychological rather than physical.

Hume duly provides 'associative principles' governing the behaviour of ideas. There must be, he says, a 'bond of union' among our ideas: 'some associating quality by which one idea naturally introduces another' (*T* 10). And the associative principles that he discovers are 'resemblance, contiguity in time or place, and cause and effect' (*T* 11). In the *Enquiry*, he gives concrete examples of the three associative principles at work:

> A picture naturally leads our thoughts to the original: the mention of one apartment in a building naturally introduces an enquiry or discourse concerning the others: and if we think of a wound, we can scarcely forbear reflecting on the pain which follows it.
>
> (*E* 24)

It is clear from these examples that the associative principles hold in virtue of the content of the associated ideas. For example, it is the contiguity of one (imagined) apartment to its neighbour in virtue of which the idea of the first naturally introduces the idea of the second, and not the contiguity of the first idea itself to the second (whatever that might mean). And in the third case, the idea of a wound naturally introduces the idea of pain because the imagined wound and pain themselves are imagined to be causally connected.

At this stage, we simply have a classification of the kinds of situation in which one idea naturally introduces another. I notice that the idea of a wound naturally introduces the idea of pain, that the idea of the sun naturally introduces the idea of heat, that the idea of one billiard ball making contact with another naturally introduces the idea of the second ball moving, and so on. What unites all these apparently disparate pairings is that in each case I also judge or believe that the first event is a cause of the second. As a matter of brute psychological fact, our minds are endowed with some sort of mechanism – I shall call it the 'associative mechanism of causation' – by means of which one idea 'attracts' another, and this mechanism somehow or other tracks our causal beliefs.[1]

16

One might naturally assume that the 'input' to the mechanism is always the first idea (of the wound or the sun or the contact of the billiard balls) together with some antecedently held causal belief (that wounds cause pain, and so on), thus generating the output: the idea of the effect (pain, heat, the movement of the black). But it will turn out that, in the most important class of cases – cases where the input is an impression (of a wound or the sun or the contact of the billiard balls) – Hume thinks that this is not what happens at all. Instead, the mechanism simultaneously generates both the idea of (in fact, belief in) the effect *and* the judgement that the first event will cause the second. In other words, in such cases the associative mechanism of causation *produces* causal judgements: causal judgements figure as output, not as input (see §3.7 and §4.6).[2]

Hume calls the three relations in virtue of which one idea 'naturally' introduces another 'natural' relations. As well as natural relations, there are 'philosophical' relations: 'any particular subject of comparison, without a connecting principle' (*T* 14). The idea here is that we can call to mind any two ideas we please and compare them with respect to a philosophical relation; that is, we can see whether one idea bears, or decide whether to place it in, a given philosophical relation to another idea. There are seven philosophical relations: '*resemblance, identity, relations of time and place* [i.e. contiguity], *proportion in quantity or number, degrees in any quality, contrariety,* and *causation*' (*T* 69).

Contiguity, resemblance and causation thus appear both in Hume's inventory of natural relations and in his inventory of philosophical relations: causation, for example, is 'a philosophical relation, as well as a natural one' (*T* 15). It is important to note that the natural/philosophical distinction is thus a distinction not between two different kinds of *relation*, where a relation is conceived merely as a relation that obtains between the contents of two ideas, but between the kinds of operation of the mind associated with the obtaining of a relation. For example, when a picture 'naturally leads our thoughts to the original' (*E* 24), resemblance is (as I shall put it) 'functioning' as a natural relation: it is the resemblance between the contents of the two ideas that is responsible for the idea of the picture's naturally introducing the idea of what it depicts. By contrast, if I am wondering whether the picture I saw yesterday is a Picasso, I might consciously and deliberately call to mind some Picassos I have seen in the past, and consider whether or to what extent they resemble the picture I am thinking of. Here resemblance is functioning as a philosophical relation. The idea of the recently seen picture does not *naturally* introduce the ideas of the other pictures; rather, I am consciously and deliberately calling those other ideas to mind and comparing each of them, under the relation of resemblance, to the idea of the recently seen picture. The relation in which those ideas (or, rather, their contents) stand is nonetheless the same relation – resemblance – as the relation that obtains, in the case where the mind is naturally led from the idea of a picture and the idea of what it depicts, between the contents of *those* ideas.

I shall argue in §4.6 that all this is crucial to understanding Hume's famous 'two definitions' of causation, where he 'defines' causation first as a philosophical relation and then as a natural relation. There has been a good deal of discussion of whether the two definitions are extensionally equivalent, as two definitions of a term, in the ordinary sense of 'definition', need to be. But the fact that the natural/philosophical distinction is a distinction concerning the operation of the mind should immediately raise the question of whether Hume is really attempting to provide two 'definitions', in the sense of necessary and sufficient conditions for the truth of causal claims.

2.2 Intuition and demonstration

Let's return to Hume's seven philosophical relations. I said earlier that we can consider any idea and see whether it bears, or decide whether to place it in, a given philosophical relation to another idea. But is it 'see whether it bears' or 'decide whether to place it in'? That depends on which philosophical relation we are considering, for philosophical relations fall into two distinct categories, which I shall call class *A* relations and class *B* relations. Class *A* relations – resemblance, contrariety, degrees in quality, and proportions in quantity and number – are those that 'depend entirely on the ideas, which we compare together' (*T* 69). For example, suppose I have before my mind an idea of The Queen and also an idea of a particular portrait of her, and consider those two ideas under the relation of resemblance (so that resemblance is functioning here as a philosophical relation). Whether or to what extent I place them under that relation is not something I can choose: whether or not one resembles the other is determined solely by the contents of those ideas. In contemporary parlance, resemblance is an internal relation.

This distinguishing feature of class *A* relations renders them capable of producing 'knowledge and certainty' (*T* 70): 'All certainty arises from the comparison of ideas, and from the discovery of such relations as are unalterable, so long as the ideas continue the same' (*T* 79). The fact that the content of the 'compared' ideas determines whether or not a class *A* relation obtains means that we can in principle *know*, just by inspecting those ideas, that the relation obtains. I can tell just by comparing the idea of navy with the idea of turquoise that navy is darker than turquoise (darkness being a 'degree in quality'), and I can tell just by comparison of the relevant ideas that $3^3 + 7 = 34$. In the former case, I am employing 'intuition': I can tell just by, as it were, inwardly inspecting the ideas that navy is darker than turquoise. In the latter case, I will need to run through several steps in a chain of reasoning, each step employing intuition; Hume calls such chains of reasoning 'demonstrations'.

The remaining, class *B*, relations, by contrast – contiguity, identity and causation – do not generate certainty. Whether I should place the idea of my computer and the idea of my fruit bowl in the relation of spatial contiguity is not settled by the content of those ideas; nor is whether I should place two fruit-bowl ideas in the relation of identity (are they ideas of the *same* fruit bowl or not?); nor is whether I should place a toe-stubbing idea and a pain idea in the relation of causation (at least when I am merely imagining, rather than actually experiencing, a toe stubbing). I can imagine a toe stubbing and a pain and either place them under the relation of causation or not.[3]

Hume does not mention philosophical relations at all in the *Enquiry*, but it is clear that he still has more or less the same underlying view in the later work. In the *Enquiry*, he divides the 'objects of human reason or enquiry' into two kinds: relations of ideas and matters of fact. He says:

> Of the first kind are the sciences of Geometry, Algebra, and Arithmetic; and in short, every affirmation which is either intuitively or demonstratively certain. . . . Propositions of this kind are discoverable by the mere operation of thought, without the dependence on what is anywhere existent in the universe. Though there never were a circle or triangle in nature, the truths demonstrated by Euclid would for ever retain their certainty or evidence.
>
> Matters of fact . . . are not ascertained in the same manner; nor is our evidence of their truth, however great, of a like nature with the foregoing. The contrary of every matter of fact is still possible; because it can never imply a contradiction, and is conceived by the mind with the same facility and distinctness, as if ever so conformable to reality. *That the sun will not rise to-morrow* is no less intelligible a proposition, and implies no more contradiction, than the affirmation, *that it will rise*. We should in vain, therefore, attempt to demonstrate its falsehood. Were it demonstratively false, it would imply a contradiction, and could never be distinctly conceived by the mind.
>
> (*E* 25–6)

It is important to get clear on exactly what Hume is up to here, because understanding his conception of the similarities and differences between 'reasoning concerning matters of fact' and 'reasoning concerning relations of ideas' is crucial to understanding his discussions of causal reasoning and the origin of the idea of necessary connection. Hume is making three distinctions: the distinction between class *A* and class *B* relations; the distinction between what can and cannot be 'demonstrated'; and the distinction between what can and cannot be known with certainty. How are we to understand all this?

The standard way to understand it is to see Hume's distinctions in the light of the kinds of distinction that are familiar in contemporary analytic philosophy: necessary vs. contingent (or analytic vs. synthetic) truths; valid vs. invalid arguments; and deduction vs. induction.[4] Seen in this light, the distinction between class *A* and class *B* relations looks like the distinction between necessary and contingent (or analytic and synthetic) truths. Those propositions that involve class *A* relations – the propositions of geometry, algebra and arithmetic, for example – are, if true, necessarily true, while propositions involving class *B* relations ('the fruit bowl is next to the computer', 'the pain in my toe was caused by my stubbing it') are, if true, only contingently so.

19

Hume seems to think that 'demonstratively false' propositions will be necessarily false, since he says that if something is demonstratively false it implies a contradiction. Correspondingly, one would expect 'demonstratively true' propositions to be necessarily true. It thus also seems natural – again in the light of familiar distinctions – to hold that Hume thinks of demonstration itself – or demonstrative reasoning – as being a matter of deductive reasoning from necessarily true premises. Thus a proposition involving a class A relation – $3^3 + 7 = 34$, say – is necessarily true, and we can be certain of this because we can deduce it, that is, demonstrate its truth, from premises that are themselves necessarily true (and, presumably, knowable to be so by intuition). By contrast, any 'matter of fact', P, involving a class B relation is contingently true, and hence its truth cannot be demonstrated: no deductively valid argument from necessarily true premises will have P as its conclusion.

However, as David Owen argues, there are good reasons to think that Hume's conception of demonstrative reasoning should not be thought of as a matter of deduction. Instead, he should be seen as offering a 'non-formal' account of demonstration, borrowed – with some modifications – from Locke.[5]

One of Owen's objections to what I shall call the 'deductivist interpretation' is that it fits badly with what Hume says about the nature of the inference from causes to effects: the inference we perform when, for example, on seeing the white make contact with the black, we come to believe that the black will move. One of Hume's central theses, for which he spends a great deal of time arguing and which I shall discuss in more detail in Chapter 3, is that 'no inference from cause to effect amounts to a demonstration' (*T* 650). In this context, Hume cannot mean that there is no valid argument from necessarily true premises whose conclusion is that the effect will occur, since this is a point that nobody disputes: it is not a necessary truth that I had a pain in my toe this morning, or that the black ball moved, and so no deductively valid arguments with such claims as conclusions can have necessarily true premises. So if we are to make sense of Hume's argument here *and* hold on to a deductivist conception of the notion of demonstration, we need to hold that Hume here takes demonstration to be a matter of deductively valid inference *simpliciter* rather than a deductively valid inference from necessarily true premises: a 'demonstration', in the causal case, would be a matter of validly inferring that the effect occurs from just the premise that the cause occurs, where that premise is itself only contingently true.

But we cannot attribute this notion of demonstration across the board to Hume, else he would elsewhere be guilty of what David Stove calls 'an error unbelievably gross and often repeated' (1973: 36). For, according to *this* conception of demonstration, it is perfectly possible to demonstrate the truth of, say, the proposition that the sun will rise tomorrow, contrary to what Hume claims (*E* 25–6): there are plenty of valid arguments with contingently true premises which have that proposition as their conclusion ('today is Thursday and the sun will rise tomorrow, therefore the sun will rise tomorrow', for example). So if we attribute a deductivist conception of demonstration to Hume, we also need to attribute to him a pervasive and apparently unnoticed ambiguity in that conception: he sometimes means 'deductively valid argument with necessarily true premises' and sometimes just 'deductively valid argument'. And it just seems implausible that Hume would have been that careless.

According to the alternative account offered by Owen, the basic units of demonstrative reasoning for Hume are not propositions but ideas; and reasoning itself, whether demonstrative or not, is a matter of comparison of ideas under some relation or other, rather than a matter of uncovering entailment relations between propositions. So, for example, the demonstrability of '4>2' is not a matter of one's being able to deduce '4>2' from necessarily true premises. Instead, it is a matter of directly *intuiting* that the idea of 4 stands in the *greater than* relation to the idea of 2.[6] Similarly, when one intuits that navy is darker than turquoise one simply does so by having those two, non-propositional, ideas before the mind and comparing them under the relation of degree in quality. What is distinctive about class *A* relations is that, at least in simple cases involving just intuition, if one has two ideas before the mind and compares them under a given relation one is *forced* either to place them in that relation or not: one cannot have the idea of 4 and the idea of 2 and, considering the ideas under the relation of proportion in quantity and number, fail to see that the first number is greater than the second.

Such simple cases involve intuition; what about demonstration? Well, demonstration is simply a chain of reasoning such that each step is itself an instance of intuition. For example, to demonstrate that $3^3 + 7 = 34$, I might start out by intuiting that $3 \times 3 = 9$ – that is, by intuiting that the idea of 3^2 and the idea of 9 stand in the relation of equality to one another; then intuit that $3^2 \times 3 = 27$, and then that $3^3 + 7 = 27 + 7$, and then, finally, having run through all these intermediate stages, that $3^3 + 7 = 34$ (see Owen 1999: 94–6).

How does Owen's interpretation solve the problem raised above for the deductivist interpretation? Well, the problem was that, on the one hand, Hume apparently holds that there can in principle be demonstrative *connections* between two matters of fact – else he would not need to argue for the claim that 'no inference from cause to effect amounts to a demonstration'. This pushes the deductivist interpretation towards the view that demonstration is a matter of deductive inference *simpliciter*. On the other hand, he denies that any matter of fact can be *demonstrated*, which pushes the deductivist interpretation towards the view that demonstration is a matter of deductive inference from necessarily true premises. But Owen's interpretation, unlike the deductivist interpretation, can allow Hume to have his cake and eat it too, since on that interpretation two matters of fact *can* stand in intuitive or demonstrative relations to one another, even though no matter of fact can be demonstrated.

To see why, consider the case where one sees four sheep in a field and infers that there are more than two sheep in the field. On Owen's interpretation, there is a demonstrative connection between the two ideas, since we can tell by intuition that the idea of four-sheep-in-a-field stands in the *greater in number than* relation to the idea of two-sheep-in-a-field; and so the inference from there being four sheep in the field to there being more than two sheep in the field 'amounts to a demonstration'. We thus have a relevant contrast to the case of causation, where a demonstrative connection is lacking: we *can* place the idea of a toe stubbing and the idea of pain under the relation of causation, but we can also refrain from doing so. Hence, on stubbing my toe I cannot predict with certainty that pain will follow, because there can be no 'demonstration' that a toe stubbing will cause pain. On the other hand, all this is entirely consistent with the claim that no matter of fact can be demonstrated. The demonstrative connection between the idea of four sheep and the idea of two sheep provides us with a demonstration that four sheep are greater in number than two sheep, but that is no matter of fact: like truths concerning Euclid's triangles, it would still be certain even if there were no sheep in nature at all.

Having argued that Owen's account makes better sense of what Hume says than does the deductivist conception of demonstration, I shall presuppose in what follows that Owen's account is broadly correct, although I shall argue in §2.4 that one element of Owen's account – the claim that intuitively related ideas are not fully distinct – needs to be rejected.

2.3 Demonstration and the genesis of knowledge

Hume's talk of knowledge and certainty might suggest that his main interest is epistemological: in drawing the distinction, in the right place, between what we can *know* to be true, or know with certainty to be true, and what we have less than conclusive reasons (if any) to believe. But I suggest that we should instead take his central concern to be genetic: in *how* it is that we get to believe what we do.[7] Introspection reveals empirical data: our mind is populated with beliefs (amongst other things). As a scientist of the mind, Hume is interested in understanding what these objects are and how the mind comes to be populated with them. We are not born with beliefs already lodged in the mind, so there must be some processes or mechanisms by which they are formed. I shall argue that if Hume really is interested primarily in understanding what these processes or mechanisms are, then there is a decisive reason to prefer Owen's account of demonstration to the deductivist account.

First, however, something needs to be said about Hume's use of the term 'belief'. We can think of (what we would consider to be) beliefs as falling into three broad categories. First, we have those beliefs that are certain. These, for Hume, are items of *knowledge*. Second, we have beliefs that are derived immediately from sensation or memory, such as my current belief that I am sitting in front of my computer and my belief, based on my being able to recollect it, that just now I was upstairs. Hume thinks that impressions of sensation and memory are *themselves* beliefs: 'the *belief* or *assent*, which always attends the memory and senses, is nothing but the vivacity of those perceptions they present. . . . To believe is in this case to feel an immediate impression of the senses, or a repetition of that impression in the memory' (*T* 86). But mostly he just calls impressions 'impressions' and reserves the term 'belief' for the third category of belief (in the usual sense): those that are neither knowledge nor immediately based on impressions, for example my belief that the black ball will move or that the sun will rise tomorrow.

In his discussion of demonstrative reasoning, Hume is interested in the first case: in items of knowledge. Let's suppose that his central concern is indeed genetic. Why does this provide a decisive reason to agree with Owen's central claim – that for Hume demonstration amounts to the grasping of relations between ideas – and to deny that it amounts to reasoning deductively from necessarily true premises?

Well, Hume's discussion of demonstrative reasoning, if it is to serve what I have assumed to be his purposes, must explain how knowledge comes about: it must explain what the mechanism is that produces it. But if his conception of demonstrative reasoning is that of deductively valid reasoning from necessarily true premises, no such explanation is forthcoming. Deductively valid reasoning from necessarily true premises is a process that takes knowledge as input and yields knowledge as output. Understanding that process does not help to explain how knowledge *in general* arises; it only explains how, given that we already have *some* knowledge, we can acquire more of it.

The traditionalist's response, presumably, would be that, at least if we trace the premises back far enough, we will be left with analytic truths: propositions that are true in virtue of meaning. But there is nothing in what Hume says to suggest that this is what he has in mind; indeed his examples of what we are able 'to pronounce at first sight, without any enquiry or reasoning' (*T* 70), are peculiarly resistant to being thought of as cases of analyticity. He says, 'tho'' it be impossible to judge exactly of the degrees of any quality, such as colour, taste, heat, cold, when the difference betwixt them is very small; yet 'tis easy to decide, that any of them is superior or inferior to another, when their difference is considerable' (*ibid.*). I can tell just by inspection of ideas that one colour (the navy I am currently imagining) is darker than another (the turquoise I am imagining). But it is hard to see how we could possibly think of this as an analytic truth, not least because we need not even be capable of attaching words to the relevant ideas in order to be able to tell that one colour is darker than the other.

Or consider the example of degrees in temperature. If we are to be able to 'pronounce at first sight' that the water in one pan (suppose this is at 60°) is hotter than the water in another (suppose this is at 30°) on the grounds that the deductivist interpretation requires, it must be because it is analytically true that 60° is hotter than 30°. Suppose we set aside the obvious problem that we can 'pronounce at first sight, without any enquiry or reasoning', that the water in the first pan is hotter than the water in the second without knowing what the temperature of either pan of water is, and so without having to formulate any analytically true proposition at all. That is, suppose that our ability to 'pronounce at first sight' that the first is hotter than the other really is a matter of its being analytically true that 60° is hotter than 30°. Even so, the deductivist interpretation is in trouble, because it now cannot explain why Hume thinks it makes a difference whether or not the difference between the two degrees of quality – in this case, temperature – is very small. For it is just as much an analytic truth that 30.01° is hotter than 30° as it is that 60° is hotter than 30°.

Jonathan Bennett notes this difficulty, but takes it to be evidence of 'how wildly [Hume] has let the subject change' from his initial concern with deductive inference from necessary truths (Bennett 1971: 259). On Owen's alternative account, however, there is no change of subject here at all. On the contrary: his account attributes to Hume just the explanatory result he needs. Recall that, according to the genetic story, intuition and demonstration ought to be important for Hume because they provide an explanation of how knowledge – one species of what we would think of as belief – comes about. If he is to get that result, he needs to conceive of demonstrative reasoning as a mental process that does not have the very item as input – knowledge – whose genesis he is trying to explain. And such a process is just what Owen's account of intuition and demonstration provides: the input to intuition, and hence to demonstrative reasoning generally, is *mere* ideas (whose origin Hume has already accounted for) – the ideas of 2 and 4, say, or the ideas of navy and turquoise. The output is knowledge of relations *between* ideas: knowledge that 4>2, or that navy is darker than turquoise, or that *this* water is hotter than *that* water. Hume thus has an explanation of how knowledge in general – and not just some particular item of knowledge – comes about: it is the result of a mental process, demonstrative reasoning (or, in basic cases, just intuition), which takes ideas, rather than knowledge, as input. And it delivers *knowledge* as output – not simply ideas but ideas to which we cannot but assent – because we have no choice but to assent to what the process delivers: we cannot imagine, and so cannot assent to, the contrary idea.

All this is important because I shall later claim that Hume's interest in the problem of induction is exactly parallel. There, he wants to explain how *belief* (in his restricted sense) comes about, and his negative discussion of the problem of induction is an attempt to show that the 'solutions' he rejects – claims about the process by which beliefs are acquired – require beliefs as input to the posited process. Such a process might in principle explain how one particular belief arises given other beliefs as input, but it cannot explain how belief *in general* arises, and so the purported explanation cannot be correct.

2.4 Demonstration and deduction

I argued in §2.3 that Owen's account of demonstration, unlike the deductivist account, coheres very well with Hume's genetic agenda. How, starting with a stock of impressions and hence ideas, do we get to *believe* anything (in the broad sense of 'believe')? Hume's account of demonstration provides an answer for a restricted class of cases: those cases where we compare two ideas under a class *A* relation. In such cases, we are compelled either to place the ideas in that relation or not, and we consequently acquire *knowledge* that the relation obtains (or that it does not obtain). Ideas constitute the input to this mental process, and the process itself is constituted by intuition, or by a chain of intuitive steps. Hume's account of causal reasoning will provide an answer in another class of cases.

However, one belief-generating mechanism now seems to have been left out of the story, namely deductive inference. While, as I argued in §2.3, deductive inference is not of central concern for Hume because it cannot generate knowledge *ex nihilo*, it does, nonetheless, generate a certain kind of *a priori* knowledge: knowledge of entailment relations, one might say. I can know *a priori*, for example, that *if* Jane went to Blackpool or Great Yarmouth, and she did not go to Blackpool, *then* she must have gone to Great Yarmouth. Indeed, as Owen points out, Hume himself uses the notion of knowledge in this connection. Hume says:

> There is no object, which implies the existence of any other if we consider these objects in themselves, and never look beyond the ideas which we form of them. Such an inference wou'd amount to knowledge, and wou'd imply the absolute contradiction and impossibility of conceiving any thing different. But as all distinct ideas are separable, 'tis evident there can be no impossibility of that kind.
>
> (*T* 87)

As Owen points out, when Hume says that such an inference would amount to knowledge, he cannot mean that we could (if the first object implied the second) know that the second object exists, since he has already established that *no* belief that something exists amounts to knowledge. According to Owen, what we would come to know is 'something like the following proposition: "Since the first thing is existent, the second thing is existent"' (1999: 82) (or, perhaps better, 'if the first thing exists, then the second thing must exist too').

Deductive inference presents a *prima facie* problem for Owen's interpretation. As we have seen, Owen characterises demonstration as a chain of intuitive steps, where each step is a matter of considering two given ideas under one of the class *A* philosophical relations and intuiting that the two ideas either do or do not stand in that relation. But how, if at all, is deductive inference to fit into that general story?

Owen's treatment of deductive inference in effect makes it count as a species of demonstration. I shall argue in this section, however, that his attempt to subsume deduction under the heading of demonstration leads him to make some claims about the nature of demonstration that fit badly with some aspects of Hume's overall position. In particular, it leads Owen to the conclusion that, for Hume, ideas that are demonstratively or intuitively related are not distinct from one another; and there are good reasons not to attribute this view to Hume. By contrast, I believe it is crucial to understanding what Hume says about causation and causal reasoning that we hold him to the view that ideas related under the class *A* philosophical relations are *distinct* ideas.

Owen characterizes deductive validity (for Hume) as a matter of there being a lack of distinctness between the premises and conclusion of an argument. Take an argument like this:

(A)   (P1)   Thomas is German
       (P2)   Germans are Europeans
       _____

       (C)   Thomas is European

Owen argues that, for Hume, our reasoning from the premises of this argument to its conclusion is a matter of forming a complex idea of (P1) and (P2) – the idea of Thomas' being German, and Germans being Europeans – and thereby being compelled to form the idea of Thomas' being European. And the reason why one is so compelled is that the ideas of being German and being European are 'not entirely distinct' (Owen 1999: 105).

Owen's account of deductive inference raises an interesting issue. As I have already said, we now seem to have *two* routes to *a priori* knowledge. The first is via the comparison of ideas under class A relations: we start out with two ideas, F and G, and, considering them under a given class A relation, we intuit (or reason via a chain of intuitive links) either that the relation obtains or that it does not. We thereby come to know *a priori* either that F bears the relation in question to G or that it does not. The second is via entailment: we hold a certain complex idea in our head (the conjunction of the two premises in argument (A), for example), and we see what (not entirely distinct) idea we are thereby compelled to form. We reason *a priori* from premises to conclusion, and thereby come to know *a priori* that the first idea (the conjunction of the premises) entails the second (the conclusion).

On the face of it, these seem to be two *different* routes to *a priori* knowledge: in the first case, we compare two ideas – ideas that are both already before the mind – under a given philosophical relation, whereas in the second case we start out with *one* (perhaps complex) idea and *infer* some *new* (though not entirely distinct) idea from it. These would seem to be two distinctively different kinds of mental process and to deliver two different kinds of *a priori* knowledge: the first delivers knowledge of class A relations and the second delivers knowledge about how (non-distinct) ideas are *inferentially* related to one another: it delivers knowledge of entailment relations.

This raises a puzzle. Hume appears to hold that all *a priori* knowledge is a matter of demonstrative reasoning. But if that is so, then demonstrative reasoning cannot be restricted to the comparison of ideas under class A relations. There are two reasons why not. First, as we have just seen, there seems to be a difference in the processes by which the relevant items of knowledge are acquired: comparing two ideas that are already before the mind, in the first case, and having one idea before the mind and inferring a second idea from it, in the second case. Second, Hume does not count entailment as a class A relation; indeed, he does not speak about a *relation* between the premises and conclusion of a valid argument at all.

I shall return to the issue of how the puzzle is to be resolved later in this section. First, I shall outline the part of Owen's account of demonstration which, it seems to me, is in a sense an attempt to subsume deductive inference under the category of demonstration.

As Owen points out, Hume sometimes deploys what has become known as the 'Separability Principle'.[8] The Separability Principle states that distinct ideas are separable: we can always imagine one without the other. Given Owen's account of deductive inference, according to which the premises of a valid argument are not entirely distinct from the conclusion, the Separability Principle gives us a straightforward test for whether a given inference is valid or not: if the mark of validity is the lack of distinctness between premises and conclusion, then we can tell whether or not an argument is valid by seeing whether we can imagine the premises being true without thereby imagining the conclusion to be true too. If the premises and conclusion are 'separable' – if we can imagine the premises without imagining the conclusion – then the complex idea formed by conjoining the premises must be distinct from the idea of the conclusion, and hence the argument cannot be valid; whereas if we cannot imagine the premises without imagining the conclusion the two ideas cannot be genuinely distinct, and the argument will be valid.

So far so good. But Owen appears to hold that the Separability Principle can be applied to intuition and demonstration too, in the sense of considering two ideas under a class A relation. He says:

> The crux of [Hume's] account of intuition and demonstration is that four of the seven philosophical relations depend entirely on the ideas and remain invariable as long as the ideas remain the same. But if all ideas are separable, how is it possible for two ideas to be so related that an intuitive or demonstrative connection is possible? To solve this problem, we must understand that Hume limits the scope of the separability claim to distinct ideas: 'where-ever the imagination perceives a difference among ideas, it can easily produce a separation' (T 10). Furthermore, Hume seems to claim 'that this is an evident consequence of the division of ideas into simple and complex' (*ibid.*). At the very least, he is committed to the claim that all simple ideas are distinct, and hence separable: 'all simple ideas may be separated by the imagination' (*ibid.*). This leaves open the possibility that, as in Locke, two ideas may not be entirely distinct if one contains or partially contains the other.
>
> (Owen 1999: 105)

Owen's claim here appears to be that 'intuitive or demonstrative connection is possible' because the ideas that are the object of intuition and demonstration are not, in fact, distinct, and hence not separable: in other words, we can 'intuit' that two ideas, P and Q, are related by a class A relation because in fact the ideas of P

and Q are not really distinct. That this is what he means is confirmed by something he says a couple of pages earlier:

> According to my interpretation of Humean demonstration, the proposition formed by comparing idea [P] with idea [Q] is demonstrable if other ideas can be interposed between them in a chain so that each idea is linked to its neighbour in a way that we can immediately intuit. Furthermore, Hume thinks he has come up with a test that will tell us in advance whether such a chain is possible. If we can conceive of one idea without the other, no such chain is possible, and we know in advance that the proposition formed by comparing the two ideas is not demonstrable.
>
> (Owen 1999: 103)

Unfortunately, however, there are clear counter-examples to Owen's claim that separability provides a test for intuitive or demonstrative connection. Consider the *darker than* relation that we can know by intuition to obtain between navy and turquoise. Colour ideas are most certainly simple ideas for Hume, so they ought to be separable. And so they are: we can easily call to mind the idea of navy without calling to mind the idea of turquoise. So the Separability Principle holds. And yet the connection between the two ideas is an intuitive one. Similarly, I can easily call to mind the idea of 4 without calling to mind the idea of 2; and yet I can know by intuition that 4>2. It seems, then, that we cannot explain the possibility of intuitive or demonstrative connection in these cases by appealing to the lack of distinctness of the ideas whose class A relationships we intuit.

From here on in, I shall generally reserve the term 'demonstrative connection' to characterize relations that can be known *a priori* to obtain between distinct ideas – so there is a demonstrative connection between the idea of 4 and the idea of 2 (namely the *greater than* relation), between the idea of navy and the idea of turquoise, between the ideas of two congruent triangles, and so on. 'Demonstration' and 'demonstrative reasoning' will similarly denote the operation of the mind – intuition, or a chain of intuitive steps – by which we come to know that two ideas are demonstratively connected. This form of reasoning contrasts with deduction: reasoning from premises to conclusion of a valid argument, where the validity of the argument is grounded in the lack of distinctness of the idea of the conjunction of the premises on the one hand and the conclusion on the other. The result of deduction is knowledge of entailment relations: knowledge that if one thing is true, then something else must be true too.

Owen, in effect, attempts to provide a unified account of *a priori* reasoning in general by thinking of both demonstrative reasoning and deduction as deriving their certainty from the lack of distinctness of the objects of reasoning: just as the conclusions of deductive arguments are not distinct from the conjunction of their premises, so the ideas whose relationships we are capable of intuiting are not distinct from one another. But his attempt at unification cannot succeed, because Hume clearly, and apparently sensibly, holds that in at least some cases of intuition and demonstration, the relevant ideas *are* distinct.

Where do we go from here? Well, let's take another look at the problem that Owen's claim about the lack of distinctness of the ideas involved in demonstration was designed to solve: 'if all ideas are separable, how is it possible for two ideas to be so related that an intuitive or demonstrative connection is possible?' (Owen 1999: 105). Owen's solution, as we've just seen, is to claim that, since Hume is only committed to the separability of *distinct* ideas, demonstrative connection is possible precisely because the connected ideas are not distinct.

Is this really a problem for Hume? I suggest that it is not – and so there is no need for Hume to take *any* demonstratively connected ideas to be non-distinct. Consider something Owen says elsewhere: 'The concept of being "intuitively related" can apply only where the two ideas involved are intrinsically related' (1999: 98). Quite so – but the question is whether being 'intrinsically related' needs to be explained in terms of lack of distinctness, and I cannot see any reason why it should. Earlier, I characterized class *A* relations as 'internal' relations: relations whose obtaining depends just on the intrinsic nature of the related objects. And internal relations just *are* relations between distinct objects. That two triangles are congruent, for example, is a fact about two *distinct* triangles; there is no pressure to attempt to explain the obtaining of the relation by claiming that the two triangles are somehow not fully distinct from one another. Similarly, it is just in the nature of navy and turquoise that the first is darker than the second. We do not need to, and Hume does not, explain this fact by appealing to lack of distinctness of the ideas of navy and turquoise; indeed, it is unclear, in both the triangle and colour cases, whether it even makes sense to say that the two ideas are not distinct.

Where does this leave the Separability Principle? Owen holds that the principle provides a test for intuitive or demonstrative connection as well as for deductive validity: 'Hume thinks he has come up with a test that will tell us in advance whether such a chain [of intuitive connections] is possible. If we can conceive of one idea without the other, no such chain is possible, and we know in advance that the proposition formed by comparing the two ideas is not demonstrable' (Owen 1999: 103). However, if, as I have argued, Hume takes intuitively connected ideas to be distinct, the Separability Principle cannot provide a test for intuitive or demonstrative connection. Does this leave Hume without a test for demonstrative connection? Not at all. The appropriate test in the case of intuition and demonstration, I claim, is not separability at all, but rather conceivability. We can know that idea *F* bears the class *A* relation *R* to *G* because we cannot conceive of *F failing* to bear *R* to *G*. And we can perfectly well be unable to conceive that and yet be able to separate the ideas of *a* and *b*. I can call to mind the idea of 4, or navy, or a particular triangle, without calling to mind the idea of 2, or turquoise, or another, congruent, triangle: for each pair of ideas, we can call to mind one without the other. But if we *do* call both ideas to mind and consider them under the relevant relation (*greater than, darker than, congruent with*) we cannot conceive of the relation failing to obtain.

To put it another way, the Separability Principle is a test for the distinctness of ideas, and hence – since the premises and conclusion of a valid argument are not distinct – a test for validity. The principle is simply silent when it comes to demonstrative connections: if we come to know that two ideas are distinct by deploying the Separability Principle, that does not tell us anything at all about whether there are any demonstrative connections between them. If we want to know that, we need to deploy the conceivability test instead: for any given class *A* philosophical relation, we need to see whether we can conceive of the ideas standing, or failing to stand, in that relation.

I want to suggest, then, that Hume at least implicitly recognizes a distinction between demonstration on the one hand and deduction on the other. The distinction has three aspects to it. First, deduction and demonstration are two different kinds of mental process, in the sense that deduction takes us from something already believed or known to something else that we thereby come to believe or know, while reasoning concerning relations of ideas produces knowledge *ex nihilo*. Second, the ideas that constitute the premises of a deductive inference are not distinct from its conclusion, while the ideas that flank a class *A* relation are distinct. Third, the Separability Principle provides the test for the validity of deductive inference – an inference is valid if we cannot form the complex idea of the conjunction of the premises and simultaneously form the idea of the negation of the conclusion – while conceivability provides the test for demonstrative connection: idea *F* stands in demonstrative relation *R* to idea *G* if we cannot conceive *F* failing to stand in relation *R* to *G*.

What this suggestion does not deliver, of course, is a unified account of demonstration and deduction; and this is problematic, not least because Hume only has one term which covers *a priori* reasoning in general, namely 'demonstration'. One might reasonably wonder why Hume does not explicitly mention the distinction I have been pressing if he really is implicitly committed to it. But a plausible reason for this oversight can be given if we focus on Hume's genetic agenda. I argued in §2.3 that Hume's interest in demonstration is a genetic interest: demonstration explains how we can end up with knowledge when we start out just with ideas. This is only true of demonstration in the narrow sense: it is only true of reasoning concerning relations of ideas. In an important sense, deduction lacks that feature. Of course, we can consider a complex idea *F*, figure out that it entails *G*, and thereby come to know *a priori* that *F* entails *G*. But that kind of knowledge isn't, just by itself, very interesting: it's not like knowing some concrete fact, like knowing a mathematical theorem or knowing that navy is darker than turquoise. Still sticking with the *a priori*, deduction only gets to perform any useful function when the input – the premises – is itself already known. (Similarly, a deductive inference with contingent premises only generates

30

belief in a matter of fact if the premises are already believed.) But, from the genetic point of view, that situation is one that Hume has no particular reason to be interested in: a mental process that can only generate substantive knowledge by having knowledge as input cannot help at all in explaining how knowledge arises in the first place.

The claim that Hume is implicitly committed to a distinction between demonstration and deduction also resolves the puzzle identified earlier: if he recognizes no such distinction, why does he not count entailment as just another philosophical relation? With the distinction in place, we can see why he would not: philosophical relations are relations between distinct ideas, and entailment therefore cannot be a philosophical relation.

The reason I have pressed the claim that Hume is implicitly committed to the existence of two distinct mental processes when it comes to reasoning *a priori* – demonstration and deduction – is that I believe it helps to make sense of his views and arguments concerning causal reasoning and the idea of necessary connection. In particular, I shall argue in §4.6 that Hume's famous 'two definitions' of causation – first as a philosophical relation and second as a natural relation – characterize causation in a way that is importantly analogous to the distinction between demonstration and deduction.

This might seem curious; after all, in rejecting the Insight Ideal as it applies to causation – roughly, the claim that we can have *a priori* knowledge about the causal structure of the world – surely Hume severs the link between causation and *a priori* reasoning in general. So how can Hume's conception of causal relations bear any relationship either to deduction or to demonstration? A short answer is that, while Hume denies that inference from causes to effects is deduction, and hence denies that causation is in any sense the same as or analogous to entailment, he still holds that, *qua* natural relation, causation (or at least our idea of it) is intimately connected to the inference we draw from causes to effects. So there is a sense in which the idea of causation is analogous to the idea of entailment, since in each case the idea is intimately connected to the process of inferring one thing from another. But, unlike entailment, causation is also a philosophical relation between distinct ideas: we can consider two distinct, arbitrary ideas and place them in the relation of causation (or not). The mental processes involved in the two cases – inferring effects from causes, and placing two ideas in the relation of causation – are distinctively different processes, just as deduction and demonstration are distinctively different processes. And this is why Hume needs to offer two different 'definitions' of causation.

Before we can begin to understand Hume's views about causation, then, we need to understand how he conceives of causal reasoning: reasoning from causes to effects. In Chapter 3 I shall argue that Hume's famous discussion of what has become known as 'the problem of induction' is best seen as an attempt to explain how causal reasoning in fact takes place. Hume's interest in that issue stems from his genetic agenda: having shown how demonstration can yield knowledge *ex nihilo* – that is, without knowledge as input – he now needs to show how causal reasoning can yield belief *ex nihilo* – that is, without belief as input. The issue Hume is interested in is not whether causal reasoning is justified; it is whether resources he has so far uncovered – impressions, ideas, demonstration and deduction – suffice to explain how belief comes about. His answer, as we shall see, is that they do not.

2.5 Reasoning concerning matters of fact and existence

Hume's central negative claim about intuition and demonstration is that they cannot, just by themselves, generate any knowledge whatsoever about anything outside the mind: 'Though there never were a circle or triangle in nature, the truths demonstrated by Euclid would for ever retain their certainty and evidence' (*E* 25). Similarly, when I know by intuition that navy is darker than turquoise, I am merely inspecting my ideas, and the knowledge thus gained is not knowledge of anything external to myself.

That demonstration cannot generate knowledge of any matter of fact is easily shown, Hume thinks, by the fact that the negation of any matter of fact is always conceivable. For any idea of something outwith the mind existing or obtaining, we can always imagine its failing to exist or obtain:

> The contrary of every matter of fact is still possible; because it can never imply a contradiction, and is conceived by the mind with the same facility and distinctness, as if ever so conformable to reality. *That the sun will not rise to-morrow* is no less intelligible a proposition, and implies no more contradiction, than the affirmation, *that it will rise.* We should in vain, therefore, attempt to demonstrate its falsehood. Were it demonstratively false, it would imply a contradiction, and could never be distinctly conceived by the mind.
>
> (*E* 25–6)

Given this, Hume now has to explain how it is that, for any given belief, *P*, concerning some matter of fact, we come to believe *P* rather than not-*P*, given that both are equally conceivable.

It is worth briefly contrasting Hume's approach to the issue with Descartes' approach in the *Meditations*. Descartes starts out with the 'method of doubt', showing that all his beliefs that are based on sense experience are dubitable. He then attempts, via *a priori* reasoning, to show how in fact reasonable belief about the external world is possible. Roughly, he proves that God exists, and argues that it is impossible, given God's benevolence, for us to be radically deceived about the nature of the world: it is impossible for our intellectual nature to be radically distorted, and so it is impossible for all or most of our empirical beliefs to be false. He then argues that *particular* empirical beliefs will be reasonable so long as we do not treat the deliverances of the senses 'as though they were absolute rules by which I might immediately determine the essence of the bodies which are outside me' (Descartes 1641: 194), for example by concluding that there are properties of objects which resemble the ideas of colours and heat.

There are three crucial aspects of Descartes' method that are starkly opposed to Hume's. First, Descartes' interest is overtly epistemological rather than genetic: Descartes is interested in the *justification* of empirical beliefs, not in how or why we come to *have* them. He does not hold that the method of destruction and reconstruction of belief pursued in the *Meditations* is one by means of which we do, in fact, come to have empirical beliefs; nor is he recommending that we *ought* to follow that method in order to acquire those beliefs. We do not need to go through the process of radical sceptical doubt and subsequent reconstruction of our beliefs in order to end up with justified beliefs about the world; rather, the fact that we *could* follow that method – that the method exists, and that by reading the *Meditations* we understand how and why it works – shows that at least some of our actual beliefs are justified. Hume, by contrast, as I have said, is primarily interested in the genetic question: how do we get to have our empirical beliefs in the first place?

Second, Descartes starts out with radical sceptical doubt, whereas Hume only deals with scepticism at the end of his investigation of human understanding: in the final part of Book I of the *Treatise* and in the final section of the first *Enquiry*. Hume's genetic interest explains this reversal: from a genetic point of view, scepticism would only need to be dealt with at an early stage if it somehow threatened to affect our ability to *form* beliefs rather than just their justificatory status. But scepticism poses no such threat: most people are not even aware of sceptical problems, and even those who are, and who hold that sceptical arguments cannot be refuted, quickly lapse back into believing more or less what the rest of us believe, despite the alleged lack of justification for those beliefs. As Hume puts it:

> And though a Pyrrhonian [sceptic] may throw himself or others into a momentary amazement and confusion by his profound reasonings; the first and most trivial event in life will put to flight all his doubts and scruples, and leave him the same, in every point of action and speculation, with the philosophers of every other sect, or with those who never concerned themselves in any philosophical researches.
>
> (*E* 160)

Finally, Descartes attempts to establish that empirical beliefs are justified by employing arguments based on the evidence of the senses together with premises that are allegedly knowable *a priori*. The genetic version of that procedure would be to show that empirical beliefs are *in fact* generated by means of *a priori* reasoning from the evidence of the senses together with premises that are themselves knowable *a priori*. In effect, as we shall see, part of the point of Hume's negative discussion of the problem of induction is to show that this cannot be how we acquire empirical beliefs.

Considered as a genetic issue, then, Hume needs to discover the sources of belief about matters of fact and existence. In fact, as we saw in §2.3, he restricts 'belief' to what is not present to the senses, with what *is* present to the senses (or memory) being a matter of impressions. And he gives, in the very early stages of the *Treatise*, an answer to the question 'how do we get to have impressions of sensation?' His answer is simply that he does not know – they arise 'in the soul originally, from unknown causes' (*T* 7) – and that is more or less all he has to say on the matter until he comes to discussing scepticism much later on.

That leaves us with beliefs, in Hume's restricted sense: my beliefs about what is going on right now anywhere outside this room, about the future, and about past events that I have not directly experienced. Beliefs must arise via some kind of mental mechanism or mechanisms. What are these mechanisms and how do they operate? Well, Hume claims that all 'reasonings concerning matter of fact seem to be founded on the relation of *Cause and Effect*. By means of that relation alone we can go beyond the evidence of our memory and senses' (*E* 26). So in fact Hume thinks that there is only one mechanism whose operation he needs to understand if he is to account for how we get to have beliefs.

In the *Enquiry*, Hume justifies this claim by giving a few examples; for instance, on hearing 'an articulate voice and rational discourse in the dark' we are assured of the presence of a person. 'Why? Because these are the effects of the human make and fabric, and closely connected with it' (*E* 27). In the *Treatise*, his approach is rather more methodical. Having identified the seven philosophical relations, which are supposed to be an exhaustive list of all the relations which two ideas can bear to one another, and having shown that four of them – the class *A* relations – 'depend entirely on the ideas, which we compare together', he is left with just the three class *B* relations: relations of time and place, identity and causation. And he proceeds to show that, of those three, only in the case of causation can the mind 'go beyond what is immediately present to the senses, either to discover the real existence or the relations of objects' (*T* 73). For example, while I can discover that Jim and Jonny are next to each other just by observing them – when both are immediately present to my senses – I will only come to hold that they are together in cases where they are *not* both present to my senses by assuming some sort of causal story about them (for example by holding that they cannot bear to be apart, or that they will both keep their promise to meet in the restaurant this evening). Similarly, the judgement that the computer I am currently observing is the very same one that was here yesterday does not arise simply by my noting their similarity, but by my assuming a causal story to the effect that the computer that was here yesterday has not been removed and replaced by a similar one. Thus it is 'only *causation*, which produces such a connexion, as to give us assurance from the existence or action of one object, that 'twas follow'd or preceded by any other existence or action' (*T* 73–4).

For Hume, then, reasoning concerning matters of fact and existence is *causal* reasoning: reasoning from causes to effects, or vice versa. The next step in his explanatory project is thus to consider how such reasoning in fact proceeds: how it is that we start out with the impression of a cause and end up with the belief that a particular effect will occur.[9] I describe how Hume pursues that project in Chapter 3.

3

CAUSAL REASONING AND THE GENESIS OF BELIEF

Hume is traditionally credited both with discovering the problem of induction and with providing a pretty convincing case for holding that the problem has no solution. In this chapter I argue that Hume is not actually interested in that problem. Indeed, his own conception of reasoning concerning matters of fact does not even fit the standard model of inductive inference, since it is not reasoning from observed to unobserved *regularities* but rather reasoning from causes to effects. And his account of that reasoning – causal reasoning – is not intended to show that it is unjustified or in any way defective (except of course in the sense that it is fallible; but that is not a controversial claim). On the contrary: Hume actually takes it for granted that causal reasoning is a 'just' form of reasoning.

In §3.1 I briefly describe the problem of induction as ordinarily understood and in §3.2 I give some general reasons to think that it is not Hume's problem. In §3.3 I introduce the context of Hume's discussion of causal reasoning in the *Treatise*: his need to 'beat about of all the neighbouring fields' in order to locate the elusive impression-source of the idea of necessary connection. Then §3.4, §3.5 and §3.6 are devoted to Hume's negative discussion of causal reasoning: his rejection of various models of causal reasoning that would render it a species of *a priori* reasoning. In §3.7 I present Hume's own account and in §3.8 I argue that according to that account causal reasoning differs from inductive inference as standardly conceived. Finally, in §3.9, I discuss Hume's attitude towards the issue of whether or how causal reasoning is justified.

3.1 The traditional problem of induction

Inductive inference is that form of inference which takes us from the observed to the unobserved. We rely on inductive inference all the time: from the fact that bread has always nourished in the past, I infer that the sandwich I am thinking of eating will nourish rather than poison me, and so I eat it. From the fact that the impact of a white ball, from a given direction, on a black ball has generally been followed by the black's moving in a certain direction, I infer, on observing the white moving towards the black, that the same thing will happen this time, rather than the black moving in a different direction or staying where it is or rising up into the air or exploding. Such inferences underlie both our claims to know, or be justified in believing, the claims of science and also our ability to survive in our everyday lives: to avoid injury by staying away from speeding cars, dangerous dogs and hot fires, and to eat, drink and walk around without worrying about the possibility that there's a lion around the next corner or that the pavement will open up and swallow us or that our dinner will inexplicably kill us.

In order for the beliefs that underlie such behaviour to count as rational, and in order for the claims of science to be justified, the form of inference that generates those beliefs – induction – must itself be rationally justified. But what justificatory story can we tell? Why, that is, are we justified in believing that past observed regularities will persist – for ever, or even in the next case?

The problem of induction starts out from the obvious fact that 'all observed *A*s have been followed by *B*s' does not entail that the next *A* will similarly be followed by a *B*: it is perfectly possible that all observed *A*s have been followed by *B*s and yet the next observed *A* fails to be followed by a *B*. The truth of the premise does not guarantee the truth of the conclusion; so what, if anything, gives us any reason *at all* to think that the conclusion is true?

The inductive sceptic maintains that, in the absence of a good, non-question-begging answer to that question, any belief about the unobserved is just as irrational as any other. The problem of induction, in essence, is the problem that whatever answer we try to give to that question will beg the question against the inductive sceptic. Suppose, for example, that we say that the inductive inference from past regularity to future regularity is justified because inductive inferences are generally reliable: they do not *guarantee* the truth of the conclusion, but, by and large, if we are careful, the conclusions of inductive arguments turn out to be true. But what is the justification for holding that inductive inferences are in general reliable? Only that they have been reliable in the past. So the claim that inductive inferences are in general reliable can only be established by appealing to induction – to get us from 'inductive inferences have been reliable in the past' to 'inductive inferences will be reliable in the future' – and hence our attempted solution to the problem presupposes what it is supposed to show.

Rather than try to show that a special kind of inference – induction – is justified, we might alternatively attempt to argue that 'inductive' arguments are in fact *de*ductive arguments with an implicit premise: 'the unobserved resembles the observed', for example. In that case, the *inference* from premises to conclusion is deductive, and hence justified. But now we need to ask what reason we have to suppose that our additional premise is true. And, again, it will turn out that in order to establish the truth of the additional premise we need to use inductive inference. For our evidence for 'the unobserved resembles the observed' is just that *in the past* the unobserved has resembled the observed. So we have no reason to suppose that our additional premise is true unless we *already* have a reason to believe the conclusions of inductive arguments – which is just what adding the premise was supposed to achieve.

If no non-question-begging justificatory story can be told for inductive infer-ence, the inevitable result appears to be that the inductive sceptic is right: no belief about the unobserved is more rational, or better justified, than any other. Arriving at a belief via inductive inference is no more rational than is employing guesswork or counter-induction or consulting the stars.

3.2 Is the problem of induction Hume's problem?

What does all this have to do with Hume? Well, it is undeniable that the main elements of the problem of induction are all to be found in Hume's discussion of reasoning concerning matters of fact in both the *Treatise* (*T* 86–94) and the *Enquiry* (*E* 25–39). But to characterize Hume as presenting roughly the argument just sketched is to misunderstand what he is doing in two important respects.

First, the account of the problem of induction sketched above makes no mention whatsoever of causation. This omission is widespread in discussions of the traditional problem of induction;[1] but, whatever the merits of that approach, it is certainly not Hume's. He says that it is 'only *causation*, which produces such a connexion, as to give us assurance from the existence or action of one object, that 'twas follow'd or preceded by any other existence or action' (*T* 73–4). It would be curious, to say the least, if he then went on to assume that such 'assurance' – if any assurance is to be had – in fact has nothing to do with causation at all.

In fact, Hume does not even use expressions like 'induction' or 'inductive inference': for him, the inference in question is explicitly inference *from* causes *to* effects. I shall call this 'causal reasoning' rather than 'inductive reasoning' or 'inductive inference' because, as I shall argue in §3.8, I do not think that what Hume thinks of as causal reasoning *is* inductive inference. This is not simply because causal reasoning (somehow or other) involves causation, while inductive inference, as traditionally conceived, does not. It is also because causal reasoning, in Hume's sense, is not reasoning from past regularities at all: 'all observed *C*s have been followed by *E*s' does not feature as a *premise* in a particular inference from *c* to *e* – or at least not in the cases in which Hume is most interested. The inference from cause to effect – from *c* to *e* – can only be accomplished if *in fact* all observed *C*s have been *E*s; but, so I shall argue, Hume does not take this fact to feature as an additional premise.

Second, characterizing Hume as primarily interested in the problem of induction casts him as primarily interested in the issue of the *justification* of beliefs about matters of fact, whereas in fact he is best seen as interested in explaining how we come to have those beliefs. This latter view of Hume is not new; it is to be found in a number of recent discussions.[2] But it is worth making the case one more time.

Suppose for the sake of the argument, then, that Hume's interest in causal reasoning *is* primarily an interest in justification or rationality. Then, given the alleged importance of the problem of induction – it threatens to undermine the rationality of all our empirical beliefs except those based on immediate experience – we would expect him either to offer a solution to the problem which is plausible by his own lights or else to hold that the problem cannot be solved and hence to be an inductive sceptic. Unfortunately, Hume does not follow either of these paths.

Let's start with the first alternative. Hume's positive account of causal reasoning is a genetic account: an account of the mental mechanism that generates beliefs about matters of fact. He claims that when we have observed past *A*s to be followed by *B*s, on observing a new *A* we come to believe that it will be followed by a *B* merely by custom or habit, rather than by *a priori* reasoning. It would be absurd to suggest that Hume might have thought that this genetic account, just by itself, constituted a solution to the problem of induction: to say that we engage in causal reasoning out of brute habit cannot, by anybody's lights, be construed as a reasonable attempt to show that such reasoning is justified.

Still, Hume does do more than this, at least in the *Enquiry*. He says, for example:

> Had not the presence of an object instantly excited the idea of those objects, commonly conjoined with it, all our knowledge must have been limited to the narrow sphere of our memory and senses; and we should never have been able to adjust means to ends, or employ our natural powers, either to the producing of good, or avoiding of evil.
>
> (*E* 55)

And on the same page:

> As nature has taught us the use of our limbs, without giving us the knowledge of the muscles and nerves, by which they are actuated; so has she implanted in us an instinct, which carries forward the thought in a correspondent course to that which she has established among external objects.
>
> (*E* 55)

One could take these remarks to point towards a reliabilist justification of causal reasoning. Causal reasoning is justified because it *works*: it generates beliefs that correspond to nature's regularities.

I think Hume does intend the reliability of causal reasoning to count as a kind of justification. I shall return to this in §3.8, but what is important for present purposes is that Hume cannot sensibly take its reliability to count as a justification of causal reasoning in the context of attempting to solve the *problem* of induction. The challenge of the problem of induction is to provide a non-question-begging justification for inductive inference. So if Hume is to be taken to be providing a solution to the problem, he must take himself to be providing a non-question-begging justification of inductive inference (or, rather, of causal reasoning). But the fact that the alleged solution currently on the table is question-begging could not possibly have escaped Hume's notice: it could not have escaped his notice that, in the absence of a prior justification for induction, the past reliability of induction gives us no reason whatever to suppose that induction will continue to carry forward our thought in a way that corresponds to the course of nature.

Hume is more usually held *not* to be offering a solution to the problem of induction; rather, he is held to be adopting the strategy 'explain where you can't justify' (Howson 2000: 20). If that is so, then Hume's positive claims about the nature of causal reasoning are not intended to be a *solution* to the problem of induction, and so Hume must be an inductive sceptic. This is our second alternative if we assume that his interest in causal reasoning is primarily an interest in justification or rationality.

There is certainly one reason why it is tempting to cast Hume as an inductive sceptic: he says that we are not 'determin'd by reason' to infer effects from causes (*T* 88), that there is 'no reason to determine us to that transition' (*T* 92), and so on. If he is not an inductive sceptic, what could Hume possibly mean here? What exactly is he denying? Without a plausible answer to that question, perhaps we ought to think that Hume really is an inductive sceptic. Fortunately, some plausible answers are available. One (borrowed from Owen 1999: ch. 6) is that Hume is denying that inference from causes to effects is the product of the *faculty* of reason – the faculty which generates knowledge in the ways described in Chapter 2. 'Reason' here contrasts with the imagination, which is the faculty that produces inference from causes to effects. And Owen's is by no means the only possible answer. Garrett argues that Hume uses 'reason', as a noun, 'quite univocally to refer to the inferential faculty – a faculty that produces two kinds of arguments, demonstrative and probable' (1997: 94). On Garrett's interpretation, Hume's claim that such reasoning is 'not produced by reason' is to be read as saying that we do not engage in it 'as a result of any piece of reasoning *about* it' (*ibid.*)[3] This is a controversy I shall avoid; my point here is simply that Hume's remarks about our not being 'determin'd by reason' to infer from causes to effects are perfectly consistent with the claim that he is no inductive sceptic. And it is worth noting that Hume never claims that causal reasoning is unjustified or irrational or unwarranted.

There are also many positive reasons to think that Hume is not an inductive sceptic. Perhaps the most decisive reason is that he describes the project of the *Treatise* and the *Enquiry* as a science of man. 'And as the science of man is the only solid foundation for the other sciences', he says, 'so the only solid foundation we can give to this science itself must be laid on experience and observation' (*T* xvi). It would be very peculiar indeed for Hume to write this knowing full well that within a hundred pages or so he would be concluding that experience and observation do not, in fact, provide a solid foundation at all (see Owen 1999: 146; Baier 1991: 55). Moreover, Hume's opposition to the Insight Ideal – to the claim that our epistemic access to the world bears some resemblance to God's, and so we can in principle have *a priori* knowledge of its causal structure – does not require that he adopt a sceptical position on induction. He needs only to establish that – as he famously puts it – '[i]f we reason *a priori*, anything may appear able to produce anything' (*E* 164). The stronger claim, that we have no reason whatever to believe that one effect rather than another will occur given the occurrence of the cause, is, from the point of view of Hume's opposition to the Insight Ideal, completely unnecessary.

Second, in his discussion of 'probability' (*T* 124–55; *E* 56–9) Hume distinguishes between 'proof' and 'probability', where proofs are 'such arguments from experience as leave no room for doubt or opposition' (*E* 56*n*.), or 'those arguments, which are deriv'd from the relation of cause and effect, and which are entirely free from doubt and uncertainty' (*T* 124). And he tells us that a 'wise man . . . proportions his belief to the evidence. In such conclusions as are founded on an infallible experience, he expects the event with the last degree of assurance, and regards his past experience as a full *proof* of the future existence of that event' (*E* 110). All this is pretty obviously in serious tension with the claim that Hume is an inductive sceptic.

A third reason to think that Hume is not an inductive sceptic comes from his view of the intimate relationship between inference from the observed to the unobserved, on the one hand, and causation, on the other: we are inclined to infer *e* from *c* just when we think of *c* and *e* as cause and effect. Hence, if he is a sceptic about causal reasoning he must be a sceptic about causation too. It would make no sense for him to hold that causal reasoning is unjustified and yet hold that the corresponding causal claims *are* justified, for to say that we are never justified in inferring effects from causes just *is* to say that we are never justified in thinking that the relevant events are causally related: it would make no sense for Hume to think that we can be perfectly justified in thinking that *c* causes *e* and yet not be justified in *inferring e* from *c*. But he displays no scepticism whatever when it comes to causation: he does not so much as mention explicitly the sceptical possibility that, by and large, our causal judgements are false (though see §5.3 and §7.1).

Indeed, in the *Treatise* Hume even provides 'rules by which to judge of causes and effects' (*T* 173–6): in effect, his version of the logic of scientific discovery. The rules are as follows:

1   The cause and effect must be contiguous in space and time.
2   The cause must be prior to the effect.
3   Cause and effect must be constantly conjoined.
4   The same cause always produces the same effect, and the same effect never arises but from the same cause.
5   Where several different objects produce the same effect, it must be by means of some quality which we discover to be common amongst them.
6   The difference in the effects of two resembling objects must proceed from that particular in which they differ.

7   If an effect increases or diminishes according to increase or diminution in the cause, we should regard the effect as a compound effect, each part of which arises from some part of the cause.[4]

8   If an object exists unchanged for a period of time without causing its effect, then it is not the sole cause of that effect; there must be an additional cause which is contiguous with the effect.

Some of these rules – specifically the first four – might be thought to be merely analytic truths (if we take Hume to hold that causation is *defined* in terms of constant conjunction, priority and contiguity). Even if that is right, it is hard to see why, as a sceptic about causation, he would restate the definition in the form of *rules* which we ought to follow in forming our causal judgements. In particular, as an inductive sceptic Hume would hold that we are *never* in a position reasonably to believe the constant conjunction requirement to be met, and so we are never in a position to meet the requirements of the rules by which to judge of causes and effects. So it is not clear why he would even bother to state them. Similarly, rules 5–8 all take for granted that the 'effect' in question really is an effect, rather than merely an uncaused event. If Hume were a sceptic about causation we would never have reason to think that the effect in question really *is* an effect, and so, again, we would never be in a position to apply the rules.

One might object to all this by appealing to the fact that Hume holds that causal reasoning is an 'instinct' that nature has 'implanted in us' (*E* 55). Whether or not Hume thinks that it is an instinct that can seriously be suppressed or over-ridden is a contentious issue; but suppose for the sake of the argument that he holds that it cannot be suppressed. Then one might argue that Hume is not bothered by scepticism about causation simply because he holds that it is psycho-logically impossible seriously to doubt that the regular course of nature will change or disintegrate, and hence psychologically impossible seriously to doubt that our causal judgements are, by and large, true – even if we recognize that such judgements are unjustified.

Even if we accept this explanation for Hume's lack of interest in the sceptical possibility that our causal judgements are mostly false, it will not do as an expla-nation for why he thinks it is appropriate to provide 'rules by which to judge of causes and effects'. For suppose we accept that our causal judgements are arrived at by blind instinct which confers no justification on those judgements. Why, in that case, should we be at all interested in the niceties of scientific methodology? Why, for example, when confronted with apparently resembling objects of kind *A* which have different effects (sometimes *E*s, sometimes *F*s), should we seek out some hidden difference in those objects (so that they divide into kinds *B* and *C*) which explains their different effects, so that we end up judging that *B*s cause *E*s and *C*s cause *F*s (rule 5)? If we do this, we will start out with no concrete judge-ments about the causal powers of *A*s, and end up with the judgement that *B*s cause *E*s and *C*s cause *F*s. But we might just as well have remained satisfied with the first situation if there is no sense in which the second situation is genuinely preferable to the first. We *can* help whether or not we judge that *B*s cause *E*s, because we can choose not to engage in the kind of scientific investigation that will result in our coming to make that judgement. Hume's rules appear to tell us that we *should* seek out hidden causes; but if he is an inductive, and hence causal, sceptic the rules lack any normative force: no purpose is served by acquiring more, or more refined, causal beliefs.

Thus there are good reasons, external to what Hume actually says in the passages in which he is traditionally thought to be raising the problem of induction, to think that this is not the problem he is raising at all. If he was interested in the problem of induction, he would surely either attempt to solve it or adopt a sceptical position with regard to causation, and, as we have seen, he does neither.

3.3 The explanation of belief in matters of fact

If Hume isn't raising the traditional problem of induction, what problem *is* he raising? The answer to that question was already suggested in §2.5. What Hume is interested in is how we get to have beliefs at all. He has already explained how we get to have *knowledge*, and he has also claimed that only causation 'gives us assurance from the existence or action of one object, that 'twas follow'd or preceded by any other existence or action' (*T* 73–4). So now he needs to discover how it is that we reason from causes to effects, since such a discovery promises to deliver an answer to the question of how we get to have beliefs about matters of fact: that the sun will rise tomorrow, that my dinner will not poison me, and so on.

In the *Treatise*, Hume begins this project by investigating causation as a philosophical relation: as a relation in which we might or might not 'place' two ideas in the mind. And he starts that investigation by examining the *idea* of causation (*qua* philosophical relation) and seeing 'from what origin it is derived. 'Tis impossible to reason justly, without understanding perfectly the idea concerning which we reason; and 'tis impossible perfectly to understand any idea, without tracing it up to its origin, and examining that primary impression from which it arises' (*T* 74–5).

He continues: 'Let us therefore cast our eye on any two objects, which we call cause and effect, and turn them on all sides, in order to find that impression, which produces an idea of such prodigious consequence' (*T* 75). This preliminary investigation reveals that 'whatever objects are consider'd as causes and effects are *contiguous*' (*ibid.*) and are also such that the cause is temporally prior to the effect. So far so good. But contiguity and priority cannot be all there is to the idea of causation, since manifestly two events can stand in those relations without the first being a cause of the second. In addition, 'there is NECESSARY CONNEXION to be taken into consideration' (*T* 77). Unfortunately, however, Hume cannot at this stage find any impression-source for *that* idea either in the 'known qualities' of objects or in the relations they bear to one another. In other words, it appears that no impression of necessary connection is revealed by our sensory inspection of causally related objects or events.

Hume therefore proposes to 'proceed like those, who being in search of any thing, that lies conceal'd from them, and not finding it in the place they expected, beat about all the neighbouring fields, without any certain view or design, in hopes their good fortune will at last guide them to what they search for'. (T 77–8). The first such neighbouring field, which I shall skip over, is the question of why we hold that every event must have a cause. The second is this: 'Why we conclude, that such particular causes must *necessarily* have such particular effects; and what is the nature of that *inference* we draw from the one to the other, and of the *belief* we repose in it? (T 78).

This second neighbouring field contains three distinct questions, and it is important to keep the first two separate in order to see clearly where Hume is taking us. It is very natural to think that an answer to the first question (why do we conclude that a given cause must necessarily have a given effect?) will provide the answer to the second (what is the nature of the inference from causes to effects?): we start out by ascertaining what the circumstances are in which we judge that a given cause must have a given effect, and, armed with that information, we will be able to use it in explaining causal reasoning – that is, explaining how it is that we infer effects from causes. After all, once we have established that c must cause e, inferring e from c looks to be a trivial matter of deduction: if c occurs and c is guaranteed to cause e, then it just follows that e will occur.

Hume, however, is going to argue that the explanatory order is in fact the other way around: we are only capable of coming to think that c is a cause of e *because* we employ causal reasoning. In other words, causal reasoning is explanatorily prior to our coming to think of events as necessarily connected to one another. This being so, Hume's positive explanatory project requires him to investigate the nature of causal reasoning *before* looking for the impression-source of the idea of necessary connection, since that impression-source is to be found in the inference from causes to effects.

Of course, Hume cannot simply give his positive account of the nature of causal reasoning straight off. If he is successfully to refute the Insight Ideal – the thought that reasoning from causes to effects is *a priori* reasoning, and hence *a priori* knowledge of the causal structure of the world is possible for us, just as it is for God – he needs to do so directly, rather than simply stating his own, rival view.

Hume's basic argument goes roughly like this:

1 The inference from causes to effects is not a matter of *a priori* reasoning from the cause, just by itself, to the effect. We need to have experience of past constant conjunction of events similar to the cause with events similar to the effect before we are able to infer the effect from the cause.

2 We cannot know *a priori* (that is, by demonstration) that unobserved instances resemble observed instances (the 'Uniformity Principle'). Nor can we come to *believe* the Uniformity Principle without employing causal reasoning – the very reasoning whose nature we are attempting to discover.

So causal reasoning cannot proceed by deductive inference from the cause, together with the Uniformity Principle, to the effect.

3   Nor can the inference proceed from the premise that the cause has a 'secret power' to produce the effect, since that premise presupposes that the cause has the same secret powers as were possessed by previously experienced events which superficially resemble the cause, and hence presupposes the Uniformity Principle, which, again, we can only come to believe by employing the very reasoning whose nature we are attempting to discover.

I shall take the three arguments in turn in §3.4, §3.5 and §3.6, returning to Hume's positive claims about the nature of the inference from causes to effects in §3.7.

3.4 Reasoning without the aid of experience

Hume's first target is the thesis that effects can be inferred *a priori* from causes just by themselves: all the resources I need in order to generate the inference from the cause, c, to the effect, e, is the impression of c, together with the belief-generating mechanisms that are already well understood, namely demonstration and deduction. Thus Hobbes, for instance, says:

> [A] CAUSE simply, or *an entire cause, is the aggregate of all the accidents both of the agents how many so ever they be, and of the patients, put together; which when they are all supposed to be present, it cannot be understood but that the effect is produced at the same instant; and if any one of them be wanting, it cannot be understood but that the effect is not produced.*
>
> (Hobbes 1656: 121–2)

Recall the distinction made in §2.4 between demonstration – coming to know *a priori* something that involves two distinct ideas and a class A relation (4>2; navy is darker than turquoise) – and deduction, which is a matter of taking an idea or collection of ideas which are already beliefs (or knowledge) and inferring something that is not distinct from the idea or collection of ideas from which it is inferred (Thomas is German, Germans are Europeans, so Thomas is European). In the *Enquiry*, I shall argue, Hume considers separately both possible routes to the belief that e occurs; and this gives some plausibility to the claim that he is committed to the distinction just described.

Let's start, as Hume does, with the deductive route. The claim that he aims to refute is the claim that I can infer e from c just by 'penetrating into the essence' of c: as Hume puts it, I can 'find' or 'discover' the effect *in* the cause (*E* 29). Call this view *PE* (for 'penetration into essences').

Recall that, according to Owen's interpretation of Hume's account of deductive inference, validity is a matter of an argument's content rather than its logical form: it is a matter of the lack of distinctness between the complex idea of the premises and the complex idea of the conclusion, so that one cannot form the first idea without thereby forming the second too. Also, according to Hume, 'the belief of the existence [of an object] joins no new ideas to those, which compose the idea of the object. When I think of God ... and when I believe him to be existent, my idea of him neither encreases nor diminishes' (*T* 94). Belief amounts simply to the idea of an object or event having 'an additional force and vivacity' (*T* 96). Given all this, *PE* amounts to the claim that we can deduce *e* from *c* because the idea of *c* somehow *contains* the idea of *e*. Hence the *impression* of *c* delivers all that is needed for me to be able to infer that *e* will occur – that is, to come to believe in *e*. Of course, strictly speaking the inference in question doesn't look much like (putative) deduction in the ordinary sense. But the important point is that deduction in this sense is inference from one (complex) idea to another idea – and we can tell that the first idea entails the second by appealing to the Separability Principle.

According to *PE*, then, given Hume's conception of deduction, the inference in question is simply the inference from *c* to *e*. However it will be more illuminating to put it into the form of an argument, like so ('APE', for 'argument from penetration into essences'):

(APE) (P1)   *c* occurs
       (P2)   *c*'s essence is such that it is guaranteed to produce *e*
       _____
       (C)   *e* occurs

The idea would be that a sensory impression of *c* can deliver both premises, and the conclusion is thus entailed by what is revealed by the impression. So our ability to infer (C) from (P1) and (P2) deductively does not involve forming a complex idea of the conjunction of (P1) and (P2); (P1) and (P2) are rather already implicit, as it were, in the impression of *c*. (APE) constitutes one possible explanation of how the belief that *e* will occur comes about – and an explanation that meets Hume's requirements in the sense that it appeals only to items that are already satisfactorily understood: the input is sensory impressions, and the mechanism is deduction.

Notice that necessity-related notions are used three times in (APE). First, there is the connection between the premises and the conclusion (entailment); second, there is the 'production' of *e* by *c*; and, third, there is the guarantee that *e* will be produced. (APE) thus manifests, in a vivid way, the thought that causal relations are analogous to entailment relations: the production of *e* by *c* mirrors the *a priori* inference from *c* to *e*. However, it is the *guarantee* that is, as it were, doing the serious work: it is by grasping that guarantee – something residing wholly in the nature of *c* – that we allegedly manage to perform the inference.

Hume's argument against *PE* is short and sweet:

> Let an object be presented to a man of ever so strong natural reason
> and abilities; if that object be entirely new to him, he will not be able,

by the most accurate examination of its sensible qualities, to discover
any of its causes or effects. Adam, though his rational faculties be
supposed, at the very first, entirely perfect, could not have inferred from
the fluidity and transparency of water that it would suffocate him, or
from the light and warmth of fire that it would consume him. No object
ever discovers, by the qualities which appear to the senses, either the
causes which produced it, or the effects which will arise from it; nor can
our reason, unassisted by experience, ever draw any inference
concerning real existence and matter of fact.

(*E* 27)

The argument is simple. If inference from causes to effects proceeded according
to (APE), we would be able to infer the effect from the cause the very first time
we were presented with the cause. But manifestly we can't do this. No matter
how closely we attend to the sensory qualities of the cause, we cannot 'discover'
the effect. So the appearance of the idea of *e* in the mind cannot be due to its
somehow being included in, and hence inferred from, the idea of *c*. And the
reason is that the ideas of *c* and *e* are distinct:

Were any object presented to us, and were we required to pronounce
concerning the effect, which will result from it, without consulting past
observation; after what manner, I beseech you, must the mind proceed
in this operation? It must invent or imagine some event, which it
ascribes to the object as its effect; and it is plain that this invention must
be entirely arbitrary. The mind can never possibly find the effect in the
supposed cause, by the most accurate scrutiny and examination. For
the effect is totally different from the cause, and consequently can never
be discovered in it. Motion in the second Billiard-ball is a quite distinct
event from motion in the first; nor is there anything in the one to
suggest the smallest hint of the other.

(*E* 29)

So much for *PE*. But there is another possibility that Hume goes on to consider
in the *Enquiry*. Having established that the 'invention' that the mind 'ascribes to
the object as its effect' must be 'entirely arbitrary' because the ideas of the cause
and the effect are distinct, he continues:

And as the first imagination or invention of a particular effect, in all
natural operations, is arbitrary, where we consult not experience; so must
we also esteem the supposed tie or connexion between the cause and
effect, which binds them together, and renders it impossible that any
other effect could result from the operation of that cause. When I see,
for instance, a Billiard-ball moving in a straight line towards another;
even suppose motion in the second ball should by accident be suggested

47

to me, as the result of their contact or impulse; may I not conceive, that a hundred different events might as well follow from that cause?

(*E* 29)

The argument here seems to go like this. The distinctness of the ideas of *c* and *e* guarantees that the idea of *e* cannot arise via deduction just from penetration into the essence of *c*, since the effect is not in fact 'discoverable' in the cause. But the distinctness of those ideas *also* rules out the possibility that, on first observing *c*, we could somehow come to believe that there is a necessary connection between *c* and *e*: distinct ideas are separable, and their separability – our ability to imagine *c* occurring without *e* – guarantees that we are unable (at least without the aid of further experience) to think of them as genuinely necessarily connected. The 'supposed tie' is 'arbitrary'. Or, to put it another way:

> When we reason *a priori*, and consider merely any object or cause, as it appears to the mind, independent of all observation, it never could suggest to us the notion of any distinct object, such as its effect; much less, show us the inseparable and inviolable connexion between them.
>
> (*E* 31)

Hume here appears to be rejecting a view that is *different* from *PE*. He is here rejecting a view according to which we can know *a priori* that there is an 'inseparable and inviolable connection' between causes and effects where our ideas of the cause and the effect are *distinct*. If so, then he cannot hold (as Owen takes him to hold) that *a priori* knowledge of philosophical relations is only possible when the related ideas are not distinct. For, if he held that, then the possibility he here appears to be rejecting would not even be so much as a coherent possibility: he could have stopped at the point where he established that the ideas of the cause and the effect are distinct, since it would follow immediately that they cannot be intuitively or demonstratively connected.

The possibility that Hume seems to be considering here, then, is the possibility that there is an intuitive connection between the *distinct* ideas of *c* and *e* – that is, the possibility that *a priori* inference from causes to effects can be effected with the aid of the demonstrative knowledge that *c* and *e* (*qua* distinct events) are necessarily connected. So the argument which Hume is attacking looks like this ('DK', for 'demonstrative knowledge'):

(DK)   (P1)   *c* occurs

          (P2)   *c* is necessarily connected to *e*

          (C)   *e* occurs

In this case, (P2) is not supposed to be established by penetration into *c*'s essence; the ideas of *c* and *e* are distinct, and so *e* cannot be 'discovered' in *c*. Rather, (P2) is supposed to be an item of demonstrative knowledge, formed by comparing the ideas of c and e and seeing that the two ideas cannot but be placed in the relation of necessary connection.

Hume is here showing that no such demonstrative knowledge is possible. The fact that we can just as well replace the idea of e with the idea of some other, incompatible event shows that we are not *compelled* to think of c and e as necessarily connected. So we do not here have a case of reasoning concerning relations of ideas: causation is (as Hume already claimed when he set up the distinction) what I called in Chapter 2 a class B relation; and feeding the *impression* of c, rather than the mere *idea* of c, in as input does not make me any more compelled to place the two ideas under the relation of causation than I am when considering the mere idea of c.

But in fact, Hume thinks, things are even worse than this. Given that we're talking about *necessary* connection here, it follows that we cannot (without the aid of experience; that is, without the aid of some sensory input additional to the impression of c) think of c and e as *necessarily* connected *at all*. Consider a parallel case involving another class B relation: the spatial relation *being behind*. Suppose I have the impression of my computer. I can consider the idea of my computer in combination with a variety of different ideas that are mutually incompatible, and in each case place the two under the *behind* relation: I can imagine that the fruit bowl is behind the computer, or that a pile of books is behind it, and so on. The fact that I can do this with a variety of incompatible ideas – incompatible in the sense that my computer isn't big enough for both the fruit bowl *and* the pile of books to be behind it – does not undermine my ability to think of any one of those items as genuinely behind the computer. But necessary connection isn't like that. Given the impression of the contact of the first billiard ball with the second (c), the mere fact that I can combine that idea with various incompatible alternatives – the second ball's rolling towards the pocket (e), its rising into the air, and so on – shows that I *cannot* think of c and e as necessarily connected. For their being necessarily connected just *would* be a matter of my being unable to conceive the combination of c and any event incompatible with e.

So the early part of Hume's discussion in the *Enquiry* lends some textual support to the claim made in §2.4 that Hume is committed to a distinction between deduction and demonstration. To reiterate: it does so because Hume *separately* addresses the possibility that we can infer effects by penetration into the essences of causes, and the possibility that we can know *a priori* that there is an 'inseparable and inviolable connection' between *distinct* events.

One reason why it is easy to gloss over this distinction is that Hume uses the Separability Principle to show that *neither* possibility obtains. Our inability to separate the idea of c and the idea of e shows *both* that we cannot deduce e from c *and* that causation is a class B philosophical relation: two distinct events cannot be known demonstratively to be causally related because we can imagine the first without the second. I argued in §2.4 that Hume does not, in general, regard the Separability Principle as a test for what can and cannot be known by demonstration. I can know *a priori* that navy is darker than turquoise even though the idea of navy is separable from the idea of turquoise: I can imagine one without the other. Rather, the appropriate test for what can be known demonstratively is conceivability: I cannot conceive navy *failing* to be darker than turquoise. The case of causation, however, is special, because my coming to know by demonstration that *c* is necessarily connected to *e would* require that the ideas of *c* and *e* be inseparable. For if the ideas of *c* and *e* are separable, then I can imagine it being the case that *c* is not necessarily connected to *e* just by imagining that *c* occurs but *e* does not.

So, in the case of causation, the separability test can be used instead of the conceivability test – or, rather, showing the separability of the two ideas is a *way* of showing conceivability: imagining *c* without *e* is one way to conceive that *c* is not necessarily connected to *e*. I *could* still apply the conceivability test without invoking separability, by imagining that both *c* and *e* occur but fail to be necessarily connected to one another. And Hume in effect shows that this test is also failed – that on first observing *c* we can conceive that it is not necessarily connected to *e* – when he says that, even if we somehow *did* come to have the idea of *e*, the idea of *c* would not 'show us the inseparable and inviolable connexion between them'.

The early part of Hume's discussion in the *Enquiry* thus raises what is, for him, the central problematic in understanding causation and causal reasoning: how can it be that we get to think of *distinct* events (or, at least, events the ideas of which are distinct) as *necessarily* connected? For it looks as though their distinctness rules out the possibility of their being so connected, if that connection is supposed to ground or explain our inference from one to the other. It is the role that necessary connection is supposed to play in inference that sets up the fundamental tension between distinctness and necessity which drives Hume's whole discussion of causation. If our ideas of causes and effects were not distinct, we could make perfectly good sense of the thought that inference from one to the other is grounded in necessary connection, since the necessary connection in question would be the kind that grounds deductive inference generally: the idea of the cause would 'contain' the idea of the effect, and we could thus infer *a priori* from the impression of the cause that the effect will follow. But, given the distinctness of the ideas of causes and effects, that model of inference is unavailable. But now, how can *necessity* play *any* role in the inference? I return to that question in Chapter 6.

3.5 The Uniformity Principle

So far, Hume takes himself to have shown that no inference from causes to effects can proceed via penetration into the essence of the cause or via demonstrative knowledge of necessary connections:

> There is no object, which implies the existence of any other if we consider these objects in themselves, and never look beyond the ideas

which we form of them. Such an inference would amount to knowledge, and wou'd imply the absolute contradiction and impossibility of
conceiving any thing different. But as all distinct ideas are separable, 'tis
evident there can be no impossibility of that kind. When we pass from a
present impression to the idea of any object, we might possibly have
separated the idea from the impression, and have substituted any other
idea in its room.

$(T\,87)$

But the failure of the attempts to explain causal reasoning considered so far
points us towards a different attempt to account for the inference. Manifestly
we *do* infer effects from causes; but, as Hume has just shown, we cannot do so on
first experiencing the cause. So the inference must somehow proceed thanks
to 'the assistance of observation and experience' $(E\ 30)$. How might that
happen?

Hume's methods for uncovering the answer to that question differ in the
Treatise and the *Enquiry*, because he has set things up differently; however the
answer itself is the same in both works. In the *Treatise*, Hume is in the process of
'beating about all the neighbouring fields' in order to try to get to the bottom of
the mysterious notion of necessary connection; he is trying to see whether
uncovering the nature of the inference from causes to effects will allow us to get
a handle on the idea of necessary connection. In the *Enquiry*, by contrast, he has
not yet explicitly raised the issue of the problematic nature of necessary connection, except insofar as he has raised the problem mentioned earlier: it is hard to
see how we can think of two events, the ideas of which are distinct, as 'inviolably
connected' with one another.

Let's start with what Hume says in the *Treatise*, and ask our question again:
how does experience 'assist' us in the inference from causes to effects? Hume's
answer is this:

> We remember to have had frequent instances of the existence of one
> species of objects; and also remember, that the individuals of another
> species of objects have always attended them, and have existed in a
> regular order of contiguity and succession with regard to them. . . .
> Without any farther ceremony, we call one *cause* and the other *effect*, and
> infer the existence of the one from the other.
>
> $(T\,87)$

Of course, this is not supposed to be a complete answer, because it doesn't tell us
how the inference proceeds; it just tells us about the circumstances under which the
inference comes to be performed. Specifically, it tells us that we need not *just*
the present impression of the cause; in addition, we need the memory of the
past observed conjunction of events similar to the cause (Cs) and events similar
to the effect (Es). But we still need to know how the inference itself works.

Before addressing that issue, however, Hume notes that:

> in advancing we have insensibly discover'd a new relation betwixt cause and effect, when we least expected it, and were entirely employ'd upon another subject. This relation is their CONSTANT CONJUNCTION. Contiguity and succession are not sufficient to make us pronounce any two objects to be cause and effect, unless we perceive, that these two relations are preserv'd in several instances.
>
> (*T* 87)

He clearly means '*observed* constant conjunction' here and not constant conjunction *simpliciter* – that is, not observed *and* unobserved constant conjunction. He is interested here in what will 'make us pronounce' that two objects are causally related; and what makes us so pronounce them is that contiguity and succession are 'preserv'd in several instances' and not that they are preserved in all instances including those we have not yet, or may never, observe.

As far as the strategy Hume pursues in the *Treatise* is concerned, then, one more piece of the puzzle has fallen into place: Hume has found a relation in addition to contiguity and succession upon which our 'pronouncing' two events to be causally related depends. He notes, however, that we are still no nearer to understanding the notion of necessary connection, since from 'the mere repetition of any past impression, even to infinity, there never will arise any new original idea, such as that of a necessary connexion' (*T* 88). But then we still have not discovered how the *inference* from causes to effects works, and so our beating about of all the neighbouring fields is not yet complete.

So how exactly does experienced constant conjunction make possible the inference from *c* to *e*? Once constant conjunction enters the picture, the possibility that reason might be the source of the inference emerges once more. Grant that reason cannot get us to belief in *e* from the impression of *c* just by itself; still, past constant conjunction might somehow help to supply a missing premise which would plug the logical gap between *c* and *e*. How might this happen? Hume says:

> If reason determin'd us [to make the transition from *c* to *e*], it wou'd proceed upon that principle, *that instances, of which we have had no experience, must resemble those, of which we have had experience, and that the course of nature continues always uniformly the same.*
>
> (*T* 89)

How would this principle, often known as the Uniformity Principle, enable reason to 'determine' us to make the transition from *c* to *e*? How, in other words, would the gap plugging work? Well, the easiest way to think of the gap plugging is as providing an additional premise in an argument, (UP), that takes us from the occurrence of *c* to the occurrence of *e*:

(UP) (P1)   *c* occurs
      (P2)   *C*s have been constantly conjoined with *E*s in my past experience
      (P3)   Instances which I have not experienced resemble those I have
               experienced

      (C)   *e* occurs

As with (APE) and (DK), in principle this argument could provide us with the explanation we are looking for. We have an account of how (P1) and (P2) are believed – a current impression and memory, respectively. And the inference is plain old unmysterious deduction. So all we need is an account of how we get to believe (P3), the Uniformity Principle. For we would then have a complete account both of how we get the input to the inference and of the nature of the inference itself. But now we need to ask what the source of the Uniformity Principle is: is it knowable *a priori* or only *a posteriori*? Or – to put it Hume's way – is it derived from 'knowledge' or 'probability'?

How might the Uniformity Principle be known *a priori*? Well, we have here two distinct ideas – the idea of instances we have experienced and the idea of instances we have not experienced – and the relation of resemblance. So if we are to know the principle *a priori* we must know it by demonstration, via the class *A* philosophical relation of resemblance: we must be able to tell, just by inspecting the two ideas, that they stand in that relation. But we cannot know this by demonstration, since we 'can at least conceive a change in the course of nature; which sufficiently proves, that such a change is not absolutely impossible' (*T* 89). In other words, I can imagine that, while all experienced instances have been *C*s followed by *E*s, the instances of *C*s that I have not experienced are *not* followed by *E*s. In that case, the relation of resemblance will not obtain between my idea of the instances I have experienced and my idea of the instances I have not experienced. And so I cannot know *a priori* that the relation obtains, since I can imagine its failing to obtain.

Perhaps we can know the Uniformity Principle *a posteriori*? Hume does not attempt to rule this possibility out; rather, he argues that the principle can only be derived from reasoning concerning causes and effects – that is, from the very form of reasoning whose nature we are trying to uncover. He says:

> Probability, as it discovers not the relations of ideas, consider'd as such, but only those of objects, must in some respects be founded on the impressions of our memory and senses, and in some respects on our ideas. Were there no mixture of any impression in our probable reasonings, the conclusion wou'd be entirely chimerical: And were there no mixture of ideas, the action of the mind, in observing the relation, wou'd, properly speaking, be sensation, not reasoning. 'Tis therefore, necessary, that in all probable reasonings there be something present to the mind, either seen or remember'd; and that from this we infer something connected with it, which is not seen nor remember'd.

> The only connexion or relation of objects, which can lead us beyond the immediate impressions of our memory and senses, is that of cause and effect; and that because 'tis the only one, on which we can found a just inference from one object to another. ... [Hence] probability is founded on the presumption of a resemblance betwixt those objects, of which we have had experience, and those, of which we have had none; and therefore 'tis impossible this presumption can arise from probability.
>
> $(T\ 89–90)$

Hume's argument, in a nutshell, goes like this. We already know that the only way to generate *belief*, when we are not engaged in discovering relations of ideas, is by starting out with an impression or impressions of sensation or memory and by reasoning from those impressions to something 'which is not seen nor remember'd'. And we already know that the only relation that will turn that trick is the relation of causation. So *anything* we believe about the world that is not present to the senses or memory – *including the Uniformity Principle itself* – must be a result of reasoning concerning causes and effects. But the Uniformity Principle was supposed to be a principle, belief in which *enables* us to reason from causes to effects. And of course belief in the Uniformity Principle cannot enable us to reason from causes to effects if belief in the principle itself requires us to have just that ability.

Hume is thus interested in explaining *how* we reason from causes to effects, and not in whether or not such reasoning is ever justified. He *is* complaining, in effect, that (UP) is circular; and of course we ordinarily take it that to complain that a valid argument is circular is to call into question whether the argument can be used to *justify* its conclusion. But *Hume's* interest in (UP) does not lie in the fact that its validity might be thought to confer justification on its conclusion, but rather in the fact that its validity might be thought to explain how it is we get to *believe* its conclusion. If I believe that Thomas is German and that Germans are Europeans, the fact that I can deduce that Thomas is European explains how it is that, starting with the first two beliefs, I can come to acquire the third. Similarly, my believing the premises of (UP) promises to explain how it is that I can come to acquire the belief that a given effect will occur on having the impression of its cause. Unfortunately, the promise cannot be fulfilled, because I can only come to believe one of (UP)'s premises – the Uniformity Principle – by means of the very process of inference whose nature (UP) is supposed to reveal.

Admittedly, Hume does not stick religiously to the genetic agenda I have attributed to him. In particular, if his agenda were *purely* genetic, one would expect him to regard it as an empirical fact that we do, actually, only ever acquire beliefs about matters of fact and existence by employing causal reasoning. But in fact he denies this. Later in the *Treatise*, he claims that a belief is simply a 'strong and lively idea' $(T\ 105)$ and spends a considerable number of pages (T 106–23) describing the various ways, apart from causal reasoning, in which an idea might become suitably enlivened – 'education', for example (by which he means rote learning and similar practices).

Given that Hume does not even seem to believe that it is an empirical *fact* that we only acquire beliefs about what is not present to the senses by employing causal reasoning, it is natural to give his frequent claims about what it is that our beliefs are 'founded on' – for example, 'probability is founded on the presumption of a resemblance betwixt those objects, of which we have had experience, and those, of which we have had none' (T 90) – a normative rather than descriptive reading. On such a reading, he is claiming in the passage just quoted that probable reasoning is *justified by* – or perhaps only purportedly justified by – appeal to the 'presumption' that the unobserved resembles the observed. And then the circularity of (UP) might be thought to be naturally read as raising a justificatory problem after all: one might *think* that probable reasoning is justified by appeal to the Uniformity Principle, but in fact it is not, because the Uniformity Principle itself can only be justified by probable reasoning.

So is Hume raising the traditional problem of induction after all, or can his epistemological language – the use of words like 'founded' and 'just' – be read in a way that is consistent with the genetic agenda I have attributed to him? I believe so. I think that, at this stage at least, Hume simply takes it for granted that reasoning from causes to effects is a 'just' form of reasoning: a form of reasoning that is justified or reasonable – something the 'wise man' of E 110 engages in – despite being a product of the imagination rather than a God-like faculty of reason. So of course he sometimes *says* that it is 'just', because that is what he thinks. But that does not at all conflict with his genetic agenda – with the search for an explanatory story about how such reasoning works, and hence how we get to have beliefs about matters of fact. As we just saw, he does not think that causal reasoning is the *only* method by which we acquire beliefs; and so he needs to provide a genetic account of other methods too – and this he does (T 106–23). But he is less interested in such other methods precisely *because* they are *not* 'just': for example, 'education', he says, 'is an artificial and not a natural cause, and as its maxims are frequently contrary to reason, and even to themselves in different times and places, it is never upon that account recogniz'd by philosophers' (T 117).

Indeed, Hume's argumentative method in his discussion of the Uniformity Principle *presupposes* that causal reasoning is 'just' reasoning. After all, why should we think that the Uniformity Principle depends on the relation between causes and effects, as Hume claims? Because that relation is 'the only one, on which we can found a *just* inference from one object to another' (T 89; my italics). As we just saw, Hume does not hold that all belief in matters of fact *in fact* arises from reasoning from causes and effects. So if he did not think that causal reasoning is 'just' inference from the observed to the unobserved he would not be in a position to claim that the Uniformity Principle depends on causal reasoning, since there are many other possible sources of the principle (see Millican 2002: 157–8). For example, I might believe that nature is uniform because I was told several times a day throughout my school years that it is uniform. In that case, the source of the principle, for me, would not involve any inferences from cause to effects, and I would therefore be perfectly capable of reasoning from causes to effects using (UP). Presumably Hume ignores this and other possible sources of belief in the Uniformity Principle because they *manifestly* do not provide a 'just' way of inferring effects from causes. Someone who acquired belief in the Uniformity Principle through rote learning would be *capable* of inferring effects from causes – we would be able to explain how it is that they came to believe that *e* would occur on observing *c*. But that belief would not be a reasonable one, since it would be founded on an unjust method of belief-formation.

The upshot of all this is that Hume is not *solely* concerned with the genetic question. If he was, then presumably he would not simply ignore alternative sources of belief in the Uniformity Principle that do not deliver a circular account of causal reasoning. But it does not follow that he is interested in whether or not causal reasoning can be justified. On the contrary: it is his *assumption* that causal reasoning is just reasoning that explains this omission.

3.6 Causal reasoning and secret powers

There is one more candidate explanation for reasoning from causes to effects in terms of past experience and *a priori* reasoning that Hume considers. This is explored briefly in the *Treatise* but at greater length in the *Enquiry*. The candidate explanation appeals to 'those powers and principles on which the influence of . . . objects entirely depends' (*E* 33) but which nature 'conceals' from us (*ibid.*). As we shall see in Chapter 7, what Hume means when he talks about such 'secret powers' is a controversial issue, as is the question of whether he is merely supposing for the sake of the argument that there are such things or is actually expressing a belief in them. But for now I shall simply assume that what he is talking about are the kinds of 'essences' that he has just shown to be impenetrable, and remain neutral about whether or not he actually believes in them.

The general idea goes like this. Hume has already established that we cannot penetrate into the essence of a cause and thereby come to discern that it is guaranteed to bring about a given effect. But the possibility he is now considering is that, even so, perhaps we can somehow *infer* that the objects we deem to be causes *do* have such essences, and, further, past experience of constant conjunction of causes and effects tells us what it is that the causes are, in virtue of their essences, guaranteed to bring about. So the potential explanation of reasoning from causes to effects goes something like this ('SP', for 'secret powers'):

(SP) (P1)   *c* occurs
      (P2)   *C*s have a secret nature, in virtue of which they are guaranteed
              to produce *E*s
      _____

      (C)   *e* occurs

Since the conclusion follows *a priori* from the premises, (SP) will deliver an explanation of how we come to believe that *e* will occur just if we can provide an account of how it is we come to believe (P2), given only the input that observed *C*s have been constantly conjoined with *E*s.

The inference from the observed constant conjunction of *C*s and *E*s to (P2) requires not one but two steps. First, we have to form the belief that, in each past instance, the *C*'s 'sensible qualities' were 'conjoined' with a secret nature, in virtue of which it was guaranteed to produce an *E*. Second, we have to infer from this that *all C*s – including the one whose sensible qualities I am currently experiencing and all the ones I have not yet experienced – have the same *E*-guaranteeing secret nature.

Interestingly, Hume does not address the first step: he grants, at least for the sake of the argument, that experience 'shows us a number of uniform effects, resulting from certain objects, and teaches us that those particular objects, at that particular time, were endowed with such powers and forces' (*E* 37). His quarrel is only with the second step:

> When a man says, *I have found, in all past instances, such sensible qualities conjoined with such secret powers*: And when he says, *Similar sensible qualities will always be conjoined with similar secret powers*, he is not guilty of a tautology, nor are these propositions in any respect the same. You say that the one proposition is an inference from the other. But you must confess that the inference is not intuitive; neither is it demonstrative: Of what nature is it, then? To say that it is experimental, is begging the question. For all inferences from experience suppose, as their foundation, that the future will resemble the past, and that similar powers will be conjoined with similar sensible qualities.
>
> (*E* 37)

Hume's procedure here is exactly the same as it was when discussing the Uniformity Principle: the inference from the past constant conjunction of sensible qualities and secret powers to their future constant conjunction cannot be *a priori*. But if it is supposed to be an inference from experience, then (SP) begs the question by illicitly appealing to the very principle, belief in which it is supposed to be explaining.

Having dispatched (SP), Hume concedes that he has not given a fully general argument for the impossibility of locating demonstration or deduction as the source of causal reasoning; he has simply shown that various different proposals turn out not to work. But in the *Enquiry* he proceeds to attempt to remove the 'suspicion, that the enumeration is not complete, or the examination not accurate' (*E* 39):

> It is certain that the most ignorant and stupid peasants – nay infants, nay even brute beasts – improve by experience, and learn the qualities

of natural objects, by observing the effects which result from them. When a child has felt the sensation of pain from touching the flame of a candle, he will be careful not to put his hand near any candle; but will expect a similar effect from a cause which is similar in its sensible qualities and appearance. If you assert, therefore, that the understanding of the child is led into this conclusion by any process of argument or ratiocination, I may justly require you to produce that argument. ... You cannot say that the argument is abstruse, and may possibly escape your enquiry; since you confess that it is obvious to the capacity of a mere infant. If you hesitate, therefore, a moment, or if, after reflection, you produce any intricate or profound argument, you, in a manner, give up the question, and confess that it is not reasoning which engages us to suppose the past resembling the future, and to expect similar effects from causes which are, to appearance, similar.

(E 39)

This passage provides further evidence for the claim that Hume is primarily interested in the genetic rather than the justificatory issue. For how could the claim that children, ignorant peasants and brute beasts do not *in fact* arrive at their expectations through 'any process of argument or ratiocination' show that no process of argument or ratiocination could ever *justify* such expectations? If that was what Hume intended to show, his point about children, peasants and beasts would simply miss the point: his opponent could legitimately retort that the issue is about the availability of a procedure for *justifying* beliefs in matters of fact, and not about *acquiring* them. The possibility that Hume's 'enumeration is not complete', if understood as an enumeration of the possible ways in which causal reasoning might be justified, is not in the least undermined by the fact that beings whose expectations might be thought to be unjustified do not have any such justificatory procedure at their disposal.

Understood as concerned with the genetic issue of how our expectations in fact arise, however, the passage is a good deal more convincing. For it is implausible (though I suppose not impossible) that the mechanism by which we acquire our expectations somehow changes, without our noticing it, at some stage early in life. So if children do not acquire their expectations through argument or ratiocination, it seems plausible to suppose that we do not either.

3.7 Hume's positive account of causal reasoning

So far, Hume has reached the negative conclusion that beliefs about matters of fact not present to the senses or memory are not the product of reason: no explanation that appeals to intuition, demonstration or deduction is satisfactory. He has also discovered the input to the mechanism that generates belief in matters of fact, namely a present impression together with past experience of constant conjunction. And what does someone with this input proceed to do?

He immediately infers the existence of the one object from the appearance of the other. Yet he has not, by all his experience, acquired any
idea or knowledge of the secret power by which the one object
produces the other; nor is it, by any process of reasoning, he is engaged
to draw this inference. . . . There is some other principle which determines him to form such a conclusion. This principle is Custom or
Habit.

(*E* 42–3)

It might be thought that Hume is here, in the *Enquiry*, introducing a completely
new mental mechanism – the 'principle' of 'Custom or Habit' – to explain the
inference from causes to effects. But in fact it is clear from his discussion of
causal reasoning in the *Treatise* that this is not what he is doing. There, his first
move towards a positive account of the nature of causal reasoning in the *Treatise*
is this:

Reason can never shew us the connexion of one object with another,
tho' aided by experience, and the observation of their constant
conjunction in all past instances. When the mind, therefore, passes from
the idea or impression of one object to the idea or belief in another, it is
not determin'd by reason, but by certain principles, which associate
together the ideas of these objects, and unite them in the imagination.
Had ideas no more union in the fancy than objects seem to have to the
understanding, we cou'd never draw any inference from causes to
effects, nor repose belief in any matter of fact. The inference, therefore,
depends solely on the union of ideas.

(*T* 92)

Recall from §2.1 that one of the fundamental building blocks of Hume's theory
of the mind is the claim that there is a 'kind of attraction' between ideas: one
idea can 'naturally introduce' another, as when, on looking at a postage stamp
with The Queen's head on it, my mind is naturally drawn to The Queen herself
because the contents of the two ideas – the picture of The Queen's head on the
one hand and The Queen on the other – resemble one another. The mind here
'associates together' the two ideas: it 'unites them in the imagination'. The case
of inference from causes to effects, Hume is claiming, is no different. He has
shown that such inference cannot be the work of the faculty of reason, since he
has failed to find any 'process of argument or ratiocination' (*E* 39) that could do
the job. And so the inference must depend 'solely on the union of ideas': on their
becoming united in the imagination.

The question Hume needs to answer, then, is this: *which* 'principle' is it that is
responsible for generating belief in matters of fact? Recall that, at the beginning
of the *Treatise*, Hume claims that there are three 'associative principles' corresponding to the three natural relations: contiguity, resemblance and causation.

As I said earlier, given the passage quoted above from the *Enquiry*, one might wonder whether Hume is now introducing an additional principle, namely 'custom or habit'. But this is not what he intends: 'custom or habit' turns out to be the very same principle as the associative principle of causation – or what I shall continue to call 'the associative *mechanism* of causation', in order to make more vivid the point that we have here a brute psychological mechanism, rather than a 'principle' to which we consciously appeal in our causal reasoning. This is the mechanism at work when, say, I have the idea of a toe stubbing before my mind and thereby come to have the idea of pain before my mind too, or vice versa. One idea 'naturally introduces' the ideas of (what we believe or imagine to be) the causes or effects of whatever the original idea represents. The mechanism will generate belief in a matter of fact, rather than simply bring one idea to mind on thinking of another, if, for example, I have an impression of a toe stubbing rather than just an idea: if I actually experience stubbing my toe rather than merely imagine doing so. In that case, the operation of the mechanism will result in my not merely *thinking* of pain but actually coming to expect it: I will come to believe that pain is about to ensue.

It might seem that there is a tension here. On the one hand, Hume, in the *Enquiry*, is saying that we immediately infer 'the existence of the one object from the appearance of the other', provided we have experienced the past constant conjunction of the two kinds of object. This inference, it seems, can take place without any appeal to causal judgements or beliefs at all. On the other hand, the associative mechanism of causation seems to require causal belief or judgement as input: when I come to think about pain on thinking about stubbing my toe, it seems that I do so precisely *because* I antecedently hold that toe stubbings *cause* pain. So if belief in matters of fact results from the operation of the associative mechanism, it looks as though Hume still owes us an account of the origin of causal belief: he has not yet explained how it is we get to believe that toe stubbings cause pain, and so he has not yet fully explained how, on experiencing a toe stubbing, I come to believe that pain will follow.

We already know, however, that Hume cannot possibly think that the belief in matters of fact in general comes about thanks to our antecedently believing some causal claim, because he would then be guilty of exactly the same kind of mistake he has been uncovering in other attempts to explain belief in matters of fact. The causal belief in question would have to either be known *a priori*, which is impossible because the ideas of the cause and the effect are always separable, or to be believed on the basis of experience – and so could not be deployed in an explanation of how belief on the basis of experience comes about.

The resolution of the tension comes from appreciating that Hume has something much more radical in mind here: the reversal of the explanatory order already mentioned in §3.3. It is not that we believe that some effect e will occur *because* we have an impression of c and already believe that c is a cause of e; rather, we come to think of c as a cause of e because, on having an impression of c, we find ourselves inferring e. Reasoning concerning matters of fact – inferring effects from causes and vice versa – is explanatorily prior to our coming to think of events as causally related.

Of course, Hume is not yet in a position to make this point, since coming to think of two events as cause and effect requires deploying the so-far elusive idea of necessary connection. Since he has not yet shown that the impression-source of that idea is the inference we draw from causes to effects, he is not yet in a position to say that the associative mechanism of causation generates not just the inference but also causal judgement itself. But he soon will be in that position, and at that point he will make exactly the claim just made on his behalf. As he puts it later on in the *Enquiry*:

> But when one particular species of event has always, in all instances, been conjoined with another, we make no longer any scruple of fore-telling one upon the appearance of the other, and of employing that reasoning, which can alone assure us of any matter of fact or existence. We then call the one object, *Cause*, the other, *Effect*.
>
> (*E* 75)

It turns out, then, that the associative mechanism of causation does rather more than Hume suggests when it is first introduced at the beginning of the *Treatise*. For, while it is true that what the mechanism does – always – is take us from the idea of a cause to the idea of its effect (or vice versa), it is *also* sometimes responsible for generating causal judgements themselves. Its input *can* be an idea (or impression) together with a causal judgement – as when I imagine a toe stubbing and my mind is drawn to the idea of pain because I think of toe stubbings as a cause of pain – but sometimes its input is a present impression together with memory of past constant conjunction. In the latter case, the mind is drawn to the idea of (or, rather, belief in) the effect *and also* comes to think of the first event as a cause of the second.

Before concluding Hume's positive account of the nature of causal reasoning, we need to say a bit more both about the nature of habit or custom, and about the nature of belief. Let's start with custom. Hume says:

> For whenever the repetition of any particular act or operation produces a propensity to renew the same act or operation, without being impelled by any reasoning or process of the understanding, we always say, that this propensity is the effect of *Custom*. By employing that word, we pretend not to have given the ultimate reason of such a propensity. We only point out a principle of human nature, which is universally acknowledged, and which is well known by its effects.
>
> (*E* 43)

In the *Treatise*, Hume makes it clear that not only do we infer *e* from *c* 'without being impelled by any reasoning or process of the understanding'; we do so in

the absence of any conscious mental process whatsoever: belief in *e* 'arises immediately, without any new operation of reason or the imagination. Of this I can be
certain, because I am never conscious of any such operation, and find nothing in
the subject [that is, the impression of *c*], on which it can be founded' (*T* 102).

What is Hume saying here? Well, the inference he is concerned with is the
kind of 'inference' we make almost all the time: the constant forming of expectations based on current experience. As I type at the keyboard, I expect on the
basis of tactile impressions that letters will appear on the screen. When I bite
into an apple, I expect a certain kind of taste. When I take a step forwards, I
expect to move in that direction rather than sink into the ground or remain
rooted to the spot. In ordinary circumstances I no more think about what will
happen when I move my feet than I think about whether I will start brushing my
top teeth or my bottom teeth first: I just, habitually, do (in the case of tooth
brushing) or come to expect (in the case of inference from causes to effects) one
thing rather than another.

Of course, as Hume says, to say that we tend to do or expect something out
of habit or custom is not to give an 'ultimate reason' why we have that tendency.
For Hume, the science of the mind has to be restricted to what is susceptible to
observation and experiment; and this restricts him, so far as the mind is
concerned, to theorizing about what we are conscious of. Given that we are not
conscious of *anything* going on in our minds in our inferences from causes to
effects, the claim that those inferences are habitual is as good an explanation as
Hume can get.

Finally, we need to know how the associative mechanism generates not just an
idea but a belief. When I have the mere idea of a toe stubbing and thereby come
to think of pain, no belief is generated: I do not come to expect my toe to start
hurting. But when I have the impression of a toe stubbing, I do come to expect
it. What does this difference consist in? Hume starts by arguing that what distinguishes a belief from a mere idea is that a belief possesses 'an additional force
and vivacity' (*T* 96). And, when the input to the associative mechanism of causation is an impression rather than an idea, that impression '*not only transports the
mind to such ideas as are related to it, but likewise communicates to them a share of its force
and vivacity*' (*T* 98). So when the input to the associative mechanism of causation
is an idea, its output – the idea the mind is drawn towards – is a mere idea; the
first idea has no force or vivacity to impart to the second. But when the input is
an impression, its force and vivacity are 'communicated' to the second idea, so
that it is not a mere idea but a belief.

What are the consequences of Hume's account for the epistemology of
reasoning concerning matters of fact? While, as I have stressed, Hume is
primarily interested in the genetic question of how we form beliefs about
matters of fact – or (what amounts to the same thing) how in fact causal
reasoning proceeds – it is worth noting just how radical his conclusion is when
contrasted with the Image of God doctrine: the thesis that our minds are comparable to the mind of God. The claim that all our beliefs about what is not

present to the senses or memory are ultimately a result of no more than brute habit takes us about as far away from the thesis that our minds are in any way comparable to the mind of God as it is possible to get. Indeed, as we have already seen, Hume holds that it is a habit we share with children and 'even brutes'.

Hume is clearly keen to stress the animal nature of the habit: both the *Treatise* and the *Enquiry* have a section entitled 'Of the reason of animals' (*T* 176–9; *E* 104–8), in which he aims to establish that 'beasts are endow'd with thought and reason as men' (*T* 176). The actions of a dog 'that avoids fire and precipices, that shuns strangers, and caresses his master . . . proceed from a reasoning, that is not in itself different, nor founded on different principles, from that which appears in human nature' (*T* 177). While one might take Hume's aim in these sections to be, as it were, talking up the mental powers of animals, he is obviously also talking down the mental powers of human beings. Hume's conception of human nature could hardly be further removed from that of the Image of God doctrine.

What about the Insight Ideal, in particular, as applied to knowledge of the causal structure of the world? Well, even if Hume does (as some sceptical realists maintain) hold that there are real necessary connections in nature, his negative arguments concerning causal reasoning show that we can have no *a priori* knowledge of them. Whatever Hume might think about the *truth* of the kinds of causal principle deployed by his predecessors, such as the principle that causes must contain as much reality as their effects and the principle that every event has a cause, his negative arguments make it clear that no such principle can be known *a priori*, for they, like the Uniformity Principle, can only be established – if at all – by appeal to *a posteriori* causal reasoning. Nor can we penetrate into the essences of causes in such a way as to reveal any metaphysical guarantee that a given event will result. So whatever Hume's views about the *nature* of causal relations, his attack on the Insight Ideal is devastating.

3.8 Causal reasoning and inductive inference

We are now in a position to see both why one might characterize Hume as providing an account of inductive inference as opposed to *causal* reasoning and why it is a mistake to do so. There is *a* sense in which Hume must hold that the notion of causation is not essential to our acquisition of beliefs about matters of fact. Hume has told us, in effect, that we come to think of events as causally related thanks to those events acquiring 'a union in the imagination' (*T* 93), although he has not yet let us in on *how* exactly their acquiring that union gives rise to the idea of necessary connection. And he has told us that it is the union in the imagination that *also* allows us to infer effects from causes. So there is a sense in which our conceiving of the united ideas *as* cause and effect may not seem hugely important. If, like dogs (presumably), we lacked the idea of necessary connection, the associative mechanism of causation would function just the same, taking a present impression and memory of past constant conjunction as input and delivering belief as output. We would still be perfectly capable of getting around in the world and engaging in scientific enquiry.

This raises the issue of what exactly our conceiving of causal reasoning as *causal* reasoning adds to our ability to infer one matter of fact from another: an ability we would have, on Hume's view, even if we lacked the idea of causation. I return to that question in §6.5. For now, I simply want to establish that causal reasoning *itself* – the inferential mechanism – is not the same as inductive inference. It is not simply inductive inference by another name: a name we can only give it because we have the idea of causation.

The difference is that inductive inference is inference *from observed regularity* to the unobserved (either to unobserved regularity or just to the next case). In other words, observed constant conjunction between Cs and Es is supposed to feature as an additional *premise* in the piece of inductive reasoning that takes us from the impression of c to the belief in e – perhaps in conjunction with the Uniformity Principle, so that the reasoning goes: 'observed Cs have been Es; the unobserved resembles the observed; c occurs; so e occurs', or perhaps in conjunction with some other premise.

Of course, on Hume's view we can only infer e from c if *in fact* we have observed a constant conjunction of Cs and Es, for it is that observed constant conjunction which brings about the union in the imagination upon which our ability to make the inference depends. But that does not entail that observed constant conjunction needs to function as a *premise* in the inference. And there are good reasons to think that Hume holds that causal reasoning is, or at least can be, what he repeatedly says it is: simply reasoning from causes to effect (or vice versa) – no additional premises required. For one thing, he says:

> [W]e may exert our reason without employing more than two ideas, and without having recourse to a third to serve as a medium betwixt them. We infer a cause immediately from its effect; and this inference is not only a true species of reasoning, but the strongest of all others, and more convincing than when we interpose another idea to connect the two extremes.
>
> (*T* 97n.)

More explicitly:

> 'Twill here be worth our observation, that the past experience, on which all our judgments concerning cause and effect depend, may operate on our mind in such an insensible manner as never to be taken notice of, and may even in some measure be unknown to us. A person, who stops short in his journey upon meeting a river in his way, foresees the consequences of his proceeding forward; and his knowledge of these consequences is convey'd to him by past experience, which informs him of such certain conjunctions of causes and effects. But can we think,

that on this occasion he reflects on any past experience, and calls to remembrance instances, that he has seen or heard of, in order to discover the effects of water on animal bodies? No surely; this is not the method in which he proceeds in his reasoning. The idea of sinking is so closely connected with that of water, and the idea of suffocating with that of sinking, that the mind makes the transition without the assistance of memory. The custom operates before we have time for reflexion.

(*T* 103–4)

There are also more general reasons to think that this really is Hume's considered view. In particular, in his negative discussion of causal reasoning he *starts* by considering the view according to which causal reasoning proceeds by penetration into the essence of the cause – a model of causal reasoning that explicitly takes as input just the impression of the cause (*PE* in §3.4). One can speculate that Hume starts with *PE* because, in an important sense, out of all the positions that he rejects it is the one that most closely resembles his own position: that causal reasoning is a matter of inference from *one* idea to another. Indeed, Hume suggests that *PE* is a pretty natural view to have:

We fancy, that were we brought on a sudden into this world, we could at first have inferred that one Billiard-ball would communicate motion to another upon impulse; and that we needed not to have waited for the event, in order to pronounce with certainty concerning it. Such is the influence of custom, that, where it is strongest, it not only covers our natural ignorance, but even conceals itself, and seems not to take place, merely because it is found in the highest degree.

(*E* 28–9)

I take Hume's point here to be something like this: the influence of custom is so strong – the transition from cause to effect seems so natural and produces such conviction – that it is easy to fail to realize that it really is custom that is at work at all. In other words, the transition from cause to effect ordinarily *seems* not to be an *acquired* habit at all. And for things to seem this way just *is* for it to seem as though we can infer effects from causes without the aid of experience – that is, *a priori*. If causal reasoning always proceeded by inference from observed regularities, the need for past experience of constant conjunction would be obvious: we could not seriously mistake it for an inference which proceeds from the impression of the cause alone.

Why does it matter whether or not Hume thinks that observed regularity need not feature as a *premise* in causal reasoning, given that he holds that we must, in fact, have observed a regularity in order to engage in it? The answer, I think, is that the fact that past experience can bring about the inference from cause to effect in an 'insensible manner' plays a large role in accounting for the *point* of the concept of causation on Hume's view. Our conceiving of causes and effects *as* causes and effects plays a role in causal reasoning for Hume, in the sense that our so conceiving of them is what makes us automatically regard inference from causes to effects as *rational* inference – though our so conceiving of them is not what *makes* the inference rational. I shall have more to say about this in §6.5.

3.9 What justifies causal reasoning?

I have argued that Hume's discussion of reasoning from causes to effects is best seen as an attempt to locate the mechanism by which that reasoning actually proceeds. I also argued that Hume takes it for granted from the beginning that such reasoning is 'just'; in fact he does not raise any properly sceptical doubts about the *justification* of such reasoning until right at the end of both the *Enquiry* and Book I of the *Treatise*.

Hume seems to hold, then, that causal reasoning is justified, even though it is the mere result of animal habit. How can this be? One way to approach the question is to replace it with the following series of questions:

(Q1) Why (if at all) ought we to engage in causal reasoning?
(Q2) Why (if at all) ought we to *prefer* causal reasoning to other belief-forming mechanisms, for example 'education'?
(Q3) Why (if at all) ought we to engage in sophisticated forms of causal reasoning, for example seeking out hidden causes? In other words, why (if at all) ought we to follow Hume's 'rules by which to judge of causes and effects'?

The point of setting the issue up in this way is to enable discussion of the kinds of justification for causal reasoning that have been offered on Hume's behalf, in particular by Owen (1999: ch. 9) and Fred Wilson (1983, 1986). In fact, I shall argue later that Hume has at his disposal a much more direct way of dealing with the issue of justification.

Let's start with (Q1): why, if at all, ought we to engage in causal reasoning? It is this question that is most obviously related to the sceptical problem of induction. We have this method of acquiring beliefs; but what *justifies* our use of that method? Wilson argues that, according to Hume, we *ought* to engage in causal reasoning because we *must* do so. He notes (Wilson 1983: 666) that, according to Hume:

> Nature, by an absolute and uncontrollable necessity has determin'd us to judge as well as to breathe and feel; nor can we any more forebear viewing certain objects in a stronger and fuller light, upon account of their customary connexion with a present impression, than we can hinder ourselves from thinking as long as we are awake, or seeing the

surrounding bodies, when we turn our eyes toward them in broad sunshine.

(*T* 183)

Hume makes the above claim, that we cannot but engage in causal reasoning, in the context of a discussion of scepticism – something he reiterates at the end of the *Enquiry*, when he says that the inductive sceptic 'cannot expect, that his philosophy will have any constant influence on the mind' (*E* 160). So it seems that Hume takes the fact that we cannot but engage in causal reasoning to constitute a response to the sceptic.

According to Descartes, 'I should hold back my assent from opinions which are not completely certain and indubitable just as carefully as I do from those which are patently false. So for the purpose of rejecting all my opinions, it will be enough if I find in each of them at least some reason for doubt' (Descartes 1641: 17).[5] So, according to what Wilson calls the 'Cartesian ethics of belief' (1983: 665), the upshot of Hume's theory of causal reasoning is that 'no one should, rationally, ever make any causal inference whatever' (*ibid.*). But on Hume's view, according to Wilson, we cannot adopt the Cartesian ethics of belief, because we cannot be rationally obliged to do what we cannot do:

> What Hume argues is that the position of the Cartesian is unreason-able. For, it requires one to do what one *cannot* do. One *cannot* cease drawing causal inferences; that is something one, as a human, *must* do. Since we cannot aim at the goal the Cartesian sets for us, it is not a goal we ought, rationally, to aim at. For all that every causal judgment is dubitable, nonetheless *there is a reason for continuing to make causal inferences*: namely, *we are forced to continue to make causal inferences*.
>
> (Wilson 1983: 666)

How plausible is the view Wilson attributes to Hume, and how plausible is it to attribute it to Hume? Well, let's start with the view itself: the view that 'must' implies 'ought'. The most obvious problem with this principle is that it does not follow from a rejection of the Cartesian ethics of belief. For to reject the Cartesian standard is to hold that 'ought' implies 'can', and the most that *this* entails is that if one cannot do X, then it is not the case that one ought to do it. In the context of causal reasoning, this establishes only that it is not the case that we ought to refrain from engaging in it. But it doesn't follow that we *ought* to engage in causal reasoning, since rejecting the Cartesian position is perfectly consistent with holding that normative evaluation of causal reasoning is simply not on the agenda at all.

A moral analogy will help to make the point. Grant that one cannot be morally obliged to do what one cannot do (that is, if one cannot do X, then it is not the case that one morally ought to do X). Imagine that someone several miles away is currently in great danger, but that there is no conceivable way I could have known about this or in any way been in a position to help them. It follows, by the above principle, that it is not the case that I ought to help them. Does it thereby follow that I *ought* to fail to help them? Surely not. My failing to help them is morally justifiable in a sense – in the sense that it is not the case that I am doing anything *wrong* – but it seems very odd to say that failing to help them is fulfilling any moral obligation. We might more reasonably judge that my failure to help the endangered person is morally neutral: it has no moral status at all.

Similarly, one might claim, for the case of causal reasoning. The norm here is a norm of rationality rather than morality, but that does not change the basic structure of the problem. One might reasonably insist that, while it is not the case that I ought *not* to engage in causal reasoning, it is nonetheless not the case that I *ought* to either. So the 'must implies ought' principle is a far from compelling one.

What about the question of whether Wilson is right to attribute the 'must implies ought' principle to Hume? Well, it seems to me that he mischaracterizes the nature of the sceptic to whom Hume is addressing himself when he invokes the 'absolute and uncontrollable necessity' of causal reasoning. According to Wilson, Hume is responding to a sceptical position according to which we *ought not* to engage in causal reasoning. But in fact the position to which Hume is responding is the position of someone who claims not to engage in causal reasoning at all, in the sense they claim not to *have* any beliefs about what is not present to the senses or memory: someone who has reasoned from the weakness of their faculties in such a way as to engender 'a total extinction of belief and evidence' (*T* 183). Immediately before making the claim about absolute and uncontrollable necessity, Hume continues:

> Shou'd it here be ask'd me . . . whether I be really one of those sceptics, who hold that all is uncertain, and that our judgment is not in *any* thing possest of *any* measures of truth or falsehood; I shou'd reply, that this question is entirely superfluous, and that neither I, nor any other person was ever sincerely and constantly of that opinion.
>
> (*T* 183)

And after the passage about absolute and uncontrollable necessity, he continues:

> Whoever has taken the pains to refute the cavils of this *total* scepticism, has really disputed without an antagonist, and endeavour'd by arguments to establish a faculty, which nature has antecedently implanted in the mind and render'd unavoidable.
>
> (*T* 183)

On Wilson's interpretation of Hume, Hume's target is someone who holds that we ought not to engage in causal reasoning. But his target is actually someone who has followed their own advice and, as a result, stopped believing anything at all. And Hume's response is to point out that there is no such person: thanks to the unavoidability of causal reasoning, the alleged opponent is a fictional character. And obviously we do not need to 'take pains to refute' a position which it is, in fact, impossible to adopt. This, it seems to me, does not so much *answer* the question of whether or not we ought to engage in causal reasoning as reveal it to be a question that is not worth asking – for, however we answer it, we will go on reasoning anyway.

So much for the attempt to save Hume from inductive scepticism by invoking the 'must implies ought' principle. Notice, however, that even if Wilson was right about that principle, we would not thereby have answers to (Q2) or (Q3). All it would show would be that we ought to engage in causal reasoning *when* in fact we have no choice in the matter; but sometimes we *do* have a choice in the matter.

Let's start with (Q2): why, if at all, ought we to prefer causal reasoning to other belief-forming mechanisms, for example 'education'? The 'must implies ought' principle would not show that we ought to *prefer* causal reasoning to other methods of belief-acquisition. For we have a choice about the *extent* to which we engage in causal reasoning; for example, I can choose whether to sign up to indoctrination by a peculiar religious cult, thereby acquiring a different set of beliefs to those I would acquire through causal reasoning. I might come to believe through brainwashing that I can communicate with the dead, or that the end of the world will come in precisely 463 days, or that standing on one's head is a good cure for heart disease, none of which I am likely to acquire through causal reasoning. The 'must implies ought' principle is simply silent on the issue of whether choosing to acquire one's beliefs through indoctrination is a less reasonable thing to do than choosing not to.

Nor would the 'must implies ought' principle show that we ought to engage in sophisticated causal reasoning by following Hume's rules by which to judge of causes and effects (Q3) – a point already made in §3.2. Since we have a choice about whether or not to engage in a search for regularities that cannot be discerned in the ordinary course of daily life, for example, the 'must implies ought' principle cannot tell us why, if at all, such searches are worth pursuing.

Wilson himself notes that the 'must implies ought' principle does not deliver the 'conclusion that one specific form of causal inferring is more justified than another' (1983: 667); he says that in the passages quoted earlier 'Hume is not . . . defending science against superstition; he is not . . . arguing that the specific practice of reasoning in accordance with "rules by which to judge of causes" is more justified than the practice of going along with common prejudice' (*ibid.*).[6] How, then, according to Wilson, does Hume defend science? Wilson's answer is that Hume aims to 'vindicate' science by showing that the norms of scientific enquiry bring about a particular end:

> A vindication requires an end to be proposed. The relevant end is introduced near the end of Book I of the *Treatise*. It is the end that is

proposed by the motive of *curiosity* (T 270), which, he tells us in Book II, is that peculiar passion otherwise known as the love of truth (T 448). This desire for truth leads us to undertake research, programmes of 'invention and discovery' (T 449).

(Wilson 1983: 670)

According to Owen, by contrast:

Hume indicates that the love of truth is not enough. The mere fact that something is true is not enough to make it appeal to us: ''Tis easy to multiply algebraical problems to infinity' and '[t]he truth we discover must also be of some importance' (T 449). Significantly, he says that those who engage in mathematical researches 'turn their thoughts to what is more useful and important' (T 450).

(Owen 1999: 219)

Owen holds that Hume's ultimate grounds for the preference of science and philosophy over superstition are moral grounds:

Reason is not the arbiter of truths; it is their means of production. But education and superstition also produce beliefs by means of properties of the imagination. Such beliefs are often 'contrary to reason'. Hume has a clear preference for reason as the source of beliefs in such cases of conflict, and the preference is grounded in Hume's conception of virtue. Those who exercise reason and give it precedence over other influences of the imagination are more pleasing and useful to themselves and others.

(Owen 1999: 223)

I want to argue that neither Wilson nor Owen locates the grounds of Hume's preference for reason over superstition – and the grounds of the normative force of the rules by which to judge of causes and effects – in the right place. Both, it seems to me, are trying to locate the grounds for Hume's preference in something inside the mind: in a passion or a virtue. But neither passion nor virtue, just by themselves, can do the job. Hume cannot ground preference for causal reasoning unless he appeals to the connection between the deliverances of causal reasoning on the one hand and the course of nature on the other.

First, Wilson. As we have seen, Wilson takes it that the scientific method is vindicated by its functioning as a means to the pursuit of truth. But wasn't the question we started with in effect the question of why we should think that the scientific method realizes that aim any better than any other available method? All Wilson takes himself to have established on Hume's behalf so far is that we are warranted in employing causal reasoning when we *must*. At best, this would allow us to infer that, on those occasions when we are compelled to reason from causes to effects, we are warranted in supposing that the beliefs delivered by our reasoning are true. But it does not allow us to infer that we are not *also* warranted in believing the deliverances of other methods of belief-acquisition, in those cases where we are in a position to choose which method we submit to, or are *better* warranted in believing the deliverances of education in those cases where the deliverances of education and causal reasoning conflict. Nor does it allow us to infer that the deliverances of sophisticated causal reasoning – our seeking out hidden causes and so on – are warranted, since our engaging in sophisticated causal reasoning is also a matter of choice. We need a reason to think that causal reasoning is a *better* means to the truth than other methods of belief-formation, and an additional reason to think that sophisticated causal reasoning is a better means to truth – or a means to a better, more complete truth – than vulgar causal reasoning. To assert that the scientific method is the best means to the pursuit of truth presupposes that we have such a reason; it does not deliver one.

Second, Owen. Owen's location of Hume's ultimate preference for reason over superstition in Hume's conception of virtue stems, I think, from the following claim:

> The faculties of the understanding, i.e. the senses, memory, and reason, were traditionally held to produce truth. If one wants truth, one will prefer the results of these faculties, when they function properly, to the results of education. But Hume has given us a non-traditional account, in terms of properties of the imagination. In spite of his claim that '[o]ur reason must be consider'd as a kind of cause, of which truth is the natural effect' (*T* 180), he cannot help himself to the notion of truth to show why it is better to prefer reason to education. All he can appeal to is belief or assent.
>
> (Owen 1999: 207–8)

It is Owen's insistence that Hume cannot appeal to truth to ground the preference for causal reasoning over education that requires him to seek an internal source for the ground: a source in how we think and feel, rather than how things are out there in the world.

I do not see why Hume cannot appeal to truth, however. What he cannot do, of course, is help himself to the thought that the senses, memory and reason *demonstrably* produce truth: he is not in a position to *guarantee* that they do so. But that in itself does not prevent him from *believing* that they do.

I therefore propose that we allow Hume to help himself to the simple answer to the question 'why prefer reason to superstition?': reason (that is, causal reasoning) generally produces truth, whereas other methods of acquiring beliefs are prone to error. And in fact I think Hume *does*, explicitly, help himself to that answer. Here is what he says at the end of his discussion of causal reasoning in the *Enquiry*:

Here, then, is a kind of pre-established harmony between the course of nature and the succession of our ideas; and though the powers and forces, by which the former is governed, be wholly unknown to us; yet our thoughts and conceptions have still, we find, gone on in the same train with the other works of nature. Custom is that principle, by which this correspondence has been effected; so necessary to the subsistence of our species, and the regulation of our conduct, in every circumstance and occurrence of human life. . . .

. . . As nature has taught us the use of our limbs, without giving us the knowledge of the muscles and nerves, by which they are actuated; so has she implanted in us an instinct, which carries forward the thought in a correspondent course to that which she has established among external objects; though we are ignorant of those powers and forces, on which this regular course and succession of objects totally depends.

(E 54–5)

What Hume is clearly saying here is that there is a *correspondence* between causal reasoning on the one hand and the course of nature on the other. As we shall see in Chapter 7, the passage, referring, as it does, to unknown 'powers and forces', plays a role in the debate about Hume's metaphysics – the issue there being whether Hume takes the correspondence to be a correspondence between our expectations on the one hand and the regularities in nature on the other, or whether he takes it to be a correspondence between our *causal* beliefs on the one hand and nature's powers and forces on the other. But I shall set that issue aside for now; either way, Hume is claiming that there is a correspondence, and that is all that is needed for present purposes.

This is significant because here Hume is expressing utter confidence in the *reliability* of causal reasoning. When we reason from causes to effects, we track (at least) the regularities in nature. That is why causal reasoning is to be preferred to education. As Hume says, education 'is an artificial and not a natural cause, and as its maxims are frequently contrary to reason, and even to themselves in different times and places, it is never upon that account recogniz'd by philosophers' (T 117). I take the point about the artificiality of education to mean that there is no possible *explanation* of why education should have any claim to track the truth (except, I suppose, insofar as those who educate us themselves acquired their beliefs through causal reasoning), whereas we *do* have an explanation of sorts for why causal reasoning tracks the truth: nature has been kind enough to 'implant' an instinct in us that is vital for our survival. And where the deliverances of education conflict with those of causal reasoning we ought to trust causal reasoning *because* we are confident that it tracks the truth.

In short, Owen is right to locate Hume's grounds for preferring reason over superstition in its usefulness; but usefulness is not (in fact, or for Hume) a notion that is internal to our practice of belief and assent. What is useful to us – what is necessary to 'the regulation of our conduct' – is a matter of how well we manage to find our way around the world by manipulating causes and predicting effects.

What about Hume's rules? Does the 'pre-established harmony' between causal reasoning and the course of nature provide us with good reason to engage in science, as opposed to merely believing and acting on the basis of those regularities we happen to stumble across in everyday life? It is certainly not obvious that it does. However, given the general reliability of causal reasoning, Hume's analysis of the nature of that reasoning in fact provides him with the resources to explain why sophisticated causal reasoning is better than the alternative.

Hume's 'beating about' in the neighbouring fields in the *Treatise* – of which his discussion of causal reasoning is the major part – has revealed, amongst other things, first, that he does not *doubt* what is sometimes called the 'causal maxim': the maxim that every event has a cause (it's just that the maxim cannot be known *a priori*); and, second, that we will only judge two events to be causally related if they have been constantly conjoined in our experience. And, of course, once we judge them to be causally related, we will thereby judge that future events of the same kinds will also be constantly conjoined. It follows from this (if our judgements are correct), together with the causal maxim, that there is 'no such thing as *Chance* in the world' (*E* 56). Every event *e* must have not just a cause but a *sufficient* cause: some event (or perhaps constellation of events) such that events of that kind are constantly conjoined with events like *e*. In other words, Hume has built up a picture of the world according to which there are far more causal truths to be had than meet the untrained eye. The scientific method is designed to uncover those truths: where similar-seeming causes give rise to different effects, look for an underlying difference in the causes, and so on.

Now in one sense this is not news; we knew all along that that's what the point of scientific method is, didn't we? And didn't I complain earlier about Wilson's attempt to ground the scientific method in the pursuit of truth? Well, yes. But what Wilson fails to explain is *why*, on Hume's view, following the scientific method gets us to (more of) the truth, for nothing in the 'must implies ought' principle entails that it will. The claim that causal reasoning is reliable, however – the claim that causal reasoning tracks the truth – *does*, in conjunction with the causal maxim and the constant conjunction requirement, imply that following the scientific method will get us to more of the truth.[7]

I claim, then, that Hume offers a reliabilist justification of causal reasoning. Causal reasoning is justified because it works: our inferential habits are in harmony with the course of nature. But what kind of a justification is this? In particular, does Hume take it to provide an answer to the sceptical problem of induction? Certainly not. At this stage – so I argued earlier – Hume has not even raised the issue of inductive scepticism. So it would be curious if he were to attempt to offer a solution to a problem that he has not yet even posed. And anyway, Hume's justification is so hopeless, construed as a solution to the sceptical problem, that it is impossible to imagine that he is addressing that problem. For of course it is an empirical claim that our inferential habits are in harmony with the course of nature, and, as Hume well knows, it is therefore not a claim that can be established without appealing to the very form of reasoning it is supposedly justifying.

What, then, *is* the status of Hume's justification of causal reasoning? Isn't it undermined by inductive scepticism? Well, perhaps so; but *Hume* does not take it to be undermined. As I said above, Hume's response to the sceptic is to refuse to answer the question: it is pointless to ask whether we *should* engage in causal reasoning when we have no choice in the matter.

Now, of course, a further issue re-emerges. When criticizing Wilson, I argued that even if we take it that causal reasoning, when unavoidable, is warranted, nothing follows for the cases where it is *not* unavoidable: nothing follows about whether we should avoid brainwashing or engage in science. So can't the same objection be raised here? I claim not. The reason is that, according to the position I am attributing to Hume, the unavoidability of causal reasoning – when it is unavoidable – plays no role in its justificatory status: its justification is based on its reliability. And that justification remains in place in those cases where we *do* have a choice in the matter.

I have argued that Hume holds that causal reasoning is justified, but that he does not think he needs to *refute* inductive scepticism in order to maintain that position. In case there is any residual doubt about whether or not Hume is an inductive sceptic, consider the following passage:

> [A]s this operation of the mind, by which we infer like effects from like causes, and *vice versa*, is so essential to the subsistence of all human crea-tures, it is not probable, that it could be trusted to the fallacious deductions of our reason, which is slow in its operations; appears not, in any degree, during the first years of infancy; and at best is, in every age and period of human life, extremely liable to error and mistake. It is more conformable to the ordinary wisdom of nature to secure so neces-sary an act of the mind, by some instinct or mechanical tendency, which may be infallible in its operations, may discover itself at the first appearance of life and thought, and may be independent of all the laboured deductions of the understanding.
>
> (*E* 55)

Hume is *so* confident that the instinct with which nature has endowed us is a reli-able one that he claims that we are in a *better* position to track the truth given causal reasoning's source in habit than we would be if that reasoning was a result of *a priori* inference. This could hardly be the view of someone who believe that an epistemological crisis is provoked by the fact that inductive inference cannot be due to the operation of the understanding.

4

THE IDEA OF NECESSARY
CONNECTION

So far, what we have is an argument for the thesis that reasoning from causes to effects is brought about by the associative mechanism of causation, and an account of how that mechanism operates. As we have already seen, in the case where the input to the mechanism is a present impression of event c plus the memory of past constant conjunction of Cs and Es, that mechanism does not simply deliver the belief in e; in addition, we come to think of c as the cause and e as the effect. But what we don't have is an account of the origin of the idea of necessary connection. All we know is that the associative mechanism *somehow* enables us to think of causes and effects *as* causes and effects. And so Hume turns his attention – in Book I, Part III, §XIV of the *Treatise* and §7 of the *Enquiry*, both entitled 'Of the idea of necessary connexion' – to tracing the impression-source of the idea of necessary connection. These sections are the focus of this chapter.

The two claims that are central to each of these sections of the *Treatise* and the *Enquiry* are a negative claim and a positive claim about the impression-source of the idea of necessary connection. The negative claim, discussed in §4.1, is that the idea of necessary connection does not have its source either in sensation or in any internal impression arising from the operation of the will. The positive claim is that the true source of the idea is the 'customary transition of the imagination from one object to its usual attendant' (*E* 75): in other words, the operation of the associative mechanism of causation. In §4.2 I ask what the exact nature of the impression of necessary connection is supposed to be for Hume, and examine Barry Stroud's proposal that the impression is a 'feeling'. In §4.3 I argue for a different view – the view that Hume actually takes the impression of necessary connection to affect *visual* experience itself. I argue that, on Hume's view, once the impression of necessary connection arises, events no longer seem 'entirely loose and separate'; they actually *seem* causally connected.

In §4.4 I note some striking differences between what Hume says about causation in Book I, Part III, §xiv of the *Treatise* and §7 of the *Enquiry*, and briefly say something about how these differences are mirrored in different interpretations of Hume. In §4.5 I turn to Hume's famous 'two definitions' of causation and describe Don Garrett's defence of the claim that they are co-extensive. In

75

§4.6, however, I argue that the two definitions are best seen as describing two different routes by which we come to think of events as causally related, corresponding to Hume's psychological distinction between natural and philosophical relations. In §4.7 I say something about where we have got to so far, before turning my attention, in the rest of the book, to the interpretative controversies surrounding Hume's semantic and metaphysical views about causation.

4.1 What is Hume looking for? Single instances of causes and effects

Let's start, as Hume does, with the negative claim about sensation – a claim for which he has already briefly argued in the course of his argument that the inference from causes to effects is not produced by reason. He says:

> When we look about us towards external objects, and consider the operation of causes, we are never able, in a single instance, to discover any power or necessary connexion; any quality, which binds the effect to the cause, and renders the one an infallible consequence of the other. We only find, that the one does actually, in fact, follow the other. The impulse of one billiard ball is attended with motion in the second. This is the whole that appears to the *outward* senses. The mind feels no sentiment or *inward* impression from this succession of objects: Consequently, there is not, in any single, particular instance of cause and effect, any thing which can suggest the idea of power or necessary connexion.
>
> From the first appearance of an object, we never can conjecture what effect will result from it. But were the power or energy of any cause discoverable by the mind, we could foresee the effect, even without experience; and might, at first, pronounce with certainty concerning it, by the mere dint of thought and reasoning.
>
> (*E* 63)

Hume is here claiming that the first time we see a certain kind of causal sequence – one ball's contact with another causing the second to move, for example – we 'only find, that the one does actually, in fact, follow the other'. In other words, as he famously puts it, 'all events seem entirely loose and separate. One event follows another; but we never can observe any tie between them. They seem *conjoined*, but never *connected*' (*E* 74). But note that he does not present this as a claim that is supposed to be phenomenologically obvious – something we would all notice if we were to reflect on the nature of our experience when observing causal sequences for the first time. On the contrary: he gives us a reason *why* we should believe the claim, namely that 'from the first appearance of an object, we never can conjecture what effect will result from it'. In other words, we cannot have any sensory impression of necessary connection or power or force on first observing a causally related pair of events, since, if we did have such an impression, we would be able to infer *a priori* from our impression of the cause what effect would follow.

While Hume is surely right on the second count, it is far from clear why we should think that this in any way justifies his claim that, on first appearance, all events seem entirely loose and separate. For surely they can 'seem connected' without their seeming connected in a way that licenses *a priori* inference from the cause to the effect. Hume is doubtless right that the first time we see, say, someone light the fuse on a stick of dynamite we cannot begin to guess what will happen next. But it does not follow that when we see the *whole thing* for the first time – from the lighting of the fuse to the explosion – we do not see the first thing producing or bringing about the second. In other words, it does not follow that the lighting of the fuse and the explosion seem entirely loose and separate.

To put it another way: we can agree with Hume that the ideas of the cause and the effect are separ*able*, and hence distinct, without agreeing that the events represented by those ideas *seem separate*. In general, two things can easily appear to be connected yet separable: we cannot tell that a boat is connected to its mooring (by a rope, say) just by looking at the boat itself, but we can if we also look at the mooring and see whether one is attached to the other. And of course our seeing that the boat and the mooring are connected does not preclude us from thinking of them as separable: I can perfectly well imagine the knot coming loose and the boat floating away. Why can't what goes for boats and moorings go for causes and effects too?

J.L. Mackie puts this worry in terms of a distinction between what he calls 'necessity$_1$,' and 'necessity$_2$':

> We should . . . distinguish the two things which [Hume's] assumption has unwarrantedly identified. We might call *necessity*$_1$ whatever is the distinguishing feature of causal as opposed to non-causal sequences, and *necessity*$_2$ the supposed warrant for an *a priori* inference, for example, the power which if we found it in *C* would tell us at once that *C* would bring about *E*.
>
> (Mackie 1974: 12–13)

The worry, then – in Mackie's terms – is that Hume infers that we have no impression of necessary connection at all from the fact that we have no impression of necessity$_2$, when in fact his argument does not establish that we have no impression of necessity$_1$.

Why, then, does Hume not consider the possibility that we might have an impression of necessity$_1$, or, as I shall generally call it, 'production'? Well, at first sight, it looks as though Hume's theory of ideas – and, in particular, the Copy Principle, according to which every idea is a faint copy of an impression – rules out the possibility of there being an impression of causation, conceived as the impression of a relation that *merely* relates two events, as opposed to something the impression of which could license *a priori* inference from the first event to the

77

second. For, consistent with that theory, wouldn't we somehow need to have, as it were, a standalone impression of the producing? That is, wouldn't we need to have an impression in between our impression of c and our impression of e, distinct from both of those impressions, that is an impression barely of the producing? And it seems plausible to say that we don't have *that*: if one were asked to picture bare production without also picturing the relata of that relation, one couldn't do it.

However, given what Hume says about the origin of our ideas of some other relations, it turns out that his standards are not as demanding as one might think. Consider what he has to say early on in the *Treatise* about the impression-sources of our ideas of space and time. Our idea of space, he says, has its impression-source in our impressions of extended objects, which are just impressions of 'coloured points, disposed [that is, arranged] in a certain manner' (*T* 34). And as for our idea of time:

> [It] is not derived from a particular impression mixed up with others, and plainly distinguishable from them; but arises altogether from the manner, in which impressions appear to the mind, without making one of the number. Five notes played on the flute give us the impression and idea of time; tho' time be not a sixth impression, which presents itself to the hearing or any other of the senses.
>
> (*T* 36)

Hume seems to be saying here that spatial and temporal *relations* are revealed in experience, even though in neither case does he require there to be a standalone *impression* (or indeed, in the case of temporal relations, any impression at all) of that relation.[1] So it seems that Hume should have no principled objection to the claim that we have an impression as of one thing producing another on first observing them. So our question remains: why does Hume not even consider this possibility?

Galen Strawson's answer (1989: 158–9) is that Hume was merely adopting, for the purposes of criticizing it, the conception of causation prevalent at the time, and that conception just is one according to which causation has what Strawson calls the '*a-priori*-inference-licensing property', or 'AP property' for short: power or energy or necessary connection is such that, if we could detect it, we would be detecting some feature of the cause itself such that we would be able to infer that the effect will occur *a priori*.[2] So he is simply not interested in whether or not there might be some weaker observable connection between causes and effects. The thought that causation has the AP property connects with the Image of God doctrine in an obvious way: if causes entail their effects, then that must be, precisely, because they have some feature, detection of which would license *a priori* inference to their effects, just as, when one proposition A entails another, B, there will be some 'feature' of A – something about its meaning or logical form – grasp of which will allow us to infer B *a priori*.

This short answer is not very satisfying, however. Hume does, after all, claim that on first observing them all events seem entirely loose and separate. If he were simply not interested in the possibility that, on first observing them, we detect a connection that fails to have the AP property – that is, the possibility that we have an impression of production – it is hard to see why he would commit himself to the 'loose and separate' claim. After all, he does not *need* to make that claim if he is only interested in refuting the view that we detect necessity$_2$; that is, something with the AP property.

A more satisfying answer is that Hume simply takes it for granted that causal necessity, *if it exists at all*, must be capable of grounding *a priori* inference from causes to effects. No relation of production revealed by sensation – no relation the sensation of which could only occur, as it were, as a package deal alongside the impressions of *c* and *e* – could possibly provide the impression-source for the idea of necessary connection (or power or whatever). For if the impression-source of that idea were the impression of production, production – that is, causation – would not be the kind of thing on which we could found causal reasoning. We would be able to make causal claims retrospectively by detecting the causal relation – by detecting that the impact of the white ball caused the black to move – but we would not be able to *predict* that the black would move in advance of its actually doing so. In other words, Hume takes it for granted that detection of causation would have to be detection of something that would generate inference from causes to effects.

From a contemporary perspective, none of this should seem terribly convincing. Hume's central claim that (1) causal connections are not revealed by sensory experience is supposed to gain its credibility from a conception of causation according to which (2) causation is the foundation of all our experimental reasoning. But our twentieth-century philosophical heritage is one according to which (2) is at best a minority view. In the great mass of literature on scientific method and the problem of induction, causation rarely gets more than a passing mention: the dominant view – a view whose ancestry traces straight back to Hume, ironically enough – is one according to which we can get by perfectly well without invoking causation at all. But if we buy into that heritage we ought to be wary of taking Hume's word for (1), since if we sever the link between causation and experimental reasoning – that is, if we take it that our inductive inferences can get along perfectly well without the need to appeal to causation – we are left with no obvious principled reason, or at least none that is offered by Hume, to deny that some relation weaker than necessary connection is revealed by sensory experience. All we have is the brute phenomenological claim that, at least on first observing them, 'all events seem entirely loose and separate', and it is far from clear why we should believe this.

Strawson notes that 'Hume's argument is now often conceived to be an argument against the possibility of detecting Causation even when Causation is *not* thought of as something detection of which . . . would give rise to the possibility of impossible *a priori* certain inferences about the unobserved' (1989: 114),[3] and comments that 'Hume might well have accepted this extension of his argument' (*ibid.*). By contrast, I am not sure that Hume would have been able to make anything of the thought that causation plays no serious role in our experimental reasoning, and hence he would not know what to make of the question of whether a causal relation that is entirely disconnected from our inferential habits is revealed to us by sensory experience. He is *so* sure of the connection between experimental reasoning and causation that it does not even occur to him that experience might reveal events to be connected in a way that does not enable one to infer the second from the first.

It is important to stress that the difference between what Mackie calls 'necessity$_1$' and 'necessity$_2$' – between what I am calling production, on the one hand, and the AP property, on the other – is not *merely* a difference in the 'strength' of the connection. An impression of production would be an impression of a genuine *relation* between events c and e, so that we would experience c-producing-e. But an impression with the AP property would not be an impression of a *relation* between c and e at all. Rather, it would be an impression of the 'power or energy' of the *cause*. If necessary connection is to license *a priori* inference from causes to effects, it cannot, on Hume's view, be a *relation* at all, in the sense of relating two distinct ideas. For no such relation could possibly ground *inference* from the first idea to the second. In order to deploy the idea of necessary connection as a way of inferring e from c, we would have to detect an AP property *in the cause itself*.

By way of contrast, consider the following remark of Harold Noonan's:

> Necessary connection, if it is to play the role Hume ascribes to it, must be capable of being presented to sense when both the connected objects are also presented *and* when only one of them is presented, so that inference to the second is possible. In this respect it must be unlike the relations of contiguity and priority in time, and indeed unlike *any* other relation. Hume's puzzlement as to how there could be such a thing in the world to be observed may now seem somewhat more understandable.
>
> (Noonan 1999: 102)

Noonan's suggestion here seems to be that Hume has set himself up in opposition to a view that is so peculiar that it is hardly surprising he manages to show that we have no impression of the relation in question. However, whatever the weaknesses are of the view Hume is attacking, the peculiarity Noonan describes is not one of them, for the view that we can somehow have a sensory impression of necessary *connection* prior to having an impression of e is not one that Hume's opponent is committed to. Instead, Hume's opponent is committed to the view that our impression of c itself reveals its e-guaranteeing nature: it is from the impression of c alone – from penetration into its essence – that we can infer that e will occur by reasoning *a priori*.

Let's get back to Hume's negative claims about the source of the idea of necessary connection, and assume, as Hume does, that what we are looking for is a sensory impression with the AP property. Manifestly no such impression is revealed by *visual* experience on one's first encounter with a given kind of event. In the *Enquiry*, Hume then goes on to argue that no such impression is revealed by attention to the workings of our minds either, in the sense that no such impression is revealed by attention to causally related mental events or to mental causes and bodily effects.

Hume gives three arguments to show that we have no impression of the 'influence' of the will on bodily movements – that is, no impression of a necessary connection between any mental cause and a physical effect – and he then repeats the arguments for the case of mental causes and mental effects (no impression of a necessary connection 'when, by an act or command of our will, we raise up a new idea, fix the mind to the contemplation of it', and so on (*E* 67). Here I shall very briefly summarize Hume's arguments in the case of mental–physical causation.

First, Hume points out that to apprehend some quality in an act of will in virtue of which it operates on the body would be, in effect, to 'know the secret union of soul and body, and the nature of both these substances; by which the one is able to operate, in so many instances, upon the other' (*E* 65). That we know no such thing Hume clearly takes to be too obvious to bother defending.

Second, he points out that our will can only influence some of our bodily organs: I can raise my arm by willing it, but I cannot effect any change in my heart or liver, no matter how strongly I will that. If I could discern in the cause – the act of will – the power by which my arm is then raised I would also be able to discern that the power is lacking in the case of the heart and liver. But of course I can detect no such difference; I cannot tell just by inspecting the act of will on its own (without the aid of prior experience of constant conjunction or lack of it) whether it will have the willed effect.

Third, Hume points out that the mechanism by which the body does what we want it to is extremely complex, involving a good number of intermediate stages (the movement of muscles, nerves and 'animal spirits'), all of which, apart from the first and last, we are completely unaware of. But if we really did have an impression of the will's power of production, we would thereby be able to tell, for example, exactly what the very next stage in the process would be; whereas, in fact, this is entirely beyond our comprehension.

The upshot of all this is that in single instances of the operation of one body on another, and the operation of the mind on the body, and the operation of the mind on mental objects:

[T]here appears not, throughout all nature, any one instance of connexion which is conceivable by us. All events seem entirely loose and separate. One event follows another, but we never can observe any tie between them. They seem *conjoined*, but never *connected*. And as we can

have no idea of any thing which never appeared to our outward sense
or inward sentiment, the necessary conclusion *seems* to be that we have
no idea of connexion or power at all, and that these words are absolutely without any meaning, when employed either in philosophical
reasonings or common life.

(*E* 74)

4.2 Locating the source: the transition of the mind

We have so far been concerned with *single* instances of causation, and discovered
that on first observing a cause–effect pair, we have no impression of necessary
connection – no impression, that is, of any feature of the cause that licenses
inference to the effect. However, Hume continues:

> But when one particular species of event has always, in all instances,
> been conjoined with another, we make no longer any scruple of fore-
> telling one upon the appearance of the other, and of employing that
> reasoning, which can alone assure us of any matter of fact or existence.
> We then call the one object, *Cause*; the other, *Effect*. We suppose that
> there is some connexion in the one, by which it infallibly produces the
> other, and operates with the greatest certainty and strongest necessity.
>
> It appears, then, that this idea of a necessary connexion among events
> arises from a number of similar instances which occur of the constant
> conjunction of these events. ... But there is nothing in a number of
> instances, different from every single instance, which is supposed to be
> exactly similar; except only, that after a repetition of similar instances, the
> mind is carried by habit, upon the appearance of one event, to expect its
> usual attendant, and to believe that it will exist. This connexion, there-
> fore, which we *feel* in the mind, this customary transition of the
> imagination from one object to its usual attendant, is the sentiment or
> impression from which we form the idea of power or necessary connexion.
>
> (*E* 75)

In this passage, Hume in effect makes two crucial argumentative moves, the first
of which completes his negative argument concerning the impression-source of
the idea of necessary connection and the second of which provides his positive
argument.

The first move starts out with the claim that the idea of necessary connection
only arises 'after a repetition of similar instances': after we have had sufficient
experience of *C*-impressions being followed by *E*-impressions. But, since our past
sensory impressions of the relevant events did not yield any impression-source
for the idea of necessary connection (as Hume takes himself to have shown
already), and since manifestly the mere fact that we have experienced 'similar
instances' before cannot suddenly enable us to discover something new in those

sensory impressions that we were previously unable to discover, it turns out that the impression-source for the idea of necessary connection cannot be a *sensory* impression at all. If the impression-source of the idea were a genuine sensory impression, then we would have been capable of having that impression, and hence inferring the effect from the cause, the first time we had a *C*-impression. But since we were not capable of doing that the first time around, the impression-source must lie elsewhere.

The second move finally locates the source. The idea of necessary connection only comes to mind after frequent repetition. And, in fact, it comes to mind at precisely the point at which the habit of inferring *E*s from impressions of *C*s kicks in. So the impression-source of the idea *must* simply be our awareness of the 'transition' of the mind from the impression of *c* to the belief in *e*.

It's important to recognize just how significant Hume's location of the impression-source of the idea of necessary connection is, in the context of his overall discussion. In the *Treatise*, it is now some ninety pages since Hume first announces:

> To begin regularly, we must consider the idea of *causation*, and see from what origin it is deriv'd. 'Tis impossible to reason justly, without understanding perfectly the idea concerning which we reason; and 'tis impossible perfectly to understand any idea, without tracing it up to its origin, and examining that primary impression, from which it arises. The examination of the impression bestows a clearness on the idea; and the examination of the idea likewise bestows a like clearness on all our reasoning.
>
> (*T* 74–5)

Now, finally, he has found what he was looking for: that without which it would be 'impossible to reason justly'. And I take it that by this he means something like the following: it is only once we have traced the impression-source of the idea of causation that we can be assured that the 'idea' of causation really is a genuine idea: a faint copy of an impression. Without that assurance, we cannot be sure that to think of events in the world *as* causes and effects is really to think anything at all, for we cannot be sure that the words 'cause' and 'effect' really have any idea – the idea of causation – associated with them. So, in effect, Hume has now vindicated our causal talk and thought; he has shown that our causal talk and thought have genuine content.[4]

This is good news for Hume, of course; but unfortunately what he says about the impression of necessary connection raises a host of tricky interpretative issues. In particular, what exactly *is* the relevant impression? There are three distinct questions here. First, what is the nature of the impression, phenomenologically speaking? Second, what is it an impression *of*, in the sense of detection: what is it that we are latching on to when the impression comes to mind? And, third, what implications does Hume take the answers to the first two questions to have for the representational content of the idea of necessary connection? It might seem as though the second and third questions must have the same answer: if (for example) the impression is *of* the transition of the mind, in the sense that it detects that transition, doesn't it just follow that the *idea* of necessary connection must *represent* that transition? In fact, this is a controversial question, and I shall leave it to one side for now, in order to get clear on Hume's answer to the first two questions. I shall call the impression that is the source of the idea of necessary connection the 'NC-impression', in order to make it clear that, at this stage at least, the impression might not be an impression 'of' necessary connection in either the detecting or the representational sense.

In the *Enquiry*, Hume says:

> This connexion, therefore, which we *feel* in the mind, this customary transition of the imagination from one object to its usual attendant, is the sentiment or impression from which we form the idea of power or necessary connexion.
>
> (*E* 75)

And in the *Treatise*, he says:

> Necessity . . . is nothing but an internal impression of the mind, or a determination to carry our thoughts from one object to another. . . .
>
> The idea of necessity . . . must, therefore, be deriv'd from some internal impression, or impression of reflexion. There is no internal impression, which has any relation to the present business, but that propensity, which custom produces, to pass from an object to the idea of its usual attendant. This therefore is the essence of necessity.
>
> (*T* 165)

This is all very puzzling. Hume seems to be saying that the transition or determination or propensity to pass from the impression of *c* to the belief in *e* – that is, the operating of the associative mechanism of causation – is, itself, an *impression*. But that cannot be right.[5] Hume's associative mechanisms are supposed to be mechanisms by which mental objects – impressions and ideas – interact; those mechanisms cannot themselves *be* simply more impressions. At best, they can only be mechanisms whose operation is attended or detected by impressions.

So perhaps Hume really means to say that the NC-impression is an impression *of* the transition, in the detection sense? That sounds odd too. For the transition would seem to be a *causal* relation between the impression of *c* and the belief in *e*, and so Hume appears to be saying that we can detect the very thing – what I earlier called 'production' – which he does not even appear to consider as a possibility during the negative phase of his argument. So it looks as though, rather than illegitimately denying that we can perceive production (in Mackie's terms, 'necessity$_1$') on the grounds that we cannot perceive AP properties (necessity$_2$), Hume is actually asserting that we *can* perceive necessity$_1$ – not between events in the world, but between our own ideas.

If this is indeed Hume's view, it raises two problems. The first is that Hume is traditionally held to believe that there is no more to causation than contiguity, priority and constant conjunction. So if, for Hume, the NC-impression really *is* an impression of production – in the sense that the impression detects a genuine causal relation between ideas – then there is something badly awry with the traditional interpretation of Hume's views about the nature of causation. The second problem is that Hume seems to be implicitly guilty of employing double standards: he does not even consider the possibility that we can detect production between external events when arguing that the source of the idea of necessary connection is not a *sensory* impression, and yet accepts that we can detect production between events in our own minds when arguing that the source of the idea of necessary connection is an impression of reflection.

The standard method for avoiding saddling Hume with both problems is, in effect, to deny that he takes the NC-impression to be an impression *of* the production of one idea by another, in the sense of *detecting* that production. For example, Stroud says:

> The impression or feeling of determination from which the idea of necessity is derived must . . . be understood as just a certain feeling that arises in the mind whenever a certain kind of mental occurrence [the impression of *c*] causes another [belief in *e*]. The impression or feeling is not an impression *of* that one event's causing the other, or *of* the causal or necessary connection between them; it is just a peculiar feeling that accompanies, or is simultaneous with, the occurrence of that second event in the mind.
>
> (Stroud 1977: 85–6)

Noonan takes a similar line:

> In fact, Hume is insistent that we can no more get the idea of necessary connection by observing causal linkages in the mental realm than we can get it by observing causal linkages in the physical realm. The 'feeling of determination' Hume refers to can, therefore, only be an *accompaniment* to the transition from the idea of an *A* to the idea of a *B*. We may try to understand it as a feeling of helplessness or inevitability that occurs in the mind when the disposition to make the transition from an idea of an *A* to the idea of a *B* . . . is activated by the occurrence in the mind of an idea of an *A*.
>
> (Noonan 1999: 142–3)[6]

It not clear that either Stroud's or Noonan's interpretation succeeds, however – or at least not without some extra help. For it is unclear what the difference is supposed to be between the NC-impression 'accompanying' the transition or 'arising whenever' one idea causes another and its being an impression *of* – its genuinely detecting – the transition. For surely just what it *is* for *X*s to detect *Y*s is for *X*s to be causally sensitive to the existence of *Y*s. Litmus paper detects the presence of acid because immersion in acid – and nothing else – reliably causes the paper to turn red. Similarly, the transition of the mind reliably causes the NC-impression; indeed, once we know that this is so, we can even consciously monitor the operation of the mechanism by keeping track of the occurrence of the impression, just as we can monitor acidity levels by noticing the colour of the litmus paper. And so it is unclear why we should not think that the NC-impression genuinely detects the transition in the mind.

Stroud and Noonan thus appear to hold that the transition of the mind is genuine production, but that the NC-impression does not detect it. But in the absence of a good reason to hold that the NC-impression *merely* accompanies the transition rather than genuinely detecting it, perhaps a better strategy would be to deny that the transition is really *production* – in the sense required for the problems mentioned above to arise – at all.

Recall from §3.7 that to say that the transition from causes to effects occurs out of habit or custom is not to provide a *complete* explanation of how the associative mechanism of causation operates; it is not to provide the 'ultimate reason' for our propensity to infer effects from causes (*E* 43). Rather, it is to give as complete an explanation as is possible given the restrictions of proper scientific methodology, namely keeping within the confines of observation and experiment, which, in the case of mental operations, restricts Hume to what we are conscious of. But Hume clearly thinks that it is the brain, and in particular the motion of 'animal spirits', that is ultimately responsible for at least some of the workings of the mind (*T* 60–1).

This being so, Hume is bound to think that there is in fact some complex process occurring in the brain when we infer effects from causes, and so we can reasonably attribute to him the view that this process also produces the NC-impression. And so he can safely hold that the NC-impression detects the operation of that process without committing himself to the claim that it detects bare *production*, for the relation between the impression of the cause and the belief in the effect is *not* bare production at all; it is some complex process in the brain whose nature we cannot discern from the nature of the impression that detects it. We can think of the NC-impression as rather like a headache: a headache *detects* some physical abnormality without intimating its nature. The upshot of all this is that Hume can hold that the NC-impression really does detect (rather than merely accompany) the transition of the mind while sidestepping both of the problems raised above, because he need not hold that what is detected is production.

86

We now have an answer to the second of the three questions raised earlier: in the detection sense, the NC-impression is an impression *of* whatever it is that goes on in the brain when we infer effects from causes. What about the first question: what is the phenomenal character of the NC-impression? As we have seen, Stroud describes it simply as a 'peculiar feeling'. But this is not enough, for two reasons. First, it just doesn't seem to be true that there *is* any such 'feeling' accompanying our formation of beliefs on the basis of current sensory experience. And, second, even if we grant that there is such a feeling, if that feeling is to count as the impression-source of the idea of necessary connection it looks as though it needs to have a distinctive, and appropriate, phenomenal character. Imagine, for example, that whenever the transition occurred we experienced a minor twinge just behind the ear. Would it then be remotely plausible to claim that the twinge was the impression-source of the idea of necessary connection? Clearly not – for what would that impression of a twinge have to do with the idea of necessary connection? A twinge would not have the kind of phenomenal character that would make such a claim intelligible.

So perhaps we need to attribute to Hume a view that is more like what Noonan suggests: perhaps we need to understand the NC-impression as 'a feeling of helplessness or inevitability' (Noonan 1999: 142). But the first objection remains. Our expectations on the basis of current experience operate pretty much all the time in our waking lives: the expectation that moving my feet in a certain way will propel me forward, that a 'k' will appear on the screen when I make a certain movement with my finger, that a pleasant sensation will result when I eat the chocolate, and so on. It just does not seem to be true that those mundane expectations are routinely accompanied by a distinctive feeling that one might describe as a 'feeling of helplessness or inevitability'.

One might object that there *is* a relevant feeling to be had, namely the feeling of expectation itself. One might claim that expectations just do have a different phenomenal character to other kinds of belief: expecting the black ball to go into the pocket feels different to believing, say, that the Battle of Hastings took place in 1066, or that today is Thursday. Well, maybe so – but the feeling we need is a feeling that *only* arises as a result of the transition of the mind from cause to effect, else the feeling will not even count as *detecting* the transition; and expectations can arise in the absence of any such transition. For example, I might come to believe, as a result of rote learning or brainwashing and not through causal reasoning, that the end of the world is nigh. In that case, *qua* expectation, that belief would have the same phenomenal character as my belief that the black ball is about to go into the pocket. So a feeling of expectation cannot do the job that needs to be done, because such a feeling will not genuinely detect, or even reliably accompany, the transition of the mind from causes to effects – it will detect or accompany something much broader than that, namely expectation, no matter how the expectation arises. Thus such an impression, if there was one, could not plausibly be held to be the impression-source of the idea of necessary connection.

4.3 Necessary connection and causal experience

It is commonly supposed that, according to Hume, 'all events seem entirely loose and separate' (*E* 74) – not just 'in single instances of the operation of bodies' (*E* 73), but in general. There are three questions raised by the sections on the idea of necessary connection in the *Treatise* and the *Enquiry* that ought to make us think again about whether Hume really does believe this. First, why does Hume only make the loose-and-separateness claim, and variants thereof, when discussing 'single instances of the operation of bodies'? Second, he spends some ten pages in the *Treatise* and seven in the *Enquiry* attempting to persuade the reader that we have no sensory impression of necessary connection. Why does it take him so long to reach that conclusion? If all events really *do* seem entirely loose and separate, why would anyone think that necessary connections can be revealed in sensory experience in the first place? And, third, why does Hume think he needs to argue for that conclusion by appealing to the (alleged) fact that an impression of necessary connection would have to license *a priori* inference from causes to effects? Again, if all events really do seem entirely loose and separate, then no such argument is necessary: he could just appeal to straightforward, introspectively available, facts about the phenomenology of experience.

There is a wider question to ask too. Grant that the epistemological views Hume has been attacking up to this point – the Insight Ideal in particular – are largely motivated by the Image of God doctrine. One can see how a philosopher might attempt to provide allegedly *a priori* arguments for the truth of the Insight Ideal (we are made in God's image, God is benevolent so would not have created us and the world in such a way as to make it impossible for us to grasp its nature, and so on); nonetheless, presumably the Insight Ideal would not have had the kind of hold it apparently had over philosophers of the time if it *manifestly* contradicted obvious facts about our experience of the world. If all events in fact seem entirely loose and separate, it is hard to see how anyone could begin to think that we can in principle penetrate into the essences of objects in such a way as to know *a priori* what effects they will produce, unless they were somehow labouring under a huge misapprehension about what experience reveals to us, which seems unlikely. If all events *seem* entirely loose and separate, it is very hard to see why anyone would come to believe that they could detect necessary connections.

The point here is this. Hume clearly does not think it is phenomenologically *obvious* that we cannot penetrate into the essences of events in such a way as to reveal what they are guaranteed to produce. But if all events seemed entirely loose and separate – not just to Hume, of course, but to all of us – it *would* be phenomenologically obvious to us. If, therefore, we were to attribute, both to Hume and to (some of) his predecessors, the view that all events do *not*, in general, seem entirely loose and separate, we would be able to explain both why the grip of the Insight Ideal is so powerful and also why Hume has to go to such lengths to refute it.

I want to argue that Hume holds that, once we have had experience of the past constant conjunction of *C*s and *E*s and hence acquired the habit of inferring *E*s from *C*s, and thereby come to have the NC-impression when we do so, *C*s and *E*s do not seem entirely loose and separate at all. On the contrary: they really do *seem* causally connected. The view I am proposing is this. For Hume, the NC-impression – the felt determination of the mind – imposes itself upon the impressions of sensation in such a way as to affect how things *appear* to us, so that, on acquiring the habit of expectation, the relevant kinds of events no longer seem entirely loose and separate.[7] Or, as I shall sometimes put it, Hume thinks there is a *phenomenal projection* of the NC-impression.

I shall offer three reasons for thinking that this is what Hume had in mind. In fact, I have already given the first reason: it explains why he goes to such great lengths to argue that the impression of necessary connection is not an impression of sensation and why he has to appeal to 'single instances of the operation of bodies'. But consider also Hume's explanation for why we are inclined to *believe* that 'power and necessity . . . are . . . perceiv'd externally in bodies' (*T* 166):

> 'Tis a common observation, that the mind has a great propensity to spread itself on external objects, and to conjoin them with any internal impressions, which they occasion, and which always make their appearance at the same time that these objects discover themselves to the senses. Thus as certain sounds and smells are always found to attend certain visible objects, we naturally imagine a conjunction, even in place, betwixt the objects and qualities, tho' the qualities be of such a nature as to admit of no such conjunction, and really exist no where.
>
> (*T* 167)

The mind's propensity to spread itself on external objects is supposed to explain why we are inclined to believe that necessity is *perceived*. But if all events seem entirely loose and separate how could we possibly be inclined to believe *that*? On the loose-and-separate view, we experience events as loose and separate, but, turning our attention inward, we notice that a new impression arises, and we somehow 'spread' that impression onto the world. What we thereby come to believe, Hume thinks, is that necessity is an impression of sensation – it is perceived – rather than reflection. It is utterly mysterious how we could make that mistake if the NC-impression did not affect how the world seems to us.

On the story I am proposing, by contrast, there is no real mystery, because in our everyday dealings with the world there is no turning our attention inward. Those causal judgements that are based on what is immediately present to the senses are formed not by looking inward and examining our own reactions to the scenes before our eyes; rather, they are formed merely by attending to those scenes themselves. When we judge how things causally *are* – whatever Hume thinks that amounts to – our judgements are based on how they *seem*.

Second, Hume's story about the psychology of causal experience is very similar to the story he tells about aesthetic experience.[8] Take what he says about beauty:

> Attend to Palladio and Perrault, while they explain all the parts and proportions of a pillar. They talk of the cornice, and frieze, and base. . . . But should you ask the description and position of its beauty, they would readily reply, that the beauty is not in any of the parts or members of a pillar, but results from the whole, when that complicated figure is presented to an intelligent mind, susceptible to those finer sensations. Till such a spectator appear, there is nothing but a figure of such particular dimensions and proportions: from his sentiments alone arise its elegance and beauty.
>
> (*E* 292)

Hume's line here is, in broad outline, the same as his line on causation. There is what sensation reveals – position, proportion and so on – and then there is an impression whose source is internal: a sentiment. For Hume, then, the impression of beauty is not, strictly speaking, an impression of *sensation* at all: when something strikes one as beautiful, one is 'staining' (*E* 294) what is revealed by sensation with an internal sentiment.

Now consider the aesthetic analogue of the traditional view of Hume on the NC-impression: the view according to which all events seem entirely loose and separate. The aesthetic analogue would be that objects would *appear* to one as devoid of aesthetic properties, since aesthetic properties are not revealed by impressions of sensation and hence not by visual experience at all. We would *think* of things as being beautiful or ugly, just as we think of objects as causes and effects. But they would not *look* beautiful or ugly.

This account of the nature of aesthetic experience is so phenomenologically inadequate that it is very hard to believe that Hume holds it. We just do, surely – on anyone's view – have genuinely aesthetic experiences: experiences as of a painting or a face looking beautiful, or a building looking ugly, and so on. We could not *think* of things as beautiful unless they *looked* beautiful. It would therefore be much more plausible to hold that Hume takes 'sentiment' to infect the nature of aesthetic experience itself: to affect how things seem or appear to us. Given the clear similarity between the aesthetic case and the causal case – there is what is revealed by uncontaminated sensation, on the one hand, and what is added by the mind, on the other – it seems reasonable to attribute the same view to him in the case of causation.

It might be objected that in another case where Hume distinguishes between what sensation reveals and what the mind contributes – the case of morality – Hume sometimes talks as though he takes precisely the opposite view to the one I am proposing. Discussing wilful murder, for example, he famously says: 'The vice entirely escapes you, as long as you consider the object. You never can find it, till you turn your reflexion into your own breast, and find a sentiment of disapprobation, which arises in you, towards this action' (*T* 468–9). But – again – Hume is not here simply offering us a straightforward phenomenological claim about how things appear to us; his conclusion is reached only after a good deal of philosophical argument. As Michael Smith notes:

> [O]ne remarkable, yet little mentioned, feature of this passage is that Hume is precisely trying to focus our attention away from where it is naturally focused when we judge a wilful murder to be wrong: that is, away from the murder itself, and on to an otherwise quite unnoticed 'calm passion' he supposes to arise in us.
>
> (Smith 1993: 246).

Third, Hume's distinction between impressions of sensation and reflection, drawn at the beginning of the *Treatise*, is not drawn on phenomenological grounds. Impressions of sensation 'arise in the soul originally, from unknown causes' (*T* 7), whereas impressions of reflection are 'antecedent to their corresponding ideas; but posterior to those of sensation, and derived from them' (*T* 8). The distinction thus concerns the origin, rather than the nature, of the impressions. Hence the NC-impression can only be *shown* to be an impression of reflection by tracing its source and showing that it is 'derived from' further impressions; and of course this is precisely what Hume does.

Where does all this leave us? Well, in §4.2 I claimed that it is phenomenologically implausible to hold that we have a 'feeling of helplessness or inevitability' when we infer effects from causes if it is those expectations themselves that are alleged to strike us as inevitable. What I am claiming here, by contrast, is that, thanks to phenomenal projection, it is the *effect* – an event in the world – that seems inevitable given its cause, and not our *belief* in the effect that seems inevitable given the *impression* of the cause. (Though of course the second case is an instance of the first in the special case where our attention is directed towards our own impressions and beliefs as causes and effects in their own right.)

If this is right, then there is a sense in which Hume does not *need* to say very much about the phenomenology of the NC-impression considered, as it were, in itself, independently of the effect which the phenomenal projection of it has on how things appear to us; in a sense, all that needs to be said is that it is that impression the having of which modifies sensory experience in such a way as to make events seem united rather than loose and separate.

4.4 Is necessary connection all in the mind?

So far, we have seen that Hume locates the impression-source of the idea of necessary connection in the transition of the mind from the impression of one event to the expectation that some other event will occur. But we need to return to the third question I asked in §4.2: what is the representational *content* of the idea of necessary connection? What do we *mean* when we say that one object is necessarily connected to another? Or, to put it another way, what (if anything) *is* necessary connection? It is at this point that the broader interpretative issues concerning Hume's views about the metaphysics of causation, briefly canvassed in §1.4, come to the fore. But at this stage I want simply to look – reasonably open-mindedly – at what Hume actually says about what we 'mean' by 'necessary connection' at this stage of the *Treatise* and the *Enquiry*. What I want to make apparent is that, despite some affinities between what Hume says in the two works, there are also some striking differences – differences that are closely connected with the different interpretative possibilities.

The most obvious similarity between what Hume says in the two works lies in his famous 'two definitions' of 'cause', which I shall discuss in detail in §4.5 and §4.6. Here are the two versions of the first definition:

> An object, precedent and contiguous to another, and where all the objects resembling the former are plac'd in a like relation of priority and contiguity to those objects, that resemble the latter.
>
> (*T* 170)

> [*A*]*n object, followed by another, and where all the objects similar to the first are followed by objects similar to the second.* Or in other words *where, if the first object had not been, the second never had existed.*
>
> (*E* 76)[9]

And here are the two versions of the second definition:

> [A]n object precedent and contiguous to another, and so united with it in the imagination, that the idea of the one determines the mind to form the idea of the other, and the impression of the one to form a more lively idea of the other.
>
> (*T* 170)

> [*A*]*n object followed by another, and whose appearance always conveys the thought to that other.*
>
> (*E* 77)

There are, however, some very large differences between the two works. First, and most noticeably, in the *Treatise* Hume straightforwardly *identifies* necessary connection with the transition of the mind:

> The necessary connexion betwixt causes and effects is the foundation of our inference from one to another. The foundation of our inference is the transition arising from the accustom'd union. These are, therefore, the same.
>
> (*T* 165)

Indeed, he *repeatedly* claims that necessity is 'something, that exists in the mind, not in objects' (*T* 165). He says that necessity 'is nothing but that determination of the thought to pass from causes to effects and from effects to causes, according to their experienc'd union' (*T* 166), that the 'efficacy or energy of causes is neither plac'd in the causes themselves . . . but belongs entirely to the soul, which considers the union of two or more objects in all past instances' (*ibid.*), that 'the efficacy of causes lie in the determination of the mind' (*T* 167), and so on.

In the *Enquiry*, by contrast, Hume does not make any claims at all to the effect that necessity is something that resides in the mind. On the contrary: insofar as he makes any claims about what necessity or power or causation *is*, what he says seems to point us in exactly the opposite direction. He claims that causation is a 'relation among objects', our ideas of which are so 'imperfect' that 'it is impossible to give any just definition of cause, except what is drawn from something extraneous and foreign to it', and he stresses 'the surprising ignorance and weakness of the understanding' (*E* 76).[10] Such remarks would appear to make little sense if he thought that necessary connection *is* the transition of the mind; for that transition is something our idea of which is not at all imperfect and reveals no ignorance or weakness.

This difference ought, I think, to make us think again about what might otherwise look like a similarity between the two works. In the *Enquiry*, Hume claims that we cannot form any idea of 'that circumstance in the cause, which gives it a connexion with its effect. We have no idea of this connexion, nor even any distinct notion what it is we desire to know, when we endeavour at a conception of it' (*E* 77). And in the *Treatise* he says that 'we have really no idea of a power or efficacy in any object, or of any real connexion betwixt causes and effects' (*T* 168). Clearly, in each case, Hume is saying that there is *something* wrong with the idea of necessary connection, considered as purporting to represent a real, mind-independent connection in nature. But the moral Hume appears to draw in the *Treatise* is that we cannot intelligibly even *think* that there are real necessary connections in nature: we 'do not understand our own meaning in talking so, but ignorantly confound ideas, which are entirely distinct from each other' (*T* 168). His moral in the *Enquiry*, however, seems to be that the connection between causes and effects lies beyond our cognitive grip – in other words, that there is something out there that we cannot grasp, and not that we cannot even intelligibly entertain the supposition that there is such a thing.

A second difference is that the conclusions of the *Treatise* are presented as considerably more shocking than those of the *Enquiry*. In the *Treatise*, Hume says, 'I am sensible, that of all the paradoxes, which I have had, or shall hereafter have occasion to advance in the course of this treatise, the present one is the most violent' (*T* 166); and 'I doubt not but my sentiments will be treated by many as extravagant and ridiculous' (*T* 167). In the *Enquiry*, Hume merely describes his conclusion as 'somewhat extraordinary' and characterizes the 'ignorance and weakness of the understanding' that he has revealed as 'surprising' (*E* 76).

It looks, then – at least *prima facie* – as though the *Treatise* and the *Enquiry* offer radically different accounts of what necessary connections or powers or forces are: in the *Treatise* Hume seems to be saying that necessary connection *is* the customary transition of the mind, whereas in the *Enquiry* he seems to be saying that it is a genuine feature of mind-independent reality, our idea of which, given its impression-source, is inadequate or imperfect. Whether or not the differences can be explained away as mere differences in style or emphasis, and, if they can, which version we should take to be the most accurate exposition of Hume's view, is a question to which I shall return in Chapter 7. In the current chapter, however, I shall stick with something the two accounts have in common: Hume's two definitions of 'cause'.

4.5 The two definitions

There has been a huge amount of interpretative discussion concerning the two definitions. Some of the discussion connects directly with broader interpretative issues; in particular, there is a dispute about what Hume *means* when he claims to be *defining* 'cause'. Defenders of the traditional interpretation of Hume on causation usually take Hume to mean roughly what contemporary analytic philosophers mean: he is claiming to provide necessary and sufficient conditions for the correct application of the concept 'cause' or, to put it another way, he is saying what it *is* for one thing to be a cause of another. However this has been disputed, especially by those who interpret Hume as a sceptical realist. Craig, for example, argues that 'a definition of cause, for Hume, is a statement of the conditions under which belief in the cause–effect relationship does in fact come about' (1987: 104). The interpretative motivation for this, of course, is that Hume's definitions make no mention of mind-independent necessary connections or powers or forces. So if Hume thinks that the truth of causal claims depends on the existence of such things, he had better think that our causal claims really do assert their existence; and so he had better *not* think that the definitions tell us what it is to *be* a cause. I return to Craig's proposal later in this section. For now, I shall stick with the traditional view of the definitions.

The major problem for the traditional view is that while Hume says that the two definitions 'are only different, by their presenting a different view of the same object' (*T* 170), they do not even appear to be extensionally equivalent, let alone necessarily so – and necessary extensional equivalence seems to be required if 'definition' is to be read in the traditional sense (see, for example, Robinson 1962).

Here, slightly paraphrased, are Hume's two definitions as they appear in the *Treatise*:

(D1)   Event *c* is a cause of event *e* if and only if *c* precedes and is contiguous with *e* and
      (1) *C*s (that is, events similar to *c*) are constantly conjoined with *E*s (events similar to *e*)

(D2)   Event c is a cause of event e if and only if c precedes and is contiguous with e and

(2)   the idea of c determines the mind to form the idea of e, and the impression of c determines the mind to form the belief in e

What's the problem? Well, for a start, whose mind is 'the' mind mentioned in (2)? My mind? Everyone's minds? The mind of someone whose associative mechanisms are working properly, that is, generating the appropriate output when and only when it has appropriate experience of constant conjunction? It had better be the latter, or the definitions do not stand a chance of being co-extensive. So let's assume so.

Even so, two events can satisfy (1) but not (2) simply by being such that *nobody* has ever observed any Cs or Es, so that nobody has had the ideas or impressions required for (2) to hold. And two events can satisfy (2) but not (1), since it might be the case that all the Cs I have observed have been followed by Es, and hence that on observing c I come to believe that e will follow, and yet it not be the case that (1) is true. In other words, I might have been unlucky enough to have observed an unrepresentative sample of Cs. Of course, this is consistent with there being nothing wrong with my *mind*; it's the world that is letting me down, not my associative mechanism.

One standard response to this lack of extensional equivalence is to claim that Hume only intends the first definition to be a genuine definition – something that specifies the truth conditions for causal claims – while the second 'definition' provides an account of either the assertibility conditions for causal claims – that is, the circumstances under which causal claims are justified – or else the conditions under which, as a matter of psychological fact, we *do* make causal claims. In other words, we do, or ought to, make causal claims just when the relevant determination of the mind occurs; but the *truth* of such claims is determined by the obtaining of (1).[11] This move effectively removes the requirement that the two 'definitions' be extensionally equivalent, since the second is not a definition at all.

However, given the fact that Hume really does seem to think of the two definitions as presenting 'a different view of the same object' (T 170), perhaps we should not give up quite so soon. One recent attempt to reconcile the definitions has been provided by Don Garrett (1997: ch. 5), who argues that, properly understood, the definitions are not just extensionally equivalent, but necessarily so. Garrett argues that each definition has a 'subjective' and an 'absolute' reading, and that the two definitions only *appear* to fail to be co-extensive because we are naturally inclined to give the first an absolute reading and the second a subjective reading. However, if we give both the same reading – whether absolute or subjective – they turn out to be necessarily co-extensive.

Let's start with the second definition, (D2). According to the subjective reading, the second definition concerns the 'determination' of the mind of a *particular* person – a person who may fail to make the transition from c to e when in fact (1) is met, because they have not observed any, or sufficiently many, past conjunctions; or who may make the transition when (1) is not met, because they have been exposed to an unrepresentative sample. Thus interpreted, (2) provides an account of the conditions under which, as Garrett puts it, 'objects function *psychologically* as causally related' (1997: 108).

However, Hume is no relativist about causation: he nowhere suggests that whether or not one thing causes another depends on the psychological state of the particular person who happens to be observing the events in question. So if (D2) is to have any credibility as a definition of causation, in something like the standard sense of 'definition', we have to read it in an 'absolute' sense: as referring not to a *particular* observer, but to 'an idealized mind or spectator – for example, one who accurately views all and only representative samples, has a well-developed human inferential mechanism, and suffers from no interfering biases such as those deriving from religion or eccentricities of the imagination' (Garrett 1997: 108–9).

Note that the notion of an idealized spectator involves both external as well as internal constraints: whether or not someone views all and only representative samples is not something that can be guaranteed by their psychology, no matter how good a scientific investigator they are. For a sample to be representative, there must be no future change in the course of nature; and this, of course, is a matter of how the world is, and not how things are solely with us. This is not, as it were, to over-idealize the notion of an idealized spectator, so that in fact no human being can *be* an idealized spectator even in principle; we *can* be idealized spectators, so long as there is in fact no change in the course of nature.

What about the first definition, (D1)? Well, that definition is standardly read in an 'absolute' sense: (1) is generally taken to refer to past *and future* conjunctions. But Garrett notes that more often than not when discussing constant conjunction Hume actually means only *past* conjunctions; for example, 'we have no other idea of this relation than that of two objects, which have frequently been *conjoined* together' (*E* 159). Indeed, just before the first definition as it appears in the *Enquiry*, Hume says, '[s]imilar objects are always conjoined with similar. Of this we have experience' (*E* 76). In this case, the first sentence *seems* at first sight to refer to past-and-future conjunctions, but in fact, given Hume's subsequent claim that we have experience of the conjunction, it seems he must be referring only to past conjunctions. This generates a subjective reading of (D1): one that refers to the past experience of some actual observer.

Garrett claims that, so long as we apply the same reading, either subjective or absolute, to each definition, (D1) and (D2) will, after all, be necessarily co-extensive. The idealized spectator will infer *e* on observing *c* if and only if *C*s and *E*s are constantly conjoined in the absolute sense; so, read absolutely, (2) holds if and only if (1) holds. And a normal, non-idealized spectator will infer *e* on observing *c* if and only if *C*s and *E*s have been constantly conjoined in their experience; so, read subjectively, (2) again holds if and only if (1) holds.

In fact, however, the definitions are not quite co-extensive when read subjectively, at least if by a 'normal' observer we just mean anybody, independently of whether their associative mechanism is functioning properly. We need to take the 'normal' observer, like the idealized spectator, to have a 'well-developed human inferential mechanism' and suffer from no 'interfering biases', else equivalence on the subjective interpretation will fail; for example, if the associative mechanism malfunctions, someone who has observed Cs to be conjoined with Es may not make the transition from c to e; or else they may make the transition in the absence of past constant conjunction. So the difference between the 'normal observer' and the 'idealized spectator' lies solely in the fact that the idealized spectator has experienced all and only representative samples of events: for any event types F and G, the idealized spectator has experienced a past constant conjunction of Fs and Gs if and only if in fact all Fs are Gs.

Given that understanding of the 'normal' observer, Garrett's interpretation seems to give us what we wanted – the extensional equivalence of the two definitions – and so leaves the way open for us to think of the definitions, read absolutely, as genuine definitions of 'cause' in the sense of providing necessary and sufficient conditions for the truth of causal claims. In fact, however, at one point Garrett himself characterizes the two definitions rather differently:

> [W]e can define 'cause and effect' either in terms of the *constant conjunction* that in fact produces the determination or transition of psychological association and inference, without specifying the psychological process to which it gives rise, or we can define 'cause and effect' in terms of the *association* and *inference*, without specifying the features of objects that in fact give rise to it.
>
> (Garrett 1997: 106)

Unfortunately, this characterization is inconsistent with Garrett's 'absolute' reading. For on that reading (D1) is to be read as referring to *universal* constant conjunction, as opposed to *experienced* constant conjunction. But universal constant conjunction is not 'the constant conjunction that in fact produces' the transition in the mind of the idealized spectator: the idealized spectator has observed a representative sample of Fs and Gs, and not *all* the Fs and Gs.

We could fix the problem by further idealizing the idealized spectator, by making her so that she has observed absolutely everything; but that would be rather too much idealization: the idealized spectator would then not be recognizably human; she might have had to observe and remember infinitely many events, for example. And anyway she would have no need for the associative mechanism of causation; having directly experienced all the matters of fact there are, she has no use for an inferential faculty.

There is a more natural way to fix the problem. Recall that Garrett takes the subjective reading of (D2) to deliver an account of the conditions under which 'objects function *psychologically* as causally related' (1997: 108). But we might extend the notion of objects 'functioning psychologically as causally related' in such a way that it covers both definitions on both the subjective and the absolute readings. In that case, (D1) would tell us the external circumstances in virtue of which two objects function psychologically as causally related to the normal observer (subjective reading) or the idealized spectator (absolute reading), with 'constant conjunction' meaning 'observed constant conjunction' in both cases – the difference between the readings being simply that the idealized spectator, unlike the normal observer, is guaranteed by stipulation to have observed all and only representative samples of events. Similarly, (D2) would tell us the internal circumstances – the psychological process – in virtue of which two objects function psychologically as causally related, again to the normal observer (subjective reading) or the idealized spectator (absolute reading).

The proposed amendment is significant because we now have an interpretation of the two definitions which both gets us extensional equivalence *and* is completely neutral on the issue of whether the definitions should be seen as genuine *definitions*, in something close to the contemporary sense, or whether they should be seen as *merely* specifying the conditions under which causal judgements are made, either for the normal observer or for the idealized spectator.[12] For example, for all that has been said so far, it might be that the conditions under which an idealized spectator comes to *judge* that *c* caused *e* do not specify the *content* of that belief at all. Imagine, by way of an analogy, that we wanted to specify the conditions under which an idealized spectator comes to believe that some unobservable entity, *o*, exists. Those conditions, *C*, will not, of course, include the the observation or detection of *o*, since not even an idealized spectator – a spectator who has *human* perceptual capacities – can detect *o*. It does not follow that *C* specifies the *content* of that belief; for that to follow, we would have to wheel out a semantic principle to the effect that the content of belief – the meaning of '*o*' – is determined by the circumstances under which the idealized spectator comes to believe in *o*. In other words, we would have to commit ourselves to a particular, empiricist view about meaning. In the absence of such a view, the fact that *C* specifies the conditions under which an idealized spectator comes to believe in *o* is logically independent of whether or not *o* exists: *o* might exist but (for example) have no observable effects whatsover, so that not even an idealized spectator would get to believe that it exists; conversely, the world might in principle be arranged in such a way that the observable phenomena are exactly *as if o* exists, and yet *o* does not exist.

The point here is that the necessary co-extensiveness of the two definitions, just by itself, leaves open the question of whether or not Hume intends them to tell us what causation *is*. For all that has been said so far, Hume might hold that what we (including the idealized spectator) *mean* by saying that one thing causes another outruns the evidence that we – including the idealized spectator – have to go on. In particular, when the idealized spectator believes that *c* caused *e*, she might believe *that c* and *e* are mind-independently necessarily connected, even though she can only acquire that belief thanks to past constant conjunction plus the transition of the mind.

So we do not yet have an answer to the question 'are the two definitions supposed to tell us what causation *is*'? In §4.6 I argue that the answer is no.

4.6 Causation as a natural and philosophical relation

Just before providing the two definitions in the *Treatise,* Hume says:

> There may two definitions be given of this relation, which are only different, by their presenting a different view of the same object, and making us consider it either as a *philosophical* or as a *natural* relation; either as a comparison of two ideas, or as an association betwixt them.
>
> (*T* 170)

Recall that a philosophical relation is 'that particular circumstance, in which, even upon the arbitrary union of two ideas in the fancy, we may think proper to compare them' (*T* 13), whereas a natural relation is 'that quality, by which two ideas are connected together in the imagination, and the one naturally introduces another' (*ibid.*). We know from what Hume says at the beginning of the *Treatise* (*T* 15) that he takes causation to be both a philosophical and a natural relation. We can consider any two ideas and place them (or, rather, what they represent) in the relation of causation. In addition, thanks to the associative mechanism of causation, one idea will 'naturally introduce' the idea of its effects. Hume's claim here, to be considering causation first as a philosophical relation and second as a natural relation, fits extremely uneasily with standard attempts to understand what Hume intends the two definitions to achieve.

Consider Garrett's characterization of the two definitions. As we saw in §4.5, Garrett holds that 'we can define "cause and effect" either in terms of the *constant conjunction* that in fact produces the determination or transition . . . or we can define "cause and effect" in terms of the *association* and *inference*' (1997: 106). Craig takes a similar view: the definitions characterize the 'circumstances under which belief in a causal connection arises, one concentrating on the outward situation, the other on the state of the believer's mind that those outward facts induce' (Craig 1987: 108).

Both Garrett and Craig thus characterize the two definitions as two different ways of describing how the associative mechanism of causation works. The first definition describes the input to the mechanism, or the 'outward situation' – observed constant conjunction – and the second definition describes what the associative mechanism does with that input: 'the state of the believer's mind that those outward facts induce'; that is, the inference from cause to effect. So, according to Garrett and Craig's accounts, *both* definitions are describing causation considered as a *natural* relation, since the associative mechanism of causation just *is* that mechanism by which the impression of the cause 'naturally introduces' belief in the effect, and, at the same time, by which we 'call the one object, *Cause*, the other, *Effect*' (*E* 75). But this is flatly incompatible with what

Hume says when he says that in the first definition he is considering causation as a philosophical relation: he is expressly *not* attempting to characterize causation as a natural relation in his first definition.

A similar problem arises for the more traditional view of the two definitions, according to which the first definition tells us 'what is going on in the world, independently of its effect on any observer', and the second tells us 'what goes on in the mind of an observer who is prompted to apply the concept of causation to the world' (Noonan 1999: 150–1). On this view, the first definition tells us – as it is often put – what causation 'in the objects' is: what it is in itself, 'independently of its effect on any observer'. In the same vein, Stroud says that the first definition 'describes all the objective relations that hold between the things we designate as causes and effects' (1977: 88–9). But, despite the prevalence of this view of what Hume is doing, it does not seem to explain what the connection is supposed to be between what causation 'in the objects' is, on the one hand, and causation's being a philosophical relation, on the other.

A philosophical relation, Hume tells us, is 'that particular circumstance, in which, even upon the arbitrary union of two ideas in the fancy, we may think proper to compare them' (*T* 13). A philosophical relation is thus not conceived by Hume as a relation that obtains between objects as they are in themselves, independently of any observer; after all, the circumstances under which *we* think it proper to compare two *ideas* can hardly be a mind-independent matter. To put the point another way, Hume's distinction between natural and philosophical relations is a distinction between two kinds of mental activity: between the 'natural' introduction of one idea by another, on the one hand, and the comparison of two arbitrary ideas, on the other. Why should this correspond to a distinction between 'what is going on in the world, independently of its effect on any observer', and 'what goes on in the mind of an observer who is prompted to apply the concept of causation to the world' (Noonan 1999: 150–1)?

A second worry for both of these interpretations of the two definitions arises from something Hume says earlier on in the *Treatise*. At the end of his discussion of causal reasoning – just after he has established that reasoning from causes to effects is brought about by the associative mechanism of causation – he says:

> Thus tho' causation be a *philosophical* relation, as implying contiguity, succession, and constant conjunction, yet 'tis only so far as it is a *natural* relation, and produces an union among our ideas, that we are able to reason upon it, or draw any inference from it.
>
> (*T* 94)

Just as with the two definitions themselves, Hume is here considering causation separately as a philosophical and a natural relation; but he is additionally claiming that we can only 'reason upon' causation considered as a natural relation.

100

Why does this create a problem for the interpretations of the two definitions considered above? Well, let's start with Garrett's and Craig's suggestion that the first definition corresponds to the input to the associative mechanism and the second corresponds to its operation. If that were right, then in the passage quoted above Hume would merely be making the point that in order to acquire beliefs in matters of fact – to 'reason upon' causation – we need not only to have the input that is required in order for the associative mechanism to operate; we also actually need it to *operate*. But, in context – at the end of a seven-page discussion of the means by which we infer effects from causes – this is such a trivial point that it is hard to see why Hume would bother to make it. Similarly, if we think of the first definition as providing an account of causation as it is in the objects, independently of any observer, Hume is again making a trivial point: that events' being *in fact* constantly conjoined will not, just by itself, generate belief. Given that the quoted paragraph concludes Hume's entire discussion of the origin of belief in matters of fact, we would expect him to be saying something rather more substantive than this.

Let's set these interpretations aside and concentrate on the distinction between causation considered specifically *as* a philosophical and as a natural relation. Seen in this light, what sense can we make of the two definitions? Well, causation considered as a philosophical relation is defined in terms of contiguity, priority and observed constant conjunction. Do those conditions identify 'that particular circumstance, in which, even upon the arbitrary union of two ideas in the fancy, we may think proper to compare them' – that is, think of the events represented by any two arbitrarily selected ideas *as* causally related? Yes they do. Hume excludes the transition or determination of the mind from his definition of causation considered as a philosophical relation not because he wants to define causation as it is in the objects, or because for some reason he wants to consider separately the input to the associative mechanism, but because he is concerned with identifying a relation under which we can 'compare' two *arbitrarily selected* ideas. And if two ideas we choose to consider have not become united in the imagination, then of course our taking them to be causally related cannot be due to the transition of the mind from one to the other.

This conception of Hume's first definition might be thought to raise a problem for Hume: if two compared ideas have not acquired a union in the imagination, doesn't that mean that one cannot genuinely think of them as necessarily connected and hence causally related, given that it is the union in the imagination that generates the idea of necessary connection? The answer, I think, is no: once we have acquired the idea of necessary connection, thanks to the impression arising from the operation of the associative mechanism, we can presumably deploy it in cases where the impression is absent, just as we can deploy any other idea in the absence of its impression-source. I can perfectly well believe that the tomatoes in the fridge are red and round without actually looking at them, and hence without having the relevant impressions. Similarly, if I can recall sufficiently many instances of Cs being conjoined with Es, or if, for example, a reliable source of information tells me that in their experience *C*s and *E*s have been constantly conjoined, I can perfectly well think it proper to place the idea of *c* and the idea of *e* in the relation of causation.

What about causation considered as a natural relation: '[*a*]*n object precedent and contiguous to another, and so united with it in the imagination, that the idea of the one determines the mind to form the idea of the other, and the impression of the one to form a more lively idea of the other*' (*T* 172)? A natural relation is 'that quality, by which two ideas are connected together in the imagination, and the one naturally introduces another' (*T* 13). At first sight, the definition of causation as a natural relation now looks curiously unilluminating. The fact that causation is a natural relation, just by itself, already guarantees that the idea of the first object naturally introduces the idea of the second; so Hume's saying that the first object is 'so united in the imagination' with the second that the 'idea of the one determines the mind to form the idea of the other' doesn't seem to add anything. But what it certainly does do is distinguish causation, considered as a natural relation, from the other natural relations – contiguity and resemblance – since (for one thing) neither in the case of contiguity nor in the case of resemblance does the *impression* of one object determine the mind to form a *belief* in the second.

There is a parallel here between the two definitions and the view I attributed to Hume concerning *a priori* reasoning in §2.4. There I argued that Hume recognized two distinct kinds of *a priori* reasoning: demonstration and deduction. Demonstration involves the comparison of two distinct ideas under a given (class *A*) philosophical relation, while deduction involves deductive *inference* from one idea to another, non-distinct idea. Each kind of *a priori* reasoning delivers *a priori* knowledge: the first delivers knowledge of class *A* philosophical relations and the second delivers knowledge of entailment: knowledge that one thing follows from something else.

According to the interpretation of the two definitions suggested above, there are also two distinctive kinds of *causal* reasoning, each of which delivers causal judgement: we have the comparison of two ideas under the relation of causation (causation considered as a philosophical relation) and *inference* from one idea to another (causation considered as a natural relation). The difference between *a priori* reasoning and causal reasoning (aside from the obvious differences: causal reasoning is not *a priori* and does not deliver certain knowledge) is that, in the case of causation, it is the very same relation – causation – that features in the judgements delivered by both routes, while in the case of *a priori* reasoning, the 'relations' involved are not the same: class *A* philosophical relations in the case of demonstration, and entailment in the case of deduction.[13]

This is what Hume means, I think, when he says that the two definitions 'are only different, by their presenting a different view of the same object' (*T* 170). The two definitions provide accounts of two distinct routes to causal judgement, and nothing stops Hume from holding that the *content* of that judgement – its 'object' – is the same, no matter which route we follow. If Hume's definitions themselves tell us nothing about the content of causal judgements but only how we come to make them, they really can be seen as presenting different views of the same object.

It's worth reflecting briefly on an often-noted feature of the two definitions about which I have said nothing up to now. Hume's definitions appear at the end of a project Hume has been pursuing, off and on, for a hundred pages in the *Treatise*. 'To begin regularly', he says at *T* 74, 'we must consider the idea of *causation*, and see from what origin it is deriv'd'. His search for the missing element – the origin of the idea of necessary connection – having finally been satisfactorily concluded, Hume proceeds to provide the two definitions. But, curiously, those definitions make no mention whatever of the very idea he has spent so long worrying about. Why would he be so concerned to trace the impression-source of the idea of necessary connection, if in fact we can perfectly well 'define' causation without appealing to it?

One possible answer is that his search for the origin of the idea of necessary connection has a purely negative purpose: to show that there is something illegitimate or incoherent about the idea of necessary connection, and so we must revise our concept of causation in such a way as to rid it of that idea, since its presence threatens the intelligibility of our causal talk. Another possible answer is that Hume is actually attempting to *reduce* the idea of necessary connection to that of constant conjunction: he is claiming that to think of c and e as necessarily connected just *is* to hold that Cs and Es are constantly conjoined. As I shall argue in Chapter 5, neither of these answers is satisfactory; in any case, neither is available if, as I have been arguing, Hume's definitions are intended as specifications of the routes by which we come to make causal judgements rather than specifications of the content of those judgements.

So why *does* Hume 'define' causation in a way that makes no mention of the very idea whose impression-source he has taken such pains to locate? The answer is in fact quite straightforward. The point of locating the impression-source was to vindicate our causal talk and thought: it is 'impossible to reason justly, without understanding perfectly the idea concerning which we reason' (*T* 74) and 'impossible perfectly to understand any idea, without tracing it up to its origin, and examining that primary impression, from which it arises' (*T* 74–5). The location of the impression-source confirms that the word 'cause' stands for a genuine idea, and hence confirms that we do genuinely mean *something* when we engage in causal talk and thought. Without having established this, providing an account of how it is we get to make causal judgements would be rather pointless: we need to know that talk of causes and effects is legitimate before it is worth stating the conditions under which we employ that talk. And Hume does not mention the idea of necessary connection in the definitions themselves simply because that would render them rather unilluminating. To say that we judge c to be a cause of e just when we judge c to be prior to, contiguous with and necessarily connected to e would not be utterly vacuous, but it would fail to explain *how* we get to judge that c is necessarily connected to e. Since Hume now has an account of how we get to judge this at his disposal, he deploys that account in the definitions.

Let's tie up some loose ends. First, where does this leave the issue of extensional equivalence? Well, the two definitions, conceived as providing accounts of two different routes by which we make causal judgements, still deliver something close to extensional equivalence in Garrett's sense. Imagine a properly functioning human being, S, who is told by a trusted witness that Cs have always been followed by Es in the past. S will thereby be in a position to judge that Cs cause Es, or that a particular c is a cause of a particular e, given the first definition. S will not be in a position to avail herself of the route to causal judgement specified by the second definition, however, since she has not herself observed the past constant conjunction, and so the idea of a C will not naturally introduce the idea of an E. Nonetheless, she will be such that if she *had* experienced the past constant conjunction, rather than having to take it on trust, she *would* be capable of judging that Cs cause Es by means of the route specified by the second definition: her causal judgement will accord with that of her informant, in whom the ideas of C and E have acquired the requisite union in the imagination.

Similarly, someone who satisfies the conditions of the second definition is also in a position to satisfy the conditions of the first definition. It might seem that such circumstances could not arise; after all, if I have acquired the habit of inferring Es from Cs, wouldn't I automatically think of an E on thinking of a C, and so not be in a position to, as it were, dispassionately *decide* to place the two ideas in the relation of causation? Not necessarily. Hume is surely not committed to holding that *every* time we imagine a C our minds are unavoidably drawn to imagining an E, for every pair of kinds of events such that we have acquired the habit of inferring one from the other. If that were the case, our minds would be endlessly and pointlessly running through successions of ideas. Presumably I can perfectly well imagine *just* the white ball being hit by the cue stick, without thinking about its causes or effects. And so there will be circumstances in which, despite my having acquired the habit of inference, I can imagine a C and, separately, an E, and place them in the relation of cause and effect.

The second loose end concerns the question of whether there is any reason to think that the first definition 'describes all the objective relations that hold between the things we designate as causes and effects' (Stroud 1977: 88–9). Well, maybe so, but we do not yet have any reason to suppose that it does, for we do not yet have any reason to suppose that the conditions under which we place two arbitrary ideas under the relation of causation – constant conjunction, contiguity and temporal priority – are all the relations there *are* between causes and effects. For one thing, Hume seems to mean only *past* constant conjunction in the first definition, and we would hope that at least some of the things we designate as causes and effects manage to be constantly conjoined *simpliciter*, else all our causal judgements will turn out to be false.[14] And, for another, nothing in the account offered above rules out the possibility that Hume takes our causal talk to reach out to real, mind-independent necessary connections in nature. As I have said, the two definitions are silent on the question of what our causal judgements

104

mean, and so they are similarly silent on whether there is more to causation than contiguity, priority and constant conjunction.

If the above account of the two definitions is correct, then, they do not (*pace* Garrett and Craig) describe the associative mechanism of causation, first in terms of its input and second in terms of its operation. Nor does the first definition provide a definition of causation as it is in the objects. Instead, the first definition describes the conditions under which one considers two arbitrary ideas and comes to hold that they are causally related, and the second describes the conditions under which we 'naturally' come to think of two events as causally related. What, then, is Hume's purpose in providing the two definitions? I suggest that his underlying purpose is epistemological.

For Hume, as we have already seen, causation underpins all our reasoning concerning matters of fact. But those 'reasonings' can be more or less sophisticated. At one end of the scale, they can be due to the brute, instinctive operation of the associative mechanism of causation – a mechanism we share with other animals. At the other end, they can be sophisticated and complex pieces of scientific reasoning. Hume's account of reasoning from experience – which covers the whole spectrum – is one that needs causation considered *both* as a natural relation and as a philosophical relation.

We need causation considered as a natural relation – we need the associative mechanism of causation – in order to draw *any* inferences concerning matters of fact at all: without that mechanism, we would form no expectations whatsoever. I take this to be the point that Hume makes when he says that it is 'only so far as [causation] is a *natural* relation . . . that we are able to reason upon it, or draw any inference from it' (*T* 94). This is a statement of Hume's central claim concerning causal reasoning: comparison of ideas, just by itself, can generate no new beliefs about matters of fact. It is only because we have the associative mechanism that causation considered as a *philosophical* relation can generate any causal judgements at all – not just because without the associative mechanism we would not have the idea of necessary connection, but because without the associative mechanism we would have no way of coming to believe that any past regularity will continue to hold, and so no way of coming to believe any causal claim whatever. But if we are to engage in properly scientific reasoning, we need more than blind instinct; we need to be able to consider, test, and accept or reject causal hypotheses, and for this we need causation considered as a philosophical relation.

This comes out clearly in Hume's 'rules by which to judge of causes and effects', which follow closely on the heels of the two definitions in the *Treatise*. Here, for example, is the fourth rule:

The same cause always produces the same effect, and the same effect never arises but from the same cause. This principle we derive from experience, and is the source of most of our philosophical reasonings. For when by any clear experiment we have discover'd the causes or effects of any phaenomenon, we immediately extend our observation to every phaenomenon of the same kind, without waiting for that constant repetition, from which the first idea of this relation is deriv'd.

$$(T\ 174\text{--}5)$$

Hume is here clearly stating that we can arrive at a causal judgement in the absence of the operation of the associative mechanism – that is, without waiting for the 'constant repetition' that would set up a union in the imagination. By 'we immediately extend our observation', he cannot be referring to the natural transition of the mind, since that would commit him to holding that, contrary to what he has consistently argued up to this point, we do *not* need experience of constant conjunction in order to acquire the habit of inference. Hence the need for causation as a philosophical relation: we sometimes need to be able to 'place' the relevant phenomena in the relation of causation despite not having acquired the habit of inference.

In fact, what Hume says here might seem rather puzzling, for surely, given his definition of causation as a philosophical relation, we cannot place two particular events in the relation of causation on the basis of *one* experiment. But presumably Hume does not mean by 'a clear experiment' simply any old case of observing one event, *a*, being followed by another, *b*. A *clear* experiment would presumably be a case where there are tightly controlled experimental conditions, so that no other plausible possible causes of *b* are present. This is confirmed by what Hume says earlier in the *Treatise* when he explains how it is possible to 'attain the knowledge of a particular cause merely by one experiment' (*T* 104): we can do so 'provided [the experiment] be made with judgment, and after a careful removal of all foreign and superfluous circumstances' (*ibid.*).

More generally, Hume's rules tell us what conclusion we *ought* to draw, given various kinds of experiential or experimental data: they provide the normative standards by which causal claims are to be judged. And, by and large, in the context of scientific investigation those causal claims will not arise because of the associative mechanism of causation; for example, when we find different effects proceeding from like causes we 'must conclude that this irregularity proceeds from some difference in the causes' (*T* 175). As we saw in §3.9, no such conclusion will arise from the operation of the associative mechanism just by itself; the 'must' here is a normative 'must' and not the 'must' of psychological compulsion.[15]

One might wonder at this point whether the move from 'is' to 'ought' here is rather too quick. I claimed earlier in this section that Hume's definitions describe the circumstances which in fact generate causal judgement. But if, as I also claimed, his purpose in providing the two definitions is epistemological, is he not deriving a claim about how we *ought* to go about making causal judgements – enshrined in the rules – from a claim about how we *do*, in fact, make them?

In effect, that question was answered in Chapter 3. Hume takes it for granted that causal reasoning tracks the course of nature and is therefore 'just' reasoning. We saw in §3.5 that he in fact accepts that causal reasoning is not the only way of acquiring beliefs about matters of fact; he holds instead that it is the only *just* way of acquiring them. His interest is thus genetic and epistemological at the same time: he wants to discover the mechanism that generates *reasonable* belief. The same point applies to the two definitions. The second definition states explicitly what was already implicit in Hume's positive account of causal reasoning (see §3.7): the associative mechanism not only generates beliefs in matters of fact; it is also responsible for generating causal judgement. And, given that the beliefs in matters of fact thus generated are reasonable – and reasonable *because* they are generated by a mechanism which tracks nature's regularities – the *causal* judgements that the mechanism simultaneously generates are *also* reasonable. The first definition shows us how reasonable causal judgements can be made in the absence of the operation of the associative mechanism. So the two definitions do not exhaust the *possible* means by which we can come to make causal judgements; we can succumb to education and superstition in the case of causal judgement just as much as we can in the case of beliefs about matters of fact. Instead, they exhaust the *reasonable* means by which we can come to make causal judgements.

4.7 Conclusion

One thing I hope to have established in this chapter and Chapter 3 is that given his genetic and epistemological concerns, Hume is not – and does not need to be – especially interested in either the semantics of 'cause' or the metaphysics of causation. His major arguments against rival views are arguments against epistemological views: the view that effects can be inferred *a priori* from causes and the related view that there are *detectable* necessary connections in the world.

His major positive claims are that the inference from causes to effects is due to an associative mechanism, that causal judgement is made possible by the existence of the impression which that associative mechanism generates, and that reasonable causal judgements derive (in the genetic sense) either from the operation of the associative mechanism or from the comparison of ideas of events which have been found by experience to be constantly conjoined. Those positive claims can all be established in the absence of any particular view about what our causal claims *mean* or about what causation in the objects *is*. If the argument of §4.6 is correct, Hume has much less to say on these semantic and metaphysical issues than is often assumed, because neither of his 'definitions' is supposed to make a claim either about what we mean by 'cause' or about what causation in the objects is.

Of course, this is not to say that Hume has *nothing* to say about the semantic and metaphysical issues, or that his overall philosophical position does not commit him to particular semantic and metaphysical views about causation. But the fact that Hume does not *need* to take a stand on these issues in order to drive home his central epistemological arguments might perhaps go at least some way towards explaining why it is so difficult to pin his semantic and metaphysical views about causation down. Still, that is what I shall try to do in the rest of this book.

5

THE TRADITIONAL
INTERPRETATION

We saw in Chapter 4 that one component of the idea of causation, for Hume, is the idea of necessary connection; and we also saw that Hume holds that the source of that idea is a 'transition' in the mind: the transition the mind makes when, on observing one event, we infer or come to believe that some other event will follow. The central interpretative question, when it comes to attributing a view to Hume about the semantics of 'cause' and the metaphysics of causation, is this: how do we put these two claims together in such a way that they can be reconciled both with Hume's theory of meaning and with what he actually says about the meaning of 'cause' and the nature of causation? Unfortunately, Hume's theory of meaning itself is an area of interpretative controversy, as is what he actually says about the nature of causation. (For example, he appears to say *both* that necessity is all in the mind *and* that there are secret powers in objects whose nature we cannot penetrate.)

In this chapter, I begin to work through the major interpretative dispute surrounding Hume's views on causation – the dispute about his semantic and metaphysical views – by focussing on what I am calling the 'traditional interpretation'. As we shall see, 'the traditional interpretation' turns out to encompass a variety of views; but they share a common core, and that is why I have lumped them together under a single interpretative heading. The core consists of a positive claim and a negative claim. The positive claim is that Hume holds that causation in the objects is a matter of temporal priority, contiguity and constant conjunction: our causal talk and thought cannot succeed in describing or referring to any more in the world than these features. The negative claim is that it is illegitimate or incoherent to apply the idea of necessary connection to external events.

These two claims by themselves suffice to distinguish the traditional interpretation from its rivals, since, as we shall see in Chapters 6 and 7, the projectivist interpretation denies the second claim, while sceptical realism denies the first (though sceptical realists differ amongst themselves with respect to the status of the second claim). But the two claims do not suffice to determine a unique interpretative position, for they do not determine a unique view about what ought to be done in the face of the alleged defectiveness of the idea of necessary connection.

One might, for example, take Hume's considered view to be that the ordinary, necessary-connection-involving idea of causation ought to be *revised* in favour of a cleaned-up, empirically respectable concept: one that involves just priority, contiguity and succession. I take this to be Mackie's position. Or one might hold that Hume recommends no such revision, so that we are effectively stuck with a defective concept of causation: a concept that has no legitimate application to the world, but which we nonetheless cannot help deploying. I take this to be Stroud's position. Or one might hold Hume to the view that our ordinary concept of causation does not in fact involve illegitimately thinking of events as necessarily connected at all; it merely represents events as standing in the relations of priority, contiguity and constant conjunction. On this view, there is nothing wrong with our ordinary concept of causation, and so no need for conceptual revision. I take this to be Garrett's position. Finally, one might hold that Hume takes priority, contiguity and constant conjunction to constitute the *truth* conditions for causal claims, but that, somehow or other, the idea of necessary connection – correctly deployed – plays a role in the *assertibility* conditions of causal claims. I take this to be Beauchamp and Rosenberg's and Wilson's position.

Whichever more specific view the traditional interpreter takes, the foundation of the traditional interpretation lies in what Garrett calls Hume's 'conceptual empiricism', and this is the claim with which I start in §5.1: with an account of how conceptual empiricism is supposed to lead to the traditional interpretation. My focus will be on how the traditional interpreter might reasonably read Hume's claim that the mind has a 'propensity to spread itself' on the world – a propensity that has come to be called 'projection'. For it is this claim in particular that is supposed to lead to the claim that we cannot legitimately apply the idea of necessary connection to events in the world. I argue that there is a plausible account of projection to be had, which one can reasonably attribute to Hume and which serves the traditional interpreter's cause. I shall argue in Chapter 6, however, that some relatively small, and equally plausible, modifications to this account deliver a projectivist interpretation.

In §5.2 I make a defensive move on behalf of the traditional interpretation concerning the following question: does the claim that causation in the objects is merely a matter of priority, contiguity and constant conjunction require Hume to hold that the nature of reality cannot outrun our capacity to conceive it? Both Edward Craig and Galen Strawson hold (roughly) that since Hume could not possibly hold the latter view he cannot hold the former view either. I shall argue that Hume can happily accept the former claim while denying the latter, and that what he says about necessary connection in the *Treatise* provides evidence that that is indeed his position. Again, I have one eye on the projectivist interpretation here, since both the traditional and projectivist interpretations agree that causation in the objects amounts to no more than priority, contiguity and constant conjunction.

In §5.3 I describe some versions of the traditional interpretation and argue against Stroud's position. According to Stroud's Hume, our causal talk is irredeemably defective, since we cannot help thinking of events as necessarily connected when in fact they could not possibly be so.

In the rest of the chapter, I criticize the view that Hume is a naïve regularity theorist about causation; that is, the view that he holds that to say that c caused e is to say that the constant conjunction, contiguity and temporal priority conditions are met. In §5.4 I argue that the two definitions themselves provide no evidence for this interpretation. In §5.5 I argue that there is no evidence that Hume takes it to be a conceptual truth that causes are contiguous and constantly conjoined with their effects. I also argue that the naïve regularity interpretation leaves it unexplained why Hume is so unconcerned with possible counter-examples to the naïve regularity theory as to fail to even mention them. (I shall argue in Chapter 6 that the projectivist interpretation solves both of these problems.) Finally, in §5.6, I raise what has become a familiar problem for the naïve regularity theory. If Hume is a naïve regularity theorist, he cannot distinguish between causal regularities ('As cause Bs') and accidental regularities ('As happen to be constantly conjoined with Bs'). I argue that Beauchamp and Rosenberg's and Wilson's attempts to solve the problem on Hume's behalf by appealing to epistemic considerations either fail or else commit them to a projectivist interpretation. The upshot of the chapter as a whole, then, is that the traditional interpretation, in all its various guises, is implausible.

5.1 Conceptual empiricism and projection

Hume holds that simple ideas are 'faint images' of simple impressions (T 1). This thesis is usually known as the 'Copy Principle', and Hume states it thus:

> [A]ll our simple ideas in their first appearance are deriv'd from simple impressions, which are correspondent to them, and which they exactly represent.
>
> (T 4)

> [A]ll our ideas or more feeble perceptions are copies of our impressions or more lively ones.
>
> (E 19)

Most commentators agree that the Copy Principle is a genetic thesis – a thesis about how we come to have ideas.[1] But it is also generally taken to have *semantic* consequences, since it is ideas that provide the ingredients for thought. If I lack a particular impression – suppose, for example, that I am congenitally blind and so lack the impression of *red* – I will lack the corresponding idea, and so cannot genuinely have any thoughts that involve the concept *red*. I might be able to utter perfectly good sentences involving the *word* 'red' – 'pillar boxes are red' and so on – but because the word 'red' is not associated with any idea in my mind I cannot really *think* that pillar boxes are red: I cannot understand the *meaning* of the sentence. The Copy Principle thus leads naturally to what Garrett calls 'conceptual empiricism': 'the view that the semantic content of thought is always fully derived from things or features of things as they have been encountered in sensory or reflective experience' (Garrett 1997: 33).

Now, this by itself does not get us very far in understanding what exactly it is that ideas are supposed to represent or how they get to do it. In the *Treatise* statement of the Copy Principle, Hume says that ideas 'exactly represent' impressions. But if we take him at his word here, he seems to be saying that ideas do not represent external *objects* (or their features) – trees, chairs, dogs – at all; rather, they represent purely mental items, namely impressions. But Hume is no Berkeleian idealist; he clearly holds that our beliefs about trees and chairs are beliefs *about* objects that exist independently of our experience.[2] So it looks like what Hume must really think is that sensory impressions themselves represent external objects, and ideas inherit their representational content from the representational content of impressions. An impression of a tree represents a tree just as a *picture* of a tree does; and so the idea of a tree, being a faint copy of the impression of a tree, also thereby represents a tree.

Let's suppose that this is a rough version of what Hume thinks. Now, what is the problem supposed to be when it comes to the idea of necessary connection? Well, the problem is supposed to derive from the fact that the impression-source of that idea – what I have been calling the 'NC-impression' – is not a *sensory* impression but an impression of reflection. As we saw in Chapter 4, Hume holds that the NC-impression does not *detect* any mind-independent necessary connections. Instead, in thinking or saying that *c* is necessarily connected to *e*, we *project* something internal – the felt determination of the mind – on to the world, where of course it cannot belong. And so it seems that the NC-impression, and hence the *idea* 'of' necessary connection, cannot successfully *represent* any mind-independent necessary connections. If it represents anything at all, it must represent what it does detect, namely the transition of the mind from one idea to another – that is, the inference from cause to effect.

This is (allegedly) a problem because when we think or say that two events *c* and *e* are causally, and hence necessarily, connected we do not take ourselves to be thinking or saying *that* the transition in the mind is occurring; rather, we take ourselves to be thinking or saying that *c* and *e* really are, mind-independently, necessarily connected. But, according to the view just described, either this is not something that we *can* intelligibly think or say, so that '*c* is necessarily connected to *e*' fails to express a genuine thought, or else it does express a genuine thought but represents the world as being a way it cannot in fact be, since the felt determination of the mind is a feature of us and not a feature of external objects.

Now, it is a matter for debate whether the account of representation sketched above really is anything like Hume's actual view. John Wright, for example, argues that the internal impression-source of the idea of necessary connection is no bar to that idea's genuinely representing the world in a way that it in fact is –

as a world of mind-independent necessary connections. According to Wright, it is only a bar to the idea's *adequately* representing the world; that is, capturing the true *nature* of necessary connections. I shall leave that dispute to one side, however (I return to it in Chapter 7), because I think there are grounds for rejecting the traditional interpretation that do not depend on agreeing with sceptical realists about Hume's theory of meaning.

Certainly a lot of what Hume says in the *Treatise* – especially in the section on the idea of necessary connection – does strongly suggest that it is illegitimate to ascribe mind-independent necessary connections to events. As we saw in §4.4, he repeats several times the claim that necessity resides in the mind and not in objects. More explicitly, in response to the charge that his view is a 'gross absurdity' he says:

> I can only reply to all these arguments, that the case is here much the same, as if a blind man shou'd pretend to find a great many absurdities in the supposition, that the colour of scarlet is not the same with the sound of a trumpet, nor light the same with solidity. If we really have no idea of a power or efficacy in any object, or of any real connexion betwixt causes and effects, 'twill be of little purpose to prove, that an efficacy is necessary to all operations. We do not understand our own meaning in talking so, but ignorantly confound ideas, which are entirely distinct from each other. I am, indeed, ready to allow, that there may be several qualities both in material and immaterial objects, with which we are utterly unacquainted; and if we please to call these *power* or *efficacy*, 'twill be of little consequence to the world. But when, instead of meaning these unknown qualities, we make the terms of power and efficacy signify something, of which we have a clear idea, and which is incompatible with those objects, to which we apply it, obscurity and error begin then to take place, and we are led astray by a false philosophy. This is the case, when we transfer the determination of the thought to external objects, and suppose any real intelligible connexion betwixt them; that being a quality, which can only belong to the mind that considers them.
>
> (*T* 168)

Hume appears to be offering us a dilemma here. We *can* use words like 'power' and 'efficacy' to signify qualities in objects with which we are 'utterly unacquainted'. If we do so, however, we 'do not understand our own meaning', because we do not have a 'clear idea' of what we are attempting to talk about. (I shall have more to say about this in §5.2.) Or we can use words like 'power' and 'efficacy' to 'signify something, of which we have a clear idea'. But if we do *that* we will not in fact be 'signifying' any 'real intelligible connexion' between objects. So neither option gives us what we would like to have: a 'clear idea' of a necessary connection between external objects.

It is important to be clear about what exactly it is, according to most versions of the traditional interpretation, that we ascribe to the world in our ordinary causal talk and thought. Traditional interpreters who grant that our ordinary causal talk involves deploying the idea of necessary connection take it that that talk involves committing an error – an error that can only be avoided by eschewing the idea of necessary connection. As we are about to see, different interpreters have different views about what, exactly, the error consists in. But one thing that all sides agree on is that Hume locates the *source* of the error in what has come to be known as 'projection'.

As we saw in §4.3, Hume provides the following explanation for why we ordinarily suppose that 'power and necessity' are 'perceived externally in bodies' (*T* 166):

> 'Tis a common observation, that the mind has a great propensity to spread itself on external objects, and to conjoin them with any internal impressions, which they occasion, and which always make their appearance at the same time that these objects discover themselves to the senses. Thus as certain sounds and smells are always found to attend certain visible objects, we naturally imagine a conjunction, even in place, betwixt the objects and qualities, tho' the qualities be of such a nature as to admit of no such conjunction, and really exist no where.
>
> (*T* 167)

And, he says, 'that same propensity is the reason, why we suppose necessity and power to lie in the objects we consider, not in our mind, that considers them' (*ibid.*).

As far as the traditional interpretation is concerned, the issue about what it is that we (erroneously) ascribe to the world in our ordinary causal talk and thought can be seen as an issue about what Hume means by 'quality' in the passage quoted above. Notice that he starts by saying that the mind has a propensity to 'conjoin' *impressions* with external objects, and ends by saying that we naturally imagine a 'conjunction, even in place', between the objects and *qualities*. There are two ways we might read this. First, we might read 'qualities' to mean just 'impressions'. In that case, in imagining the 'conjunction in place' between objects and qualities, we in effect imagine that objects possess the impressions themselves, so that in saying '*a* is necessarily connected to *b*' we in fact only succeed in saying that the NC-impression itself somehow resides between *a* and *b*. And of course this is nonsense.

This is the view that Noonan attributes to Hume. He says:

> What Hume has in mind, in talking about the mind's spreading itself on the world, is . . . what we might call . . . *literal* projectivism . . . it is what would be involved if someone thought a sad song was *feeling sad*, or a wilful murder was itself *feeling a sentiment of disapprobation*, or a beautiful painting was itself *feeling pleasure*.

Of course, these are not intelligible thoughts, because the objects in question could not possibly possess the properties being ascribed to them. But the same is true, Hume seems to want to say, of necessity considered as a quality in bodies.

(Noonan 1999: 148–9)

Thus, according to Noonan's Hume, there are 'no genuine . . . thoughts we can achieve by "spreading our minds on the world". There is only confusion' (*ibid.*). So, on Noonan's view, Hume is telling us that we cannot succeed in so much as *thinking* that *a* is necessarily connected to *b*. We can of course utter the sentence '*a* is necessarily connected to *b*', to ourselves or out loud, but the sentence does not correspond to a genuine thought.

The problem with this interpretation, however, is that the 'conjunction in place' between object and quality is supposed to be one that we 'naturally' imagine. What the traditional interpretation needs is thus an account of projection that not only renders our ordinary causal talk and thought illegitimate or mistaken, but also explains why we are inclined to engage in that talk and thought in the first place. Noonan's interpretation fails to satisfy this second constraint. We are not at all naturally inclined to imagine that external objects are literally endowed with impressions; it is *obviously* nonsensical to attribute feelings to songs, pictures and murders, and it is not something we actually do.

A.H. Basson offers a strategy that Noonan rejects, but which is in fact much more promising. Here is Basson's analogy:

A clear case of projection occurred during the late war, when people wrote to the newspapers complaining of the gloomy and despondent note put forth by air-raid sirens. Why, they asked, could not the authorities have arranged for these to play some cheerful and encouraging tune, like 'Britannia Rules the Waves'? The answer was, of course, that the note of the sirens was not despondent or alarming, but its acquired associations induced despondency in the hearer. Even if they had played 'Britannia Rules the Waves', people would soon have complained of a hitherto unsuspected menace in that tune. The projection was in fact nearly complete for most people: the warning note was actually felt as menacing, and the note at the end of a raid really sounded cheerful.

(Basson 1958: 76)

Noonan claims that the cases of the despondent note and necessary connection are not analogous for Hume. He says:

It is, of course, clear what mistake was being made by the writers to the newspapers in this entertaining story. They thought that the note made by the siren produced feelings of despondency in them, and would have done so even if it had *not* been associated, as it was, with the prospect of imminent death and disaster. So they thought the note had a certain dispositional property: being such as to produce certain effects in human hearers. And their mistake was in thinking that this dispositional property was possessed by the note independently of its association with wartime circumstances.

(Noonan 1999: 147)

This being so, the mistake involved in the case of the despondent note simply amounts to being mistaken about 'the dispositions of external objects to affect human beings':

> [F]inding something disgusting or boring, I might naively think that everyone will so do, that is, that the object has a disposition to produce that effect in every human being. . . .
>
> Similarly, given that there is an impression of necessary connection which is produced in one's mind in the circumstances Hume supposes (that is, when one has encountered a constant conjunction of *A*s with *B*s and is currently aware of an *A*) it would be possible to think that that impression of reflection had a less complex cause – for example, the mere observation of an *A*. And this mistake *would* be parallel to the mistake made by the newspaper writers. . . .
>
> But this is not the mistake Hume has in mind when he speaks of 'spreading our minds on the world'. For this mistaken belief, like that of the newspaper writers, *could* have been true. For Hume, however, the ascription of necessity to objects is as absurd as the ascription of spatial location to sounds and tastes.

(Noonan 1999: 148)

In fact, I think Noonan misrepresents Basson's position: the mistake Basson attributes to the writers to the newspapers is not the mistake Noonan attributes to them at all. After claiming that 'on experiencing *A*, *we feel compelled* to expect *B*', Basson says:

> It is this feeling of compulsion, that we have to expect *B* on the occurrence of *A*, which is projected [on] to the events themselves, and is as it were seen as a compulsion on *A* to produce *B*. The sense of compulsion in us appears as a necessary relation between external objects, just as the despondency in us appears as an intrinsic quality of the siren's warning note.

(Basson 1958: 77)

Basson's claim, then, is that despondency 'appears as an intrinsic quality of the siren's warning note' to the writers to the newspapers; and so, presumably, the

115

writers believe that despondency *is* an intrinsic quality of the note. And of course this is a different mistake to that of thinking that the siren's note is disposed to produce feelings of despondency independently of its association with wartime circumstances, since this latter mistake would not involve attributing any intrinsic qualities to the siren's note. Analogously, Basson takes Hume to hold that we ordinarily take necessary connection to be an intrinsic quality of – or, rather, relation between – objects. But necessary connection is not, and could not be, an intrinsic quality of objects, any more than despondency is. In other words, when Hume says that we 'naturally imagine a conjunction, even in place, betwixt the objects and qualities, tho' the qualities . . . really exist no where' he is not, according to Basson, saying that we naturally imagine that the *impression* of necessary connection (or despondency, or whatever) resides in objects. Rather, he is saying that we naturally imagine that the relevant impressions *represent* qualities that reside in objects. And, of course, that, on the traditional interpretation, is a mistake: the relevant impressions do not represent any quality that does or could reside in objects.

Now in fact the claim just made on Hume's behalf is ambiguous, for there are two distinct mistakes we might be making here. First, our causal talk might genuinely represent the world as containing real, mind-independent necessary connections, so that the mistake is to think that the world could actually be the way we thereby represent it as being. In that case, we do genuinely express a thought when we say '*a* is necessarily connected to *b*'; but it is a thought that could not possibly be true. Or, second, we could be mistaken in thinking that our causal talk succeeds in representing the world *at all*, so that '*a* is necessarily connected to *b*' does not express a genuine thought – but we mistakenly suppose that it does.

Actually we still have not exhausted the interpretative options. In §6.1 I shall argue for a slightly different option, which leads Hume towards a projectivist view of causation; and in §7.5 I shall describe how a version of sceptical realism can be derived from yet another conception of what we do when we 'spread' the idea of necessary connection on to the world. According to both of these additional accounts, Hume thinks there is nothing wrong with our ordinary, necessary-connection-involving causal talk and thought at all. The current project, however, is to find an interpretation of Hume's 'spreading' metaphor that is consistent with the traditional interpretation, and hence consistent with the claim that there *is* something irredeemably wrong with our ordinary, necessary-connection-involving causal talk and thought.

So, relative to that aim, which of the two possibilities just described should we attribute to Hume? Following Stroud (1977: ch. 4), I think we should attribute the first view to Hume: the view that our ordinary causal talk really does ascribe *necessary connection* to objects, in the sense that it represents the world as being a world of mind-independent necessary connections.

As we saw in §4.2, Stroud takes Hume to hold that the impression 'of' necessary connection is merely a peculiar feeling that accompanies, or is simultaneous with, the expectation that some event will occur, when that expectation is generated by the associative mechanism of causation (1977: 86). That feeling is thus not an impression *of* – in the representational sense – anything internal to the mind. Rather, Stroud says, the idea of necessity 'will simply be an idea of whatever it is we ascribe to the relation between two events when we believe them to be causally or necessarily connected. And for the moment we can only say that it is *necessity* that we so ascribe' (*ibid.*).

Stroud goes on to say:

> Although that is perhaps disappointing, it is important to see that we are in no better position with respect to any other simple idea. We get our simple idea of red from an impression of red, but if we ask what our idea of red really is an idea of, we can say only that it is an idea *of red*. It is an idea of whatever it is we ascribe to a ripe apple when we believe that it is red. And there still seems to be nothing to say if we ask why that impression from which the idea of red is derived is an impression *of red*, or why the impression that arises when we see a ripe apple is an impression *of red*. Again, there seems to be nothing to say. But that does not imply that we have no idea of red, or that it is only an idea of something that happens in our minds.
>
> (Stroud 1977: 86)

The view Stroud ascribes to Hume is thus this:

> [I]t is really *necessity*, and not just something that happens in the mind, that we project onto the relations between events in the world. In believing that two events are necessarily connected we believe only something about the way the world is, and nothing about our own minds, although we believe what we do only because certain things occur in our minds. And so it can be said after all that we really do believe (albeit falsely, according to Hume) that necessity is something that 'resides' in the relations between objects or events in the objective world.
>
> (Stroud 1977: 86)

Stroud thus gives projection a semantic role: it is thanks to the projection of the idea of necessary connection that we come genuinely to believe *that there are* objective necessary connections between events rather than simply having a certain kind of 'feeling' when we infer from an impression of *c* that *e* will occur.

This is a better view to attribute to Hume than the other possible view described earlier in this section – the view that our ordinary causal talk does not succeed in *representing* the world at all, so that we are incapable of genuinely *thinking* that one event is necessarily connected to another – because it fits better with what Hume says. For example, he says that the propensity of the mind to spread itself on external objects 'is the reason, why we suppose necessity and power to lie in the objects we consider, not in our mind, that considers them' (*T* 167). Hume is here more naturally read as saying that we really *do* literally suppose or think or believe that necessity lies 'in the objects' than read as saying that we cannot, in fact, suppose or think or believe any such thing.

Unfortunately, Stroud (2000) thinks that Hume cannot, in fact, coherently maintain the position just described: the view that 'we really do believe . . . that necessity is something that "resides" in the relations between objects or events in the objective world'. 'What is especially problematic for Hume', Stroud says, is that this is not the 'ordinary kind of falsehood or delusion' (as when I hallucinate a unicorn or erroneously believe that unicorns exist):

> The world as he conceives of it does not just happen to lack causal connections, virtuous characters and beautiful objects. He does not just think that if things had been different in certain intelligible ways, those qualities and relations would have been there. There is no coherent place for them in any world which he conceives of. What is problematic is therefore to explain how we can have intelligible thoughts or percep-tions which do not represent 'any thing, that does or can belong' to the way things 'really stand in nature', if we take the ways things could 'really stand in nature' to exhaust the range of what could be so.
>
> (Stroud 2000: 27)

The problem here, then, is this: how can we genuinely *think* that *P* (that a painting is beautiful, that *c* and *e* are necessarily connected, and so on), when '*P*' could not possibly be true? Surely if '*P*' could not possibly be true, that precludes the possibility of our genuinely *representing* the world as being such that *P*? After all, doesn't the fact that round squares could not exist or the fact that murders cannot have feelings prevent us from even imagining, let alone believing, that there are round squares or that murders have feelings?

I want to claim that there is no real problem here. As I said earlier, on Stroud's interpretation projection plays a semantic role in our ordinary causal talk and thought: it is thanks to projection that our causal thoughts get to (erro-neously) represent the world as a world of necessary connections. Now, why is it a problem for this view that, as it turns out, the world could not be the way we represent it as being? It *would* be a problem if the fact that the world cannot be that way were something that was *obvious* to us. It's obvious to us that the world could not contain round squares and that murders cannot have feelings, and so we cannot represent the world in those ways: we cannot so much as imagine that the world is like that. But the fact that nature could not contain necessary connections is not, on Hume's view, something that is *at all* obvious to us; if it were, he would not say that his conclusions 'will be treated by many as extrava-gant and ridiculous' (*T* 167).

Hume holds that we ordinarily assume that we *perceive* necessary connections. Indeed, I argued in §4.3 that he thinks that (once the associative mechanism is up and running) we experience events *as connected*: that is how they *seem* to us. And that is *why* we ordinarily assume that we can perceive necessary connections. One way to go with that thought (though I shall suggest another way in Chapter 6) would be to say that experience itself *represents* the world as being a world of necessary connections and that our causal talk simply inherits its representational content from experience, in just the way that the idea of a tree inherits its representational content from the impression of a tree. On that way of understanding Hume's view, it is entirely unmysterious how we could find ourselves representing the world as being a way that, as it turns out, it could not possibly be: we are systematically misled by the nature of our experience, and it takes a considerable amount of careful philosophical investigation to reveal that experience misleads us. Consider an analogy with colour. The view that there is an intrinsic quality of objects that our impression, and hence our idea, of red represents is a perfectly natural view for someone with little scientific knowledge to have. And it is a perfectly natural view to have because it *seems* to us that redness is an intrinsic feature of objects. Experience presents objects *as red*, just as Basson's writers to the newspapers' experience presented the siren note *as despondent*.

I claim, then, that Stroud's interpretation of Hume's 'spreading the mind' metaphor is viable: we can sensibly take Hume to hold that our ordinary causal thought represents the world as a world of necessary connections, but that it thereby represents the world in a way it cannot be. Hume's conceptual empiricism (allegedly) explains why the world cannot be that way, while phenomenal projection explains why we ordinarily suppose that it is.

5.2 Necessary connections and unknown qualities

Let's return to a passage from the *Treatise*:

> I am, indeed, ready to allow, that there may be several qualities both in material and immaterial objects, with which we are utterly unacquainted; and if we please to call these *power* or *efficacy*, 'twill be of little consequence to the world. But when, instead of meaning these unknown qualities, we make the terms of power and efficacy signify something, of which we have a clear idea, and which is incompatible with those objects, to which we apply it, obscurity and error begin then to take place, and we are led astray by a false philosophy. This is the case, when we transfer the determination of the thought to external objects, and suppose any real intelligible connexion betwixt them; that being a quality, which can only belong to the mind that considers them.
>
> (*T* 168)

119

In §5.1 I was concerned with what we do when we 'transfer the determination of the thought to external objects'. But it is worth saying something about what, from the perspective of the traditional interpretation, would be involved in calling 'qualities . . . with which we are utterly unacquainted . . . *power* or *efficacy*'.

The point I want to press in this section is that we can attribute to Hume the view that our necessary-connection talk cannot represent 'how things really stand in nature', as Stroud puts it, without attributing to him the view that there could not possibly be any objective connection of any sort between events. Hume has often been interpreted as holding both views; 'If Hume is right', according to Kripke, 'even if God were to look at [causally related] events, he would discern nothing relating them other than that one succeeds the other'.[3]

This particular interpretative claim has prompted a line of objection against the traditional interpretation, which runs roughly as follows. The view that there are no objective relations other than succession binding causes and effects together is obviously absurd. Moreover, it results from a kind of arrogance: it results from the view that what there is is constrained by what human beings can imagine or conceive. But Hume would not, of course, hold a view that is absurd. Moreover, he manifestly does not hold that what there is is constrained by what human beings can imagine or conceive. And so Hume cannot be a regularity theorist about causation: he cannot hold that causation is just a matter of constant conjunction, temporal priority and contiguity.

The way to block the objection is, of course, to press the point suggested above: that we can coherently hold Hume to the view that our causal talk cannot latch on to real necessary connections, or indeed to connections of any sort, in nature, while denying that 'there is nothing relating [effects and causes] other than that one succeeds the other'. This is a line that has been taken by some commentators who are sympathetic to the traditional interpretation. For example, Kenneth Winkler says that 'Hume's scepticism may consist in a *refusal to affirm* the existence of real powers' (2000: 67). Garrett agrees that 'for Hume there is no contradiction in the general supposition that there are things or qualities (nature unspecifiable) that we cannot represent. And he never denies, needs to deny, or seeks to deny, that there may be such things or qualities in causes' (1997: 114).

In this section, my aim is to get clear about exactly what view is being attributed to Hume here, and so I shall take it for granted that Hume does think that our necessary-connection talk cannot represent how things really stand in nature, and that causation in the objects amounts to no more than temporal priority, contiguity and constant conjunction. What needs to be shown is that that view does not entail – and Hume, characterized as holding that view, shows no inclination to endorse – the claim that there could not be any objective connection of any sort between events.

Here, then, is a reasonable way to read Hume's claim that 'there may be several qualities . . . with which we are utterly unacquainted; and if we please to call them *power* or *efficacy*, 'twill be of little consequence to the world'. There may well be more to nature than we are capable of detecting and hence representing. And we can, if we like, give an arbitrary name to whatever might exist that we cannot represent. But doing so serves no useful purpose, since in doing so we do not even succeed in representing some specific quality.

By way of an analogy, consider Basson's example of despondency in the air-raid siren's note. The people who wrote to the newspapers were complaining that the siren note was despondent – meaning that the note really did have an intrinsic quality that their feelings of despondency, and hence their idea of despondency, represented. And of course they were wrong about this: there is no such intrinsic quality. But now imagine that, having had this pointed out to them, someone insisted that, while their idea of despondency admittedly does not represent a genuine quality of the note (which is to say, it does represent the note as being despondent, but the note could not in fact really *be* despondent), there is nevertheless an 'unknown' quality of the note – a quality that their idea of despondency does *not* represent. And suppose they insisted, rather misleadingly, on calling this quality 'DESPONDENCY'.

Now, they might in principle be right that there *is* an unknown quality in the note. It might even be the case that that quality is typically present when, on listening to sounds, people get despondent feelings. It might even *cause* people to get despondent feelings. Tandy (2000) argues that infrasounds – very low frequencies which human beings cannot hear – can produce certain kinds of emotional responses, for example feelings of unease or fear. In principle, then, there could be some frequency that typically produces feelings of despondency. So it could, in some sense, be true that the mind-independent quality of DESPONDENCY exists. But, because we do not actually have any *idea* of DESPONDENCY – 'DESPONDENCY' is just an arbitrary name attached to an unknown quality – the claim that DESPONDENCY exists is an extremely unspecific claim. It is no more than the claim that some quality or other exists and is present in certain sorts of situation.

Of course, because 'DESPONDENCY' and 'despondency' have the same spelling, it would be easy to think that 'there is a mind-independent quality of 'DESPONDENCY' and 'there is a mind-independent quality of despondency' say the same thing. But they don't. The former claim attaches an arbitrary name to an unknown quality which may or may not exist and could be true: it could be true that there are unknown intrinsic qualities of sounds that produce feelings of despondency in us. The latter claim ('there is a mind-independent quality of despondency'), by contrast, deploys a *clear* idea – we are perfectly well acquainted with its impression-source – but could not possibly be true, because that idea does not represent a way the world could be. This difference is masked by the fact that we picked the name 'DESPONDENCY' to refer to the unknown quality. We might as well, and just as informatively, have called it 'the X factor'; and that would have been less misleading, since we would not have been at all inclined to confuse talk about the X factor with talk about despondency.

It makes perfectly good sense to attribute the same view to Hume when it comes to 'power', 'efficacy', 'necessary connection' and the like, and to claim that this is just the view he is expressing in the passage quoted at the beginning of this section. This is an important point because it seems that some authors – specifically Craig and Strawson – take it for granted that to hold Hume to the view that causation in the objects is no more than constant conjunction is to cast him as a crazy embryonic positivist; and of course nobody ought seriously to think that Hume has a *crazy* view.

Let's start with Craig, who wants to 'dislodge' the 'logical positivist's encampment on Humean territory' (1987: 128). He quotes Schlick:

> We must say that a question is meaningful, if we can *understand* it, i.e. if we are able to decide for any given proposition whether, if true, it would be an answer to our question. And if this is so, the actual decision could only be prevented by empirical circumstances, which means that it would not be *logically impossible*. Hence no meaningful problem can be insoluble in *principle*. . . . This is one of the most characteristic results of our empiricism. It means that in principle there are no limits to our knowledge. The boundaries which must be acknowledged are of an empirical nature and, therefore, never ultimate . . . there is no unfathomable mystery in the world.
>
> (Schlick 1936: 352; quoted in Craig 1987: 129)

Craig says of this passage:

> This is an amazing paragraph. The verification principle tells us that what we cannot know, we cannot understand either – the second inability follows upon the first. The way in which Schlick, by adding one *inability* to another, with such massive self-confidence conjures our potential omniscience into being is a show-piece of human self-deception. . . . Schlick's conclusion, 'in principle, there are no limits to our knowledge', no very distant relative of the Image of God doctrine, is not so much Hume's teaching as his target. Hume's heirs indeed!
>
> (Craig 1987: 129–30)

Well, of course it *would* be a mistake to attribute to Hume the very view that he is attempting to undermine. But – while I am not equipped to enter into a dispute about the interpretation of Schlick – one need not read the claim that 'in principle, there are no limits to our knowledge' or the claim that there is 'no unfathomable mystery in the world' in the way Craig reads them. Craig takes these claims to be statements of our 'potential omniscience', and hence to express a view that is a close relative of the Image of God doctrine. But one can instead read them as an expression of humility: a recognition of our limitations.

Our cognitive resources are so limited, Schlick might be saying, that we cannot so much as understand a question to which we cannot in principle provide an answer. This is not to say that a being with better sensory apparatus, and hence more cognitive resources, could not ask – and answer – lots of questions that *we* can neither ask nor answer. Such a being would know more than we do. But – limited beings that we are – we are not even capable of wondering what those questions might be, and if somehow presented with one we would not be capable of understanding what it was asking.[4]

Thus characterized, Schlick's view would, in broad outline, not be so very different to the view attributed to Hume above, in the sense that both hold that 'we do not understand our own meaning' when we use words to which no clear idea attaches and claim that we thereby represent some specific unknown quality (though that is not to say that Hume employs anything like the Verification Principle). But neither would bear even a faint resemblance to the Image of God doctrine: neither Hume nor Schlick would be committed to the claim that our lacking the idea of any particular 'unknown quality' guarantees that there *are* no unknown qualities.

Strawson adopts a similar line of objection. He says that the view '(O1) [that] all that causation actually *is*, in the objects, is regular succession' is 'wildly implausible', and that, since (O1) makes 'a positive assertion that something definitely does not exist', it 'is very seriously at odds with [Hume's] strictly non-committal scepticism with regard to knowledge claims about the nature of reality' (Strawson 1989: 11). The point I have been pressing is that Hume can in principle perfectly well agree with (O1) – wildly implausible or not – without making any 'positive assertion that something definitely does not exist'. We can coherently hold Hume to the view that our idea of necessary connection does not correspond to any necessary connection in nature without holding him to the view that, as Kripke puts it, there is 'nothing relating [effects and causes] other than that one succeeds the other'. For our idea of necessary connection is just that: *our* idea, derived from the operation of *our* psychological processes. Some other being might, conceivably, be genuinely able to detect some unknown (by us) quality of the cause, or an unknown relation between causes and effect, that we cannot detect, and so be capable of forming an idea of such a quality. But their idea would not be ours, even if in fact that quality were present in just those situations in which we use the term 'cause' – just as the existence of DESPONDENCY would not enable *us* to refer to it using the idea of despondency.[5]

This is not, of course, to say that the traditional interpretation is home free. On the contrary: in the rest of this chapter I shall argue that it is, in fact, untenable. My point is simply that this particular line of objection, if it succeeds at all, succeeds only against a version of that interpretation which holds Hume to the claim that there are not or could not be any objective connections at all between causes and effects; and there is no need to hold Hume to that claim.

5.3 Different versions of the traditional interpretation

As I said at the beginning of this chapter, the core that is shared by different versions of the traditional interpretation consists of a negative claim and a positive claim. The negative claim is that the idea of necessary connection does not and could not correspond to any feature of reality, given that its source is an impression of reflection. As we have seen, there is textual evidence for his claim – particularly in those passages of the *Treatise* where Hume repeatedly says that necessity resides in the mind and not in the objects themselves. The positive claim is that causation in the objects is merely a matter of temporal priority, contiguity and constant conjunction. And there seems to be textual evidence for this too. For example, Hume says:

> As to what may be said, that the operations of nature are independent of our thought and reasoning, I allow it; and accordingly have observ'd, that objects bear to each other the relations of contiguity and succession; that like objects may be observ'd in several instances to have like relations; and that all this is independent of, and antecedent to the operations of the understanding.
>
> (*T* 168)

However, while these two claims form the core of the traditional interpretation, they do not determine a unique interpretative position, because they leave as an open question what Hume takes to follow from the defectiveness of the idea of necessary connection. In this section, I briefly describe some different answers to the question.

I'll start with Stroud. As we saw in §5.1, Stroud holds that in our ordinary causal talk and thought we represent the world as being a way that it could not possibly be: we represent events as being necessarily connected. The consequence of this, of course, is that none of our ordinary causal claims are, or could possibly be, *true*. A natural move to make at this point, which I discuss later in this section, would be to claim that our ordinary concept of causation ought to be abandoned and replaced by a concept that *can* represent how things really stand in nature. But Stroud offers no such move on Hume's behalf.

The problem with Stroud's interpretation is that Hume shows no inclination at all towards the view that no causal claims are or could ever be true. Not only does he provide us with rules for making causal judgements, but his whole theory of the mind is causal through and through. The Copy Principle – the thesis that ideas are copies of impressions – is a causal principle (the impression *causes* the idea that is a copy of it; *T* 4–5); natural relations between ideas are causal relations (*T* 10, 169); and so on. But this employment of causal talk, and Hume's view that such talk is subject to normative constraints, is impossible to square with the claim that he thinks that all our causal claims are and must be false.

One might attempt to reply that, since we can no more help making causal claims than we can help inferring effects from causes – indeed, the two are sides of the same coin since both are products of the associative mechanism of causation – the fact that all our causal claims are false can make no difference to us: even knowing that they are all false, we cannot but continue to make them. I argued in §3.9 that Hume regards sceptical objections to causal *reasoning* as unanswerable but nonetheless idle: since nobody can genuinely fail to believe the deliverances of the associative mechanism, it is pointless to dwell on the fact that our predictions might turn out to be false. Why should he not make the same response to scepticism with respect to our causal *judgements*, which are after all delivered by the very same mechanism?[6]

By Stroud's own lights, however, the cases are not parallel. According to his interpretation, in the case of causal judgement we have good reasons – indeed decisive reasons – to think that our judgements are mistaken, whereas in the case of beliefs in matter of fact generated by the associative mechanism all we have is the mere sceptical *possibility* that a particular expectation is false, or that at some point in the future the course of nature will change, generating widespread predictive errors.

In another respect, however, the cases *are* parallel. In §3.9 I argued that the unavoidability of causal reasoning does not provide any justification for engaging in the kind of sophisticated causal reasoning described by Hume's rules. Similarly, even if one could argue on Hume's behalf that the unavoidability of causal *judgement* in general explains Hume's willingness to appeal to such judgements, it would not explain why causal judgement should be subject to the normative constraints provided by the rules. Nothing compels us to engage in sophisticated scientific investigation – to put ourselves in a position to make causal judgements that everyday experience by itself will not deliver.

Putting the point slightly differently: I argued in §3.9 that what *does* justify Hume's rules, from the perspective of causal reasoning, is the combination of the thesis that every event has a cause and the thesis that causation requires constant conjunction. Those two theses together provide a deterministic conception of the causal structure of the world and so entail that there are a lot more regularities than meet the untrained eye, since many types of event are not constantly conjoined *in our experience* with other types of event: many objects behave in ways that we can ordinarily neither predict nor retrospectively fully explain. And so we need to adopt procedures for uncovering those hidden regularities: we need to employ the scientific method.

But appealing to the fact that we cannot help thinking of the world as a world of causes and effects, just by itself, will not get us to that point, for neither the claim that every event has a cause nor the claim that causation requires constant conjunction is a claim that we are compelled, just from the everyday operation of the associative mechanism of causation, to believe. Certainly Hume himself does not regard either claim as psychologically mandatory; if he did, he would not need to argue that there is no such thing as chance, and he would not have hailed the discovery that causes and effects are constantly conjoined *as* a 'discovery' (*T* 87), reached only after a good deal of fairly sophisticated philosophical background has been put in place.

We therefore cannot hold Hume to the view that all our causal talk and thought is, and could not but be, false. This leaves the defender of the traditional interpretation with two options. First, one can attribute to Hume the view that our *ordinary* causal talk involves the 'spreading' of the idea of necessary connection onto the world, in the way described in §5.1, but combine this with the claim that he advocates a revision of our ordinary concept of causation, so that the ordinary, necessary-connection-involving concept be replaced with a concept that either does not involve the idea of necessary connection or else only involves the idea in a way that does not lead to wholesale error: that does not involve 'spreading' the idea on to the world.

This is the approach taken by (amongst others) J.A. Robinson, who says that '[i]n Hume's view it is a philosophical error to include [the element of necessity] in the analysis of the causal relation' (1962: 167), and Mackie, who says:

> When at the conclusion of the discussion in the *Enquiry* [Hume] says 'we mean only that they have acquired a connexion in our thought', etc., he is telling us what we can properly mean rather than what we ordinarily mean. He thinks that the ordinary meaning is itself mistaken, and calls for reform.
>
> (Mackie 1974: 20)

Second, one can attribute to Hume the view that our ordinary causal talk does not *really* involve the illegitimate spreading of the idea of necessary connection on to the world in the first place – or, at least, not in a way that renders all our causal talk false. I think this is Garrett's view.

Garrett's account (1997: ch. 5) starts from the thought that, for Hume, the idea of causation is an *abstract* idea. An abstract idea, for Hume as well as for Locke, is an idea that somehow manages to represent objects (or properties or relations) which do not exactly resemble each other. Thus, for example, the idea of a triangle is abstract because it represents *all* triangles, whether large or small, isosceles or equilateral, and so on. Similarly, the idea of a dog represents dachshunds, golden retrievers, collies and so on.

For Locke, an abstract idea is formed by abstraction from what differentiates all the items the idea represents, leaving only what is common to them. The abstract idea of a triangle is thus the idea of a solid figure with three sides and three angles: the idea is indeterminate with respect to sizes of angles and lengths of sides. So when we have the abstract idea of a triangle we do not have the idea of a *particular* triangle – a triangle with particular sizes of angles and lengths of sides – before the mind. Rather, the idea is indeterminate with respect to those features. Berkeley attacks Locke's account of abstraction, arguing that such indeterminate ideas are impossible – a sensible response if we think of ideas, as Berkeley does, as images, since the image of a triangle must depict the triangle as having determinate angles and lengths of sides. Berkeley argues that instead 'a word becomes general by being made the sign, not of an abstract general idea,

126

but of several particular ideas, any one of which it indifferently suggests to the mind' (1710: §11). In other words, the word 'triangle' becomes a general idea because it can suggest to the mind *any* idea of a particular triangle: on one occasion it might suggest the idea of an equilateral triangle with three-inch sides, on another occasion a scalene triangle with such-and-such specific length of sides and sizes of angles, and so on.

Hume sides with Berkeley in this debate; he says that 'all general ideas are nothing but particular ones, annexed to a certain term, which gives them a more extensive signification' (*T* 17).[7] Garrett glosses Hume's view thus:

> Upon noticing a resemblance among objects, Hume claims, we apply a single term to them all, notwithstanding their differences. The term is directly associated with the determinate idea of a particular instance. This determinate idea nevertheless achieves a general *signification* – and hence serves *as* an abstract idea – because the term also revives the 'custom' or disposition to call up ideas of other particular instances.
>
> (Garrett 1997: 103)

Garrett calls the set of particular instances to which the relevant term ('triangle', 'dog' and so on) refers its 'revival set' (1997: 103). A *definition* of an abstract idea specifies what it is that all members of the revival set have in common. For example, once I know the definition of a triangle ('an enclosed figure with three straight sides', say), I come to acquire the abstract idea of a triangle: I acquire the ability to call up any member of the revival set of the term 'triangle' – to bring to mind an idea of a particular triangle – and have it *serve* as representative of the revival set as a whole.

In the case of the abstract idea of a relation R, Garrett claims that the 'revival set' is constituted by all the pairs of objects or events (or whatever) that are related by R. So, for example, when using the term 'taller than' I call to mind the ideas of two particular objects, such that (I believe that) the first is taller than the second; and the idea of that pair of objects serves as representative of any pair of objects which stand in the *taller than* relation.

Given all this, the abstract idea of *causation* will be the idea of a particular cause-and-effect pair – <ball A strikes ball B, ball B moves>, say – such that the idea of that pair serves as representative of any pair of causally related events. A *definition* of causation is a specification of what all pairs of causally related events have in common: it is a specification such that, in coming to understand it, I learn how to identify the members of the revival set. Garrett claims that this is just what Hume's two definitions achieve: they provide two different means of identifying the members of the revival set for the abstract idea of causation. And, as we saw in §4.5, Garrett provides an interpretation of the two definitions which renders them necessarily co-extensive, which of course they need to be if we are to understand the definitions in the way Garrett proposes, since they both need to specify the members of the *same* revival set.

If we want to know what it means to say that one thing causes another, then, what we want to know, according to Garrett's account, is how to identify the members of the revival set for the idea of causation, so that the idea of any particular cause–effect pair can be made to serve as representative of any member of that set. Here is how the definitions achieve this:

> [E]ach cause-and-effect pair whose idea we become disposed to call up is such that all objects *similar to the first* have been followed by objects *similar to the second*, which results in a determination of the mind to pass *from the idea of the one to the idea of the other*. Thus, it seems that we can specify the membership of the revival set of ideas of cause-and-effect pairs in either of two ways, depending on whether we choose (i) to describe the shared (though not intrinsic) feature of the *pairs of objects* whose ideas become included in the revival set, or (ii) to describe the shared features of the *ideas of pairs* that are included in the revival set themselves. That is, we can define 'cause and effect' either in terms of the *constant conjunction* that in fact produces the determination . . . or we can define 'cause and effect' in terms of the *association and inference*. . . . These two approaches provide two different 'views of', or two different 'lights on', the revival set of ideas signified by 'cause'.
>
> (Garrett 1997: 106)

Garrett is thus clearly offering a version of the traditional interpretation: 'the revival set of ideas signified by "cause"' can be defined in terms of constant conjunction (first definition) or the determination of the mind (second definition). But Garrett nowhere suggests that Hume's definitions are intended to provide a *revised* concept of causation. I take it that the claim is thus that the definitions capture our *actual* idea of causation: while Garrett agrees that we 'mistake the internal impression [that is, the NC-impression] for the impression of a relation or quality intrinsic to individual cause-and-effect pairs, according to Hume, because we tend to "spread" this impression of necessary connection onto the objects' (*ibid.*), he appears not to hold that this 'spreading' or projection infects our actual, ordinary concept of causation.

So what, in that case, does the idea of necessary connection *do*? I take it that Garrett's view is that, while the NC-impression provides us with one way of acquiring beliefs about what causes what – it provides us with one way of determining which pairs of events are members of the revival set for the idea of causation – and while we might ordinarily be *additionally* inclined to believe that the pairs that are members of the revival set are related by necessary connection as well as priority and contiguity, that belief plays no role in the abstract idea of causation, since that idea is merely the idea of a pair of events that serves as representative of the relevant class.

In slightly different ways, then, Robinson, Mackie and Garrett offer interpretations which characterize Hume as something close to a naïve regularity theorist about causation: causation in the objects is no more than priority, contiguity and constant conjunction, and our causal judgements – in Robinson's and Mackie's readings, causal judgements that involve the revised rather than the ordinary concept of causation – do not involve attributing to causally related events anything over and above those three relations. The issue that will occupy the rest of this chapter is whether or not there are good reasons to attribute such a view to Hume.

5.4 The two definitions again

The central piece of evidence that Hume holds a naïve regularity view of causation is supposed to come from the two definitions – and in particular, obviously, the first definition. A pretty standard way to read the definitions, deriving from Robinson (1962), runs roughly as follows. The first definition is Hume's (revisionary) *definition* of causation, and the second 'definition' is not a definition at all: 'It is clearly an error on Hume's part', Robinson says, 'to have offered it *as a definition*' (1962: 167). According to Robinson, the function of the second definition is to *explain* why it is that we are mistakenly inclined to think that the first definition misses out something essential, namely necessary connection. We are inclined to think this because of the fact that causation is a natural relation: the impression of the cause induces us to believe that the effect will occur. Hume therefore offers in the second definition 'a "compromise" characterization of the cause–effect relation which, as it were, encapsulates' this explanation (*ibid.*).

A second reason for thinking that the second definition is not really a definition is that, characterized as a genuine definition, it is circular: it defines causation in terms of the *determination* of the mind to form the idea of the effect, given the idea of the cause. Taking the first, but not the second, definition to be a genuine definition resolves this problem: armed with a definition of causation (priority, contiguity and constant conjunction), we can apply it to the notion of determination that appears in the second definition. So to say that the mind is *determined* to form the idea of *e* given the idea of *c* is just to say that the two mental events – the presence in the mind of the idea of *c* and the presence in the mind of the idea of *e* – themselves stand in the relations of priority, contiguity and constant conjunction.

It is often thought that there is indirect evidence for this conception of the two definitions. After all, if Hume thinks that the idea of necessary connection cannot be legitimately applied to the world, then – unless he thinks that all causal claims are irredeemably false, which, I argued in §5.3, he doesn't – he *must* think that it is, as Robinson puts it, a 'philosophical error' to include the idea of necessity in the 'analysis of the causal relation' (1962: 167). But, as we shall see in Chapters 6 and 7, the claim that Hume holds that the idea of necessary connection cannot be legitimately applied to the world is highly controversial. So is there any *direct* evidence that Hume intends the definitions to be read in this way? In particular, is there any evidence that he takes it to be a mistake to include necessary connection in the definition of causation?

Robinson takes the following passage to be a crucial piece of evidence in favour of his view:

> Thus in advancing we have insensibly discover'd a new relation betwixt cause and effect, when we least expected it, and were entirely employ'd upon another subject. This relation is their CONSTANT CONJUNC-TION. Contiguity and succession are not sufficient to make us pronounce any two objects to be cause and effect, unless we perceive, that these two relations are preserv'd in several instances. We may now see the advantage of quitting the direct survey of this relation, in order to discover the nature of that *necessary connexion*, which makes so essential a part of it.
>
> (*T* 87)

Robinson says of this passage:

> The 'new' relation, now introduced over and above contiguity and succession . . . is heralded here as the sought-for missing condition which was needed to provide, with [contiguity and succession], a *sufficient* condition for *x* to cause *y*, and therefore to provide the analysis of the extra element of necessitation which was lacking when [contiguity and succession] alone had been adduced earlier.
>
> (Robinson 1962: 169)

There are several things wrong with Robinson's reading of the text, however. First, Hume is here explicitly concerned with what is 'sufficient to make us pronounce' that *x* causes *y*, and not (as Robinson claims) with a sufficient condition for *x* to *be* a cause of *y*. So Hume here means 'observed constant conjunction' rather than 'universal constant conjunction', and hence cannot be claiming to offer a sufficient condition for causation. Second, while Hume is clearly saying that the discovery of the new relation represents *progress* towards his ultimate goal of discovering the nature of necessary connection, he does not claim that he has now *reached* that goal. In fact, the very next thing he says is:

> There are hopes, that by this means we may at last arrive at our propos'd end; tho' to tell the truth, this new-discover'd relation of a constant conjunction seems to advance us but very little in our way. For it implies no more than this, that like objects have always been plac'd in like relations of contiguity and succession; and it seems evident, at least at first sight, that by this means we can never discover any new idea, and can only multiply, but not enlarge the objects of our mind.
>
> (*T* 87–8)

Hume is here saying that he has *not* yet provided 'the analysis of the extra element of necessitation': just the opposite of what Robinson takes him to be saying.

So let's turn to Garrett's conception of the two definitions. Garrett, as we saw in §5.3, rejects Robinson's account and claims that, properly understood – that is, once we disambiguate the subjective and absolute readings of each definition – the two definitions are necessarily co-extensive.

As we saw in §5.3, according to the view Garrett attributes to Hume, to have an abstract idea of X – dog, triangle and so on – is, on that view, to be able to call up a *particular* idea – the idea of Jim's terrier, say, or the idea of an equilateral triangle of a particular size – in such a way that that particular idea serves as a representative of the revival set for X, so that the idea of Jim's terrier *serves* as an idea of dogs in general, for example. In the case of the abstract idea of a binary relation, Garrett claims that the relevant revival set will consist of pairs of objects or events that stand in that relation.

Given all this, it looks as though the two definitions do provide support for taking Hume to be a naïve regularity theorist. For, on this view of abstract ideas, there just *is* no more to representing a relation as obtaining than, as it were, having the relevant revival set in one's mind – that is, being able to have the idea of a particular pair of events $<c, e>$ serve as a representative of the appropriate set. Thus Garrett says that the revival set 'constitutes' the 'representation of the causal relation' (1997: 110).

This conception of abstract ideas of relations suffers from a problem, however, for it appears to preclude the possibility of representing *any* relation as being anything more than simply a set of pairs of objects or events. Grant that we (or the ideal spectator) in fact come to think of c and e as causally related in just the way the two definitions specify. It seems that we might nonetheless still coherently have a dispute about what we mean when we say that c caused e. We might mean that c has a secret power of production which guarantees that e will occur, or that Cs and Es are constantly conjoined, or that the normal observer would be disposed to infer e if she were to observe a c, and so on. But given Garrett's conception of abstract ideas of relations, no such dispute is possible – or at least, whatever the dispute is, it is not a dispute about the meaning of 'cause'. But surely *something* is being disputed, and if it is not the meaning of 'cause' that is being disputed it is hard to see what it could be.

A second problem is that, as we saw in §4.5, Garrett himself seems to think of the two definitions as specifying the circumstances under which we come to make causal judgements, rather than the content of those judgements:

[W]e can define 'cause and effect' either in terms of the *constant conjunction* that in fact produces the determination or transition of psychological association and inference, without specifying the psychological process to which it gives rise, or we can define 'cause and effect' in terms of the *association* and *inference*, without specifying the features of objects that in fact give rise to it.

(Garrett 1997: 106)

I suggested in §4.5 that in order to square this claim with the 'absolute' reading of the first definition, we need to think of the absolute reading of the first definition as referring to constant conjunctions that have been observed by the idealized spectator: that is, to constant conjunctions that have been observed by someone who has observed all and only representative samples of events. But, as I argued, if we do this we are left with definitions that merely specify the conditions under which causal judgements come to be made (by us, or by the idealized spectator), and so they do not make any claims about the meaning of causal claims at all.

Whether or not these worries are conclusive, there are independent reasons to think that the two definitions do not provide any grounds for thinking that Hume is a naïve regularity theorist about causation. For I argued in §4.6 that the two definitions really should not be seen as specifying the meaning of causal claims. Instead, they should be seen as providing two separate accounts of the two kinds of mental operation by means of which we come to think of two objects or events as causally related – placing two arbitrary ideas under the relation of causation (first definition) and the operation of the associative mechanism (second definition). If that claim is right, then the two definitions, just by themselves, do not provide any textual evidence for or against any interpretative position concerning the meaning of 'cause'.

If there are any grounds for attributing a naïve regularity theory to Hume, then, they seem to come pretty much exclusively from the claim that the idea of necessary connection cannot be legitimately applied to the world. And while, as I argued in §5.1, we *can* attribute that view to Hume, there are, as we shall see in Chapters 6 and 7, other views concerning the application of the idea of necessary connection to the world that we can also attribute to Hume – views that do not result in conceiving him as a naïve regularity theorist.

5.5 Constant conjunction and contiguity: *a priori* truths or empirical discoveries?

A consequence of interpreting Hume as a naïve regularity theorist is, of course, that it turns out to be an analytic truth that causes are prior to, contiguous with and constantly conjoined with their effects. However, I argue in this section that, in the cases of contiguity and constant conjunction, there is no textual evidence to support that view. On the contrary: in both cases, Hume appears to regard the relevant fact as an empirical discovery.

Let's start with contiguity. Hume says:

I find in the first place, that whatever objects are consider'd as causes or effects, are *contiguous*; and that nothing can operate in a time or place, which is ever so little remov'd from those of its existence. Tho' distant objects may sometimes seem productive of each other, they are commonly found upon examination to be link'd by a chain of causes, which are contiguous among themselves, and to the distant objects; and when in any particular instance we cannot discover this connexion, we still presume it to exist. We may therefore consider the relation of CONTIGUITY as essential to that of causation.

(*T* 75)

This passage is most naturally read as claiming that the contiguity of causes and effects is a well-established scientific hypothesis and not a conceptual truth about the meaning of 'cause'. Distant objects are 'commonly found' to be linked by a chain of causes, and when we can find no chain linking them we *in fact* presume that there is one. There is no claim here that it is *inconceivable* that distant objects be causally related without being contiguous, or that we are *compelled* to think of distant causes as connected to their effects by a hidden chain.

What about constant conjunction? Well, we have already seen some instances in the text where Hume, in speaking of 'constant conjunction', is most naturally taken to mean 'observed constant conjunction' rather than 'universal constant conjunction' (see §4.5 and §5.4); in particular in the context of the first definition as it appears in the *Enquiry*. So, even if we were to take his talk about 'meanings' and 'definitions' at face value, we would be a long way from establishing that he takes *universal* constant conjunction to be part of the meaning of 'cause'. And of course if we take Hume's 'definitions' to be merely telling us the conditions under which we in fact come to make causal judgements, he *must* mean 'observed constant conjunction'.

In fact, there are very few uses of the phrase 'constant conjunction' in the text where it is at all plausible to suppose that Hume means 'universal constant conjunction'. The overwhelming majority of his uses of 'constant conjunction' explicitly or implicitly mean 'observed constant conjunction'. On almost every occasion, Hume talks of our 'finding' or 'remembering' or 'observing' that objects or events are constantly conjoined. Here are some examples taken from Hume's discussion of causal reasoning in the *Treatise*:

[T]he transition from an impression present to the memory or senses to the idea of an object, which we call cause or effect, is founded on past *experience*, and on our remembrance of their *constant conjunction*.

(*T* 88)

The idea of cause and effect is deriv'd from *experience*, which informs us, that such particular objects, in all past instances, have been constantly conjoin'd with each other.

(*T* 89–90)

133

It may, perhaps, be said, that after the experience of the constant conjunction of certain objects, we reason in the following manner.

(*T* 90)

Reason can never shew us the connexion of one object with another, tho' aided by experience, and the observation of their constant conjunction in all past instances.

(*T* 92)

When ev'ry individual of any species of objects is found by experience to be constantly united with an individual of another species, the appearance of any new individual of either species naturally conveys the thought to its usual attendant.

(*T* 93)

We have no other notion of cause and effect, but that of certain objects, which have been *always conjoin'd* together, and which in all past instances have been found inseparable. We cannot penetrate into the reason of the conjunction. We only observe the thing itself, and always find that from the constant conjunction the objects acquire an union in the imagination.

(*T* 93)

The one place in this entire discussion where Hume does not *explicitly* use 'constant conjunction' to mean 'observed constant conjunction' is right at the very end, where he says:

Thus tho' causation be a *philosophical* relation, as implying contiguity, succession, and constant conjunction, yet 'tis only so far as it is a *natural* relation, and produces an union among our ideas, that we are able to reason upon it, or draw any inference from it.

(*T* 94)

This, I think, should give us pause. Hume is here stating, for the first time, what has traditionally been taken to be the cornerstone of the traditional interpretation: he is telling us that causation, considered as a philosophical relation, 'implies' contiguity, succession and constant conjunction. Now of course it is just possible that, despite the fact that every previous time Hume has used the expression 'constant conjunction' (or similar) he has clearly and unambiguously meant 'observed constant conjunction', he here, suddenly and without warning, switches to meaning 'universal constant conjunction'. But that really does seem unlikely – not to mention incompatible with the reading of this passage suggested in §4.6.

Consider another passage that might be thought to support the traditional interpretation: Hume's third 'rule by which to judge of causes and effects'. Hume says:

> There must be a constant union betwixt the cause and effect. 'Tis chiefly this quality, that constitutes the relation.
>
> $(T\,173)$

One might think that Hume must mean 'universal constant union' rather than 'observed constant union' here, since causation surely cannot, on anyone's view, be 'chiefly' constituted merely by *observed* constant union. But now consider his fourth rule:

> The same cause always produces the same effect, and the same effect never arises but from the same cause. This principle we derive from experience, and is the source of most of our philosophical reasonings.
>
> $(T\,173)$

If causation were 'constituted' by universal constant conjunction, then the principle that the same cause always produces the same effect would not be a principle we 'derive from experience' at all; it would be an analytic truth.

I claim, then, that there is no direct textual evidence for holding that Hume takes contiguity or universal constant conjunction to be part of the meaning of 'cause'.[8] If he does have that view, it is puzzling that, having given himself every opportunity to state it clearly and unambiguously, he fails to do so.

If there is any reason at all to attribute that view to Hume, it is that it is difficult to see how he could fail to have it, given that the alternative appears to be that he takes causation to be a matter of succession, contiguity and *observed* constant conjunction; and such a view is obviously inadequate. But we already have good reasons to think that appearances are deceptive. In particular, I argued in §4.6 that Hume's first definition of causation should be read as a statement of the conditions under which it is appropriate to 'place' two arbitrary ideas under the relation of causation. So to read 'constant conjunction' in that definition to mean 'observed constant conjunction' is not to attribute to Hume the view that causation *itself* requires only observed constant conjunction; it merely involves attributing to him the view that that is what our reasonably judging events to be causally related requires, which of course is perfectly sensible.

The point here is that Hume can perfectly legitimately hold that there is a sense in which causation in fact requires universal constant conjunction without holding that it does so as a matter of definition. For he can hold that causes and effects are in fact (but not by definition) constantly conjoined, and so hold that our causal claims are hostage to the constant conjunction requirement in the sense that, given the way the world actually is (that is, given determinism), if two kinds of event fail to be constantly conjoined, then events of the first kind cannot be causes of events of the second kind.

Attributing to Hume the view that the meaning of causal claims is exhausted by priority, contiguity and constant conjunction raises another problem too. The problem is that if priority, contiguity and constant conjunction are considered to be conceptual requirements – requirements that any pair of events must, as a matter of conceptual necessity, satisfy if one is to be the cause of the other – then the view is, at least *prima facie*, subject to some pretty obvious counter-examples which one might reasonably expect Hume to be in a position to think of. For it seems that we can imagine two events to be causally related yet be neither contiguous nor joined by a chain of contiguous events, and we can also imagine that two events might be causally related yet fail to satisfy the constant conjunction requirement: they might be merely regularly, rather than constantly, conjoined.

Of course, it could be, and sometimes is, argued that even though these seem, *prima facie*, to be coherent possibilities, they are not in fact coherent possibilities at all.[9] But the fact that they are even *prima facie* possibilities raises a problem for interpreting Hume as a naïve regularity theorist, given that he is in a position to regard them as such; for he makes no attempt at all to defend his own theory against alleged counter-examples.

I shall argue in §6.3 that the projectivist interpretation allows Hume to resist – as he appears to – the view that universal constant conjunction is part of the meaning of 'cause', while holding on to the thought that, as a matter of empirical fact, causes and effects are constantly conjoined. And I shall argue that this would also explain why he is so unconcerned by the *prima facie* counter-examples just mentioned: he is unconcerned because, as a projectivist, for him they are not even *prima facie* counter-examples at all.

5.6 The problem of accidental regularities

I now turn to a different worry concerning the plausibility of the theory of causation that Hume, *qua* naïve regularity theorist, is putting forward. Other things being equal, we ought to credit Hume with a view that is not manifestly false in a way that he is in a position to recognize. And yet the traditional interpretation does appear to do just this.

Here is the problem. Consider the following two statements:

(1)   All *A*s are followed by *B*s.
(2)   *A*s cause *B*s.

According to the naïve regularity theory, (1) and (2) have precisely the same meaning. But it seems to be just obvious that this is false, because it can easily be the case that (1) is true and (2) false: there are some regularities that are merely accidental.

Several authors sympathetic to the traditional interpretation have suggested broadly similar ways in which we might try to avoid the problem on Hume's behalf. I shall examine the suggestions of Beauchamp and Rosenberg (1981) and Wilson (1986).[10] I shall argue that, while these attempts are heading in the right direction, they are not, insofar as they are successful, consistent with characterizing Hume as a naïve regularity theorist. Instead, they push him firmly in the direction of projectivism.

Beauchamp and Rosenberg offer the most sustained defence of the claim that Hume is able to deal with the problem of accidental regularities. Strictly speaking, they do not – so they claim – hold that Hume is a naïve regularity theorist, since they take him to hold that necessity, in the sense of the felt transition of the mind, 'must play a role in any correct theory of causation' (Beauchamp and Rosenberg 1981: 32). Nonetheless, they claim that, for Hume, constant conjunction is part of the meaning of causal claims, and that it is possible to offer a 'unified and defensible Humean theory of causation' – unified in the sense of doing justice to both of Hume's definitions. They proceed to offer just such a 'unified' account, which, they say, is 'the account most faithful to the spirit of Hume's intentions' (*ibid.*).

The role the felt transition of the mind plays, according to Beauchamp and Rosenberg, is precisely that it allows Hume to distinguish between accidental and causal regularities:

> The general direction of [Hume's] thinking can be reconstructed as follows: In causal contexts, the word 'necessity' does not function to describe or to convey information about events in themselves. Rather, it marks a distinction between lawlike generalizations and accidental generalizations needed for certain uses of predictive and subjunctive expressions.
>
> (Beauchamp and Rosenberg 1981: 142)

The problem that Beauchamp and Rosenberg are addressing is thus not – or at least not directly – the problem of accidental regularities raised above: the problem that Hume appears to be committed to holding that (1) and (2) have the same meaning. Rather, the problem they address is that of distinguishing between statements like (3) and (4):

(3)   Whenever large amounts of arsenic are swallowed by humans, death ensues.

(Beauchamp and Rosenberg 1981: 136)

(4)   All U.S. Senate speeches on marine life are followed immediately by the death of a European head of state.

(Beauchamp and Rosenberg 1981: 135)

Following Beauchamp and Rosenberg, let's call the state of affairs described by (3), if it is true, as a 'universal of law', and the state of affairs described by (4), if true, as a 'universal of accident' (Beauchamp and Rosenberg 1981: 132). Traditionally, the main difference between universals of law and universals of accident has been taken to be the fact that universals of law do, and universals of accident do not, support counterfactuals: if it is a universal of law that all Fs are followed by Gs, then it is true that, for any object, o, that is not F, if o had been an F, it would have been followed by a G. (If I had drunk a large amount of arsenic last night, I would be dead by now.) By contrast, if it is merely a universal of accident that all Fs are followed by Gs, then it is not true that for any object, o, that is not F, if o had been an F, it would have been followed by a G. (It is not the case that, if there had been a U.S. Senate speech on marine life last night, a European head of state would have died just afterwards.)

Beauchamp and Rosenberg also note a related difference between lawlike and accidental *generalizations* (1981: 135). Suppose that one has past experience of a constant conjunction between drinking arsenic and death. Then one will unhesitatingly come to believe (3), and one will also unhesitatingly be prepared to assert the corresponding counterfactuals ('if I had drunk a large amount of arsenic last night, I'd be dead by now', and so on; see Beauchamp and Rosenberg 1981: 136). By contrast, suppose that one has past experience of several instances of (4) and no counter-instances. In that case, 'even if one were in a position to know that there would be several further instances and no disconfirming ones, such evidence would be regarded as insufficient for further predictions and as inadequate support for subjunctive conditional statements such as "Had there been a Senate speech on marine life yesterday, a European Head of State would have died"' (Beauchamp and Rosenberg 1981: 135).

It is this alleged epistemological difference that forms the basis of the account that Beauchamp and Rosenberg offer on Hume's behalf. Their claim is that Hume takes the difference between universals of law and accident to *derive* from the epistemological difference just described. We *treat* lawlike generalizations, and not accidental generalizations, as a basis for prediction and counterfactual reasoning; and it is our so treating them that *makes* them lawlike. And so a universal of law is a universal of law *because* we so treat lawlike generalizations: what makes (3) – if true – describe a universal of law is the fact that we treat (3) as a basis for prediction and counterfactual reasoning. In other words, the difference between universals of law and universals of accident is a difference in our epistemic attitude towards the generalizations that describe them.

How exactly does all this bear on the problem of accidental regularities as defined above; that is, on the problem of distinguishing between (1) 'All As are followed by Bs' and (2) 'As cause Bs', when, according to Hume *qua* regularity theorist, they appear to have the same meaning? Beauchamp and Rosenberg do not directly address this issue, but they appear to hold that what goes for lawlikeness goes for attributions of necessity too. They say:

Hume was clearly sensitive to the nondescriptive, inferential uses served by modal discourse in causal contexts (*E*, §32, 59, 60). Whatever the exact content of his message, his most important legacy is the claim that '*x* is necessarily connected with *y*' is not a factual statement about nature. . . . However, to say that the world can be described without modal terminology is not to say that such terminology serves no important function.

(Beauchamp and Rosenberg 1981: 143)

In other words, they appear to hold that to attribute necessary connections to pairs of events is to do just what (on Hume's alleged view) we do when we designate a given generalization as a lawlike generalization – when we take it to mark a universal of law rather than a universal of accident. That is to say, when we attribute necessary connections to pairs of events – when we say '*x* is necessarily connected with *y*' or '*x* caused *y*' – we mark our epistemic attitude to those events. We mark the fact that we take events of the first kind to be a basis for prediction and counterfactual reasoning, so that we mark the fact that we believe or are prepared to assert things like 'next time an *X* happens, a *Y* will follow' and 'if an *X* had occurred just now, a *Y* would have followed'.

I shall argue later that Beauchamp and Rosenberg are right about this. However, what is important for present purposes is the fact that this claim is utterly inconsistent with the claim that Hume holds anything remotely like a naïve regularity theory of causation, or the claim – and this is Beauchamp and Rosenberg's claim – that a 'unified' theory of causation can be constructed (1981: 32); that is, one that somehow does justice to *both* of Hume's definitions, taken in the standard contemporary sense of 'definition'.

Here's why. Suppose we take the first definition of causation to be an adequate characterization of causation – that is, we somehow simply remove the idea of necessary connection. Then there is no difference in meaning between (1) and (2) outlined earlier in this section. But suppose we take the second definition to be an adequate characterization, and so take the idea of necessary connection to be part of the idea of causation. Then, on Beauchamp and Rosenberg's view of what we *do* when we attribute necessity to pairs of events, when we say that *c* caused *e*, we do more than simply say *that* events like *c* are constantly conjoined with events like *e*. For we also mark our preparedness to treat events like *c* as a basis for prediction and counterfactual reasoning. But, in that case, that commitment – the commitment to certain kinds of predictive and counterfactual inferences – must play a part in the content of what it is we assert when we assert '*c* caused *e*'. Otherwise we will be left with a theory of causation that accords with the first definition, and we will not be in a position to draw any distinction between (1) and (2). If the commitment in question did not play a part in the content of causal claims, then the most Beauchamp and Rosenberg would be able to explain is a difference between our epistemic attitudes to accidental regularities and our epistemic attitudes to causal regularities. But that would leave the problem of accidental regularities untouched, because if we are to draw the kind of distinction we need between (1) and (2) it has to be a distinction according to which (1) can in principle be true and (2) false. No difference in our epistemic attitudes towards (1) and (2) can achieve this result unless it affects the meaning of (2).

For Beauchamp and Rosenberg's claim about differences in epistemic attitudes to do the job they want it to do, then, they need to hold that those differences make a difference to the content of causal claims. And that is precisely to ascribe to Hume something like a projectivist position, according to which causal claims are expressions of epistemic commitments. So in fact what Beauchamp and Rosenberg are implicitly suggesting is a version of the projectivist interpretation. The passage quoted earlier in this section – where they say that Hume's 'most important legacy is the claim that "x is necessarily connected with y" is not a factual statement about nature' – points us very clearly in that direction.

It is worth noting the similarity between Beauchamp and Rosenberg's approach to the problem of accidental regularities and Wilson's. Wilson says that, on Hume's view, '[o]bjectively considered ... , there is no distinction between an accidental generalization and a causal generalization: both are of the simple form "All A are B". This is Hume's first definition of "cause"' (1986: 618–19). It is the second definition which, Wilson claims, provides the distinction between accidental and causal regularities – between, as Wilson puts it, *post hoc* and *propter hoc*. 'The distinction between *post hoc* and *propter hoc* ... cannot be objective; it is rather, Hume argues, subjective. This is the thrust of the second definition of "cause", which asserts that a generalization is causal just in case we are prepared to use it in counterfactual assertions and predictions' (Wilson 1986: 619). As Wilson later puts it:

> Hume is explicitly offering [in his second definition] a subjectivist account of causation: to judge that As cause Bs *just is* to assert in a specific way the matter-of-fact generality that all As are Bs, to wit, to assert it as usable for purposes of prediction and support of the assertion of counterfactual conditionals. After all, having argued against any objectivist account of the distinction between *post hoc* and *propter hoc*, Hume has little choice but to locate the difference as one of cognitive attitude.
>
> (Wilson 1986: 623)

Again, I will later argue that there is something right about this. But again, Wilson's suggestion seems to be not *just* that the distinction between causal and accidental regularities is, at bottom, a matter of 'cognitive attitude', but that it is a matter of cognitive attitude *as opposed to* content. In other words, his suggestion seems to be that the content of 'As cause Bs' is just 'the matter-of-fact generality that all As are Bs', despite the fact that in asserting 'As cause Bs' we somehow assert that generality 'in a specific way'. But – again – that cannot be right. For if 'As cause Bs' just *means* 'all As are Bs', then the two propositions will have the same truth conditions, and there will therefore be no possible circumstances in which (1) is true and (2) false.

5.7 Conclusion

I have argued that there are serious obstacles to adopting one version or another of the traditional interpretation. The central problem is really just this. On the one hand, Hume clearly endorses our causal talk, just as he endorses causal reasoning: he does not suggest that he thinks that our ordinary causal claims are irredeemably incoherent, or indeed defective in any way. On the other hand, once we discount the alleged evidence provided by the first definition and its ilk there is no serious evidence that Hume holds a naïve regularity theory of causation. For he does not suggest that our ordinary concept of causation does not include the idea of necessary connection; nor does he suggest that our ordinary concept of causation *does* include the idea of necessary connection but should, for that reason, be revised by excluding that idea.

I have also given two further reasons to think that Hume is not a naïve regularity theorist. First, he appears to regard the fact that causation requires constant conjunction and contiguity as an empirical claim and not an analytic truth. Second, *qua* naïve regularity theorist, Hume is saddled with no way of distinguishing between causal claims (As cause Bs) and accidental generalizations (all As are Bs) – a fairly basic error, which we might expect him to have noticed.

The projectivist interpretation, which is the topic of Chapter 6, faces none of these problems. By allowing Hume to endorse our ordinary, necessary-connection-involving causal talk, the projectivist interpretation allows him to take constant conjunction and contiguity to be empirical facts about causation; it also allows him to solve the problem of accidental regularities.

6

PROJECTIVISM[1]

The purpose of this chapter is to present and motivate a projectivist interpretation of Hume on causation. While Simon Blackburn holds that Hume is a projectivist about causation (see, for example, Blackburn 1984: 210–12; 1993a: 55–7; 1993b: 178–80; 2000: 107–11) and a projectivist interpretation is sometimes mentioned by other authors (see, for example, Craig 2000), it has not, so far as I know, been either articulated or criticized in much detail. I shall talk about 'the projectivist interpretation' as though it were an established interpretative option, but in fact it is not (yet); the point of this chapter is to put some flesh on the bones.

In §6.1 I lay out the basic semantic claims of projectivism and give an account of the nature of causal experience and causal talk which coheres well with Hume's claims about the propensity of the mind to spread itself on external objects. In §6.2 I argue that there are some close parallels between what Hume says about causation and what he says about morals, and hence that, given that a projectivist interpretation is a serious contender in the moral case, it therefore ought to be a serious contender in the causal case too. In §6.3 I describe how, considered as a projectivist, Hume conceives of the relationship between causal reasoning and causal judgement. And I argue that he can hold – as I claimed in Chapter 5, he does hold – that neither constant conjunction nor contiguity forms part of the meaning of causal claims. In §6.4 I show how the projectivist interpretation solves the problem raised for Hume considered as a naïve regularity theorist concerning the distinction between causal and accidental regularities. Finally, in §6.5, I show that the projectivist interpretation makes good sense of the thought that Hume takes the idea of necessary connection to play an important role in our conception of the world.

6.1 Projection and projectivism

Recall the account of the role of projection that I offered on behalf of the traditional interpreter in §5.1. The account goes roughly as follows. Thanks to the phenomenal projection of the NC-impression, our experience represents the world as a world of necessary connections. Our *idea* of necessary connection thus inherits that representational content, so that when we say or think that *c*

142

caused *e*, we represent *c* and *e* as being mind-independently necessarily connected. Unfortunately, *c* and *e* cannot stand in any such relation: since the source of the idea of necessary connection is the transition of the mind from the idea of *c* to the idea of *e*, there could be no intrinsic relation between *c* and *e* to which the idea of necessary connection corresponds, any more than there could be an intrinsic quality of Basson's siren note to which our idea of despondency corresponds.

Plausible though that account is, in the sense that it coheres well with what Hume says about the mind's propensity to spread itself on the external world, it cannot be quite right. For if that is Hume's view, then, as we saw in Chapter 5, he must hold that our ordinary causal talk is and must be false. But he appears to hold neither that our causal talk is in principle illegitimate nor that our ordinary concept of causation should be replaced with a concept that eschews the idea of necessary connection.

Fortunately, however, the view just described can be modified in such a way that it still coheres well with what Hume says about projection but does not saddle him with the view that our ordinary causal talk is irredeemably false. Roughly, the idea is that our (necessary connection-involving) causal talk does not purport to *represent* the world as a world of necessary connections. Nor does it purport to represent our own mental responses – the transition of the mind. Rather, that talk is non-representational or non-descriptive: in speaking and thinking causally, we express our habits of inference and project them on to the world.

Following Blackburn, let's say that 'we *project* an attitude or habit or other commitment which is not descriptive onto the world, when we speak and think as though there were a property of things which our sayings describe, which we can reason about, know about, be wrong about, and so on' (1984: 170–1). (Blackburn goes on to claim that projecting so defined is 'what Hume referred to when he talks of "gilding and staining all natural objects with the colours borrowed from internal sentiment"' (1984: 171).) To be a projectivist about causation is thus to claim that we speak and think as though causation were a mind-independent relation, even though in fact our so speaking and saying really involves projecting some sort of attitude or habit or commitment on to the world. Moreover, that projection is 'not descriptive', which is to say that it does not involve representing the world either as containing mind-independent causal relations or as being such that it *produces* that attitude or habit or commitment in us (or in ideal spectators, or whatever).

What attitude or habit or commitment is it that we project on to the world? Recall that, for Hume, in basic observational cases like watching someone sink the black our thinking of one event as cause and another as effect arises just when, on observing the first event, the associative mechanism responsible for causal reasoning kicks in and leads us to expect the second event to occur. So, clearly, if Hume is a projectivist about causation the relevant 'attitude or habit or commitment' will be something like the habit of inferring that an *E* will occur on observing that a *C* has occurred. I shall have more to say about this later.

What is it to 'speak and think as though' causation were a mind-independent relation? It is important to realize that, given the above characterization of projection, this does not involve our mistakenly *assuming that* there are mind-independent causal relations. The non-descriptive semantics of our causal talk would rule out the possibility of our even being capable of making this assumption: to think *that* there are mind-independent causal relations requires that the meaning of 'causal relations' is descriptive, which of course is what is being denied. What *would* be a mistake, on the projectivist view, would be to hold that the meaning of 'cause' is descriptive, and hence to hold that our causal talk so much as purports to be talk *about* mind-independent causal relations.

On a projectivist view, to 'speak and think as though' causation were a mind-independent relation is to speak and think in such a way that the habit or commitment in question takes on what Blackburn calls 'propositional behaviour' (1993a: 55). In the case of ethics (to put it rather crudely), 'Murder: Boo!' and 'Murder is wrong' express the same ethical attitude, but the second, and not the first, has propositional form. Similarly, the attitude expressed by 'Manslaughter: Boo! Murder: *BOO!*' takes on propositional form when one says instead, 'Manslaughter is bad, but murder is worse'. Such propositions, Blackburn says, 'stand at a needed point in our cognitive lives – they are objects to be discussed, rejected, or improved upon when the habits, dispositions, or attitudes need discussion, rejection or improvement. Their truth corresponds to correctness in these mental states, by whichever standards they have to meet' (*ibid.*).

Here is another way to put the point, this time borrowing from Huw Price (1998). Imagine teaching a novice speaker to use colour language. Two habits need to be instilled. The first is simply the habit of using the word 'red' (say) in *prima facie* appropriate circumstances, namely circumstances in which the novice speaker has red-experiences. The second is – as Price puts it – 'the habit of taking redness to be something that falls under the objective mode of speech'. Price continues:

> Against the general background of assertoric practice, the way to combine these lessons will be to teach novices to describe their redness experiences in terms of the notions of perception and belief – ordinary, world-directed perception and belief, of course, not any introspective variety. In treating the distinctive redness response as defeasible perceptual grounds for a corresponding belief, we open the way to such comments as 'You believe that it is red, but is it *really* red?' This in turn may call into play the standard methods of rational reassessment. In virtue of their acquaintance with the objective mode *in general*, speakers will be led into the practice of subjecting their colour judgements to reflective scrutiny by themselves and others. The objective mode brings with it the methods and motives for rational enquiry.
>
> (Price 1998: 125–6)

What about the causal case? Well, as with the ethical and colour cases, the basic idea would be that our coming to speak and think in causal terms – our expressing our inferential habits in propositional form, or adopting the 'objective mode of speech' – brings with it the resources for thinking of those habits as susceptible to critical scrutiny: as habits that can be refined, rejected, warranted or unwarranted and so on. In Hume's case, the relevant standards against which the expressed commitment is to be judged will be his 'rules by which to judge of causes and effects' (T 173–5).

Care is needed here, for it might seem as though to say that we cannot so much as think *that* there are mind-independent causal relations, as I did above, is tantamount to giving up on the thesis that we 'do really think of objects as causally or necessarily connected' (Stroud 2000: 21) – when part of the point of a projectivist interpretation of Hume is precisely that it allows him to endorse our ordinary causal talk and thought. The two claims are not really incompatible, however. To say that we cannot so much as think *that* there are mind-independent causal relations means, in this context, to say that we cannot genuinely think or say of two events that they stand in a mind-independent relation of causation to one another. As Hume says, we are 'led astray . . . when we transfer the determination of the thought to external objects, and suppose any real intelligible connexion betwixt them; that being a quality, which can only belong to the mind that considers them' (T 168). By contrast, to say that we do really think of objects as causally or necessarily connected is to say that we are *not* led astray – we are not making any kind of mistake – when we 'speak and think as though' causation were a mind-independent relation, in the sense just described. For so to speak and think is merely for the expressed commitment to take on 'propositional behaviour' – for us to adopt the 'objective mode of speech'. On the projectivist view, the propositional behaviour of our causal talk and thought does not amount to our genuinely representing the world as being a world of mind-independent causal relations, but it *does* amount to our really thinking of events as causally related.

Well, that's the basic semantic position that I am calling 'projectivism'. What exactly does attributing such a position to Hume amount to? Here is the beginning of an answer. I argued in §4.3 that for Hume, phenomenologically speaking, we experience paintings *as* beautiful or ugly, murders *as* vicious and, once the associative mechanism kicks in, events *as* causally related. In §5.1 I suggested on behalf of the traditional interpreter that Hume can reasonably hold that our experience, and hence our causal talk and thought, thereby *represents* events as necessarily connected. I now need to spin that story slightly differently, since on the projectivist interpretation our causal talk does *not* represent events as causally related. But I think this can be done. On a projectivist view, to *judge* a painting to be beautiful is to express the sentiment of pleasure which the perception of the painting produces and to 'think as though' beauty is a property of the painting in the sense described above. We can say the same when it comes to *experiencing* a painting as beautiful: this, too, involves projecting something non-descriptive on to the painting itself. The ingredients of thought are ideas, and the ingredients of experience are impressions (or sentiments), and so experiencing the painting as beautiful stands to judging it to be so just as impressions stand to ideas generally. Similarly in the case of causation: to experience a sequence of events as causal is to project something non-representational on to the sequence, just as judging it to be causal is.

I said 'project something' rather than 'project the NC-impression' for a reason. Discussion of projection in the context of Hume's talk of the mind's propensity to spread itself is typically conducted in terms of the projection of the *impression* of necessary connection; indeed, I have been talking in those terms up to now. We saw in §4.2 that, thus characterized, Hume faces a problem: it looks as though the NC-impression has to have the right kind of phenomenal character in order to make it plausible to claim that the projection of the impression results in our thinking of events as *causally* connected. If the operation of the associative mechanism produced a tickle behind the right ear, for example, projecting *that* impression on to the world would not result in our thinking of events as causally connected.

In §4.4, I claimed that the way to solve the problem is to think of the NC-impression as affecting visual experience, so that we do not simply *judge* events to be causally connected on the basis of visual experience that reveals only loose and separate events; rather, visual experience itself presents events *as* causally connected, thanks to the NC-impression.[2] This, by itself, makes it look as though we have, as it were, a self-standing impression, and we project *that impression* on to the objects. But I now want to make a slightly different claim. It is the *transition of the mind* that is projected, and not the NC-impression: the NC-impression just *is* the modification of visual experience that we undergo when the transition takes place.

Let's start with a recap of what has already been established. On first observing a *C* and an *E*, we experience them as loose and separate. Once we acquire the habit of inferring *E*s from *C*s, the nature of our visual experience changes: we no longer experience *C*s and *E*s as loose and separate, but rather as causally connected. That difference in experience, given Hume's arguments, cannot be due to the perception of any mind-independent relation between them, and so it must be due to the associative mechanism that generates the inferential habit.

It's at just this point that Hume starts getting himself in a bit of a muddle. In particular, he seems to confuse the transition of the mind with the impression it produces:

> Necessity . . . is nothing but an internal impression of the mind, or a determination to carry our thoughts from one object to another.
>
> (*T* 165)

> There is no internal impression, which has any relation to the present business, but that propensity, which custom produces, to pass from an object to the idea of its usual attendant.
>
> (*T* 165)

This connexion, therefore, which we *feel* in the mind, this customary transition of the imagination from one object to its usual attendant, is the sentiment or impression from which we form the idea of power or necessary connexion.

(*E* 75)

This just looks like a crass error on Hume's part – not the sort of thing he is usually guilty of, and certainly something one might have expected him to have fixed before he wrote the *Enquiry*.

Hume may be a little confused here, but I want to suggest that at least he is not simply making a crass mistake. I want to claim that he is trying (and failing) to articulate a thought that his own conception of impressions cannot quite allow him to make, and that is why what he actually says is rather mangled.

Our experience undergoes a change once the associative mechanism kicks in: events used to seem loose and separate, and now they seem necessarily connected. Now, Hume has no option here but to hold that there is an *impression* 'of' necessary connection, for he has no other way to articulate the thought that events seem, and so we judge them to be, necessarily connected. Given that there must *be* an NC-impression, and given that Hume has located its source (the transition of the mind), it really ought to be possible to, as it were, turn our attention inwards and focus on the impression itself, thereby getting a grip on its phenomenal character independently of the effect it has on our experience of the external world.

But now, when we turn our attention inwards, what do we find? Do we find a *feeling* of determination or helplessness or inexorability? I don't think so. And, unless my inner life is very different to Hume's, neither does he. Certainly he makes no attempt to persuade us that we find any impression with the right phenomenal character. Of course, we know what's in there: the associative mechanism is doing its thing. But, I suggest, Hume (like me) finds no introspective *awareness* of its operation at all.

This, I claim, is what leads Hume to run together the propensity 'to pass from an object to the idea of its usual attendant' and the 'internal impression' – the NC-impression. He has to put the difference the transition makes to our experience in terms of its producing an impression, but the impression it produces can only be found when we are attending to what is happening in the world.

If all this is right, then the NC-impression is not a distinct impression which we can isolate and 'feel' when we turn our attention inward, and which we project on to our sensory experience. Rather, it is the transition of the mind that is projected. The NC-impression just *is* the modification of experience that arises from our projecting the transition: the inference from one idea to another is felt *as* a union between the objects themselves.

I have dwelt on this claim because it is an important one in the context of motivating a projectivist interpretation of Hume. I argued in Chapter 5 that the major deficiency of the traditional interpretation is that it cannot characterize

Hume as someone who both endorses our causal talk and thought and holds that our thinking of the world in terms of causes and effects is importantly different to – and better than – our thinking of the world merely in terms of regularities. I have yet to make the case that the projectivist interpretation succeeds where the traditional interpretation fails, but that case will depend upon the claim that our thinking of the world as a world of causes and effects is more than simply a matter of projecting a 'feeling' on to it. What is needed is the claim that it really is our inferential habits that we project. I return to this issue in §6.3 and §6.5.

It might be objected that, if the account presented above is correct, then we cannot explain why Hume thinks that the mind's propensity to spread itself gives rise to an *error* – since, on the projectivist interpretation, no error is involved in our idea-of-necessary-connection-involving causal talk and thought at all. In particular, we cannot explain why Hume says that we are 'led astray by a false philosophy' when we 'transfer the determination of the thought to external objects' (*T* 168), since, on the projectivist interpretation, the transfer of the determination of thought does not lead to error.

The answer lies in the fact that Hume says we are led astray when we transfer the determination of thought to external objects 'and suppose any real intelligible connexion between them'. Hume can be interpreted as referring *not* to an error that is enshrined in our ordinary causal talk and thought, but to a *philosophical* error: the error of supposing that talk *represents* the world and so enshrines the supposition that there is 'any real intelligible connexion' between events. Hume is endorsing our ordinary causal talk and thought but rejecting a certain – representational – conception of the commitments of that talk and thought. And it is easy to explain why we make that mistake, if that is the mistake Hume is referring to: it is easy to assume that we perceive, and hence represent in our experience, mind-independent necessary connections because our experience is just as though we *are* perceiving them.

It might be thought that there is a problem lurking here for the projectivist interpretation. I have described causal experience as being such that events 'seem causally connected' rather than loose and separate. But I also just said that our everyday experience is just as though we are experiencing real, mind-independent necessary connections. But wouldn't the phenomenology of causal experience, described in the latter way, be such that it renders us unable to imagine the cause without the effect? Hume is clearly not committed to *that* claim, because of course he does think that we can imagine the cause without the effect. After all, his whole argument for locating the impression-source of the idea of necessary connection where he does – in the transition of the mind – hinges on the separability of the idea of the cause and the idea of the effect.

The claim made above – that our everyday experience is just as though we are experiencing real, mind-independent necessary connections – does not really commit Hume to the claim that causes and effects ordinarily seem not just united but inseparable, however. For we can say that, from a phenomenological point of view, the everyday experience of ordinary people does not discriminate between their detecting necessary connections and their projecting their habits of inference on to the world. Only careful reflection of the kind that Hume engages in reveals that we are doing the latter rather than the former. As Peter Kail puts it, 'the phenomenology . . . does not intimate to the subject its best explanation' (2001: 27). But that is not to say that the phenomenology of causal experience is itself, by its very nature, inherently misleading – that the phenomenology intimates to the subject the *wrong* explanation. The phenomenology is what it is; it is only when we reflect on how that phenomenology is to be explained that we are prone to the error of thinking that we are detecting a feature of the cause which licenses *a priori* inference to the effect. And of course we will only be prone to that error if we fail to notice that it is possible to imagine the cause without the effect.

While I have generally avoided saying that events *seem necessarily connected* according to Hume *qua* projectivist, and instead have mostly said only that they 'seem causally connected', we are now in a position to see that the two claims really amount to the same thing, so long as 'seeming necessarily connected' is read in the right way. In the context of projectivism, to say that events seem necessarily connected is just to say that our inferential habits are projected on to them, so that we 'call one object, *Cause*; the other, *Effect*' (*E* 75). It is not, in this context, to say that it seems to us *that* there is a mind-independent connection between them, such that the impression of the cause licenses *a priori* inference to the effect. Insofar as we are inclined to suppose that there *is* such a mind-independent connection between causes and effects, which is represented by the idea of necessary connection – insofar as we are capable of having a genuine thought when we attempt to make that supposition – we are led astray not by the phenomenology of experience just by itself, but by a false philosophy, the false philosophy of the Insight Ideal.

It is important to stress the fact that Hume, *qua* projectivist, is not committed to holding that there is definitely no more to the world itself than regularity. He is committed to holding, first, that the features of the world to which our causal talk responds are no more than contiguity, priority and constant conjunction; and, second, that we cannot manage to represent the world as a world of mind-independent necessary connections, given that the semantics of the expression 'necessary connection' render that term non-representational. But, as with the version of the traditional interpretation discussed in §5.2, Hume can still perfectly well 'allow, that there may be several qualities . . . with which we are utterly unacquainted; and if we please to call these *power* or *efficacy*, 'twill be of little consequence to the world' (*T* 168). Again, calling such unknown qualities 'power' or 'efficacy' would be akin to calling an unknown quality of Basson's siren notes 'DESPONDENCY'. Whether or not 'power' or 'efficacy' understood in this sense – as expressions that purport to refer to unknown qualities – genuinely succeed in referring is irrelevant to what we ordinarily mean when we use those expressions.

6.2 Causal, ethical and aesthetic projectivism

Direct textual support for the projectivist interpretation is admittedly thin, and this might be thought by some to constitute a decisive objection to it. However, one moral that I hope has been clear from Chapters 3–5 is that, given Hume's central concern with the genesis and epistemology of belief in matters of fact – that is, with causal reasoning – and his corresponding concern with the genesis of the idea of necessary connection, there is not much direct textual support for *any* view about what Hume thinks about the *meaning* of 'cause'. That this is so becomes even clearer once we appreciate that even when Hume is apparently explicitly talking about the 'meaning' of 'cause', and providing 'definitions', the fact that he appears to mean by 'constant conjunction' only 'experienced constant conjunction' should lead us to conclude that he is not intending to be 'defining' causation in the sense of saying what we really *mean* when we say that one thing caused another. The motivation for adopting one interpretation rather than another thus has to come from a more general conception of what Hume is trying to do.

A large part of the motivation for the projectivist interpretation comes from seeing a parallel between Hume's views on causation and his views on ethics and aesthetics, where a projectivist interpretation more clearly has some textual support, most notably in Hume's claim that '*taste* . . . gives the sentiment of beauty and deformity, vice and virtue. [It] has a productive faculty, and gilding or staining all natural objects with the colours, borrowed from internal sentiment, raises in a manner a new creation' (*E* 294). In this section, I shall argue that there is enough of a parallel between the causal and ethical cases to make a projectivist interpretation of Hume on causation at least a *prima facie* viable option.

Hume's views on ethics are, of course, no less a matter for interpretative dispute than are his views on causation. However the difference between the viable interpretative positions in the case of ethics is more subtle than in the case of causation: it is generally agreed that Hume is what Mackie calls a 'sentimentalist' about ethics (1980: ch. 5), and this rules out the possibility that Hume intends either a reductionist analysis of vice and virtue or a realist view according to which vice and virtue are mind-independent features of characters or actions. Hence in the case of ethics a projectivist interpretation, being a variety of sentimentalism, is more obviously a serious interpretative option, along with (amongst other options) a secondary-quality view (what Mackie calls 'dispositional descriptivism'), emotivism, and what Mackie calls 'the objectification theory', according to which moral features are 'fictitious, created in thought by the projection of moral sentiments onto the actions (etc.) which are the objects of [moral] sentiments' (1980: 74).

As we saw in §5.1, Stroud holds Hume to an 'objectification theory', so defined, in the case of causation. He also argues, in effect, that Hume holds the objectification theory in the case of ethics (Stroud 1977: ch. 8) and that this interpretation 'coheres better than any alternative with [Hume's] general philosophical aims' (1977: 185):

More of Hume's aims would be served by a theory of moral judgments that follows the same general lines as I suggested for the case of necessity. I contemplate or observe an action or character and then feel a certain sentiment of approbation towards it. In saying or believing that X is virtuous I am indeed ascribing to X itself a certain objective characteristic, even though, according to Hume, there really is no such characteristic to be found 'in' X. In that way virtue and vice are like secondary qualities. In saying that X is virtuous I am not just making a remark about my own feeling, but I make the remark only because I have the feeling I do. In 'pronouncing' it to be virtuous I could also be said to be expressing or avowing my approval of X. Hume thinks that approval is a quite definite feeling, so for him it would be expressing my feeling towards X.

(Stroud 1977: 184)

As we saw in §5.1, Stroud later expresses the worry that the view thus ascribed to Hume cannot, in the end, be made to work. The problem, remember, is that we cannot intelligibly 'ascribe to X itself a certain objective characteristic' – that is, *represent* X as possessing that characteristic – if our doing so involves 'gilding or staining' X with a feeling or impression. The projectivist interpretation solves that problem in the case of causation by denying, on Hume's behalf, that 'ascription' amounts to representation; and of course the same move can be made in the ethical case. In fact, Stroud comes slightly closer to projectivism in the ethical case than in the causal case, because he holds that in the ethical case 'in "pronouncing" it to be virtuous I could *also* be said to be expressing or avowing my approval of X' (1977: 182; my italics). But he rejects an 'emotivist' interpretation on the grounds that Hume 'thinks of a moral conclusion or verdict as a "pronouncement" or judgment – something put forward as true' (*ibid.*). Again, a projectivist interpretation solves this problem, since according to projectivism the projection of sentiment does indeed involve our putting forward moral conclusions, pronouncements or judgements: that is what 'adopting the objective mode of speech' (to use Price's phrase) amounts to.

Of course, a full defence of a projectivist interpretation of Hume on ethics requires more than merely showing that it solves Stroud's problem. But suppose that Stroud's argument for the claim that the objectification theory coheres better with Hume's aims than do any of the other alternatives that he canvasses is correct. (Stroud does not consider the projectivist interpretation.) If so, we do have reason to think that the projectivist interpretation is the best interpretation. This is partly because it solves Stroud's problem, but also because it allows Hume not only to make sense of our moral pronouncements, but to endorse them. According to the objectification theory, our moral pronouncements are all, strictly speaking, false: we ascribe to actions or characters features which they do not possess. But Hume does not suggest that he thinks this. He does not suggest that there is anything defective about our moral pronouncements, or that any

moral pronouncement is as legitimate as any other. Instead, he seems straightforwardly to endorse some moral pronouncements and reject others. Hence, at least
prima facie, the projectivist interpretation makes very good sense of what Hume
says about our moral thought and talk.

Unfortunately, there appear to be some significant disanalogies between what
Hume says about virtue (and beauty), on the one hand, and what he says about
causation, on the other. So, even assuming the viability of a projectivist interpretation in the moral case (and the aesthetic case), there are *prima facie* grounds for
suspicion that Hume does not endorse a projectivist view of causation. I shall
argue, however, that the differences are not as great as might be thought.

Perhaps the most significant problem is that Hume explicitly contrasts the
'boundaries of *reason* and of *taste*' (*E* 294). Reason 'conveys the knowledge of
truth and falsehood', while taste 'gives the sentiment of beauty and deformity,
vice and virtue'; reason 'discovers objects as they really stand in nature', while
taste 'has a productive faculty' which 'raises in a manner a new creation'; the
standard of reason is 'founded on the nature of things', while the standard of
taste arises 'from the internal frame and constitution of animals' (*ibid.*). 'Reason'
here should presumably be understood to include reasoning from experience –
that is, causal reasoning – since reason in a narrower sense (reasoning
concerning relations of ideas) discovers nothing about how objects 'really stand
in nature': it reveals no truths whatever concerning matters of fact. So surely
Hume holds that causal judgements stand on the side of reason rather than
taste: surely he holds that causal judgements express beliefs about 'matters of
fact', while moral judgements do not. But if Hume had more or less the same –
projectivist – view about causation as he has about beauty, deformity, vice and
virtue, then he would surely have to hold that causal judgements stand on the
side of taste rather than reason.

A second problem, related to the first, is that Hume asks, right at the beginning of his discussion of ethics in the *Treatise*, '*[w]hether 'tis by means of our ideas or
impressions we distinguish betwixt vice and virtue, and pronounce an action blameable or
praise-worthy*' (*T* 456); and his answer is 'impressions'. This sets up a second
apparent difference between his treatment of vice and virtue on the one hand
and necessary connection on the other. As Stroud says:

> In the case of necessity we are said to have an *idea* of necessity that we
> employ in formulating our *belief* that two events are necessarily
> connected, but Hume nowhere mentions a corresponding *idea* of virtue
> or goodness and he never talks explicitly about moral *beliefs*.
>
> (Stroud 1977: 185)

Instead, Stroud points out, Hume tends to talk about moral 'pronouncements'
and 'judgements'.

So it seems that Hume is drawing a clear distinction between, on the one
hand, belief, reasoning and matters of fact; and, on the other, 'pronouncements'

and matters of taste. And it seems that he intends causation to fall into the first category, while vice and virtue fall into the second category. I shall argue, however, that it is not at all obvious that Hume *does* take causation to fall into the first category.

Consider, first, Stroud's claim that 'we are said to have an *idea* of necessity in formulating our *belief* that two events are necessarily connected'. Well, Hume undeniably does say that we have an idea of necessity. But, so far as I can tell, he nowhere talks about the 'belief' that two events are necessarily connected. Instead, he says that 'we call the one [event] *cause* and the other *effect*' (*T* 87; see also *E* 75), and that we 'pronounce . . . two objects to be cause and effect' (*ibid.*).

In fact, given Hume's restrictive sense of 'belief', this is just what we should expect: Hume restricts 'belief' to what is inferred on the basis of a present impression (of sensation or memory) together with past experience of constant conjunction (see *T* 94–8). So whatever it is we do when we 'pronounce' *a* to be a cause of *b*, the only candidates for being the objects of *belief* here are *a* and *b*. One might therefore object that Hume's unwillingness to talk about our believing *that a* caused *b* is merely a by-product of his somewhat idiosyncratic use of the term 'belief'. But this would be unwarranted, for Hume's notion of 'matter of fact' is similarly restricted. 'Reasoning concerning matters of fact', for Hume, is reasoning *from* one matter of fact *to* another; that is, from cause to effect. He does not need to think, and nowhere says, that *a*'s *being* a cause of *b* is an *additional* matter of fact.

What I am suggesting here is that Hume's explicit contrast between reason and taste can be read as a contrast between the *objects* of reason (including causal reasoning) on the one hand – what reason leads us to *believe* – and the 'objects' of taste on the other. Reason leads us to form beliefs about matters of fact: beliefs about 'objects as they really are in nature'. In the case of ethics, by contrast, there are no such matters of fact to represent. There are no 'objects' of moral thought, since such thought does not attempt to represent matters of fact: it does not attempt to capture objects as they really are in nature. Moral thought, unlike reasoning, does not deliver belief in matters of fact; rather, it involves moral 'pronouncements', in which sentiment plays an ineliminable role. *This* contrast between reason and taste is one that makes no implicit claim about causal thought – as opposed to the objects of causal reasoning – at all. Hume need not think of causation as an *object* of reason, in the sense that our causal pronouncements or judgements are themselves beliefs that purport to represent matters of fact. So the contrast is entirely compatible with the claim that causal pronouncements, like moral pronouncements, are not beliefs in matters of fact, do not discover objects as they really stand in nature, and 'raise in a manner a new creation'.

This still leaves us with a version of the difference noted by Stroud, however. While I have denied that Hume holds that we have causal *beliefs*, strictly speaking, he nonetheless does appear to think that the *idea* of necessary connection plays a role in our causal thought, whereas in the case of moral thought it is the *impressions* of vice and virtue that are supposed to play the role: in his discussions of ethics, he does not talk about the *ideas* of vice and virtue.

However, we can resolve the apparent discrepancy between causal and moral thought by pushing Hume towards the view that there *are* ideas of vice and virtue, which play a role in moral thought, even though he does not say that there are. There are three reasons for thinking that Hume can be pushed towards that view. First, at the beginning of the *Treatise*, Hume talks quite freely about 'the ideas of passion and desire' (*T* 7) and 'the idea of pleasure or pain' (*T* 8). And he goes on to say that these ideas in turn produce 'the new impressions of desire and aversion, hope and fear' which 'again are copied by the memory and imagination, and become ideas' (*ibid.*). If Hume thinks we have ideas of desire, aversion and the like, he has no principled reason to deny that we have ideas of vice and virtue. Indeed, in the aesthetic case, Hume explicitly says that we *do* have 'an idea of the perfect beauty' (1757: 234).

Second, as Stroud points out, the fact that Hume denies that the idea of virtue or goodness plays a role in our moral pronouncements presents him with a problem: 'what could a moral "pronouncement" be? It would seem to consist only of an impression or feeling, but how do we employ that very feeling in formulating a "pronouncement"?' (Stroud 1977: 185). Stroud goes on to say that what Hume *ought* to do here is to say what he says in the case of necessary connection: 'I make the distinction [between vice and virtue] on the basis of my impression or feeling, but I use an *idea* of viciousness or virtuousness in making my pronouncement' (Stroud 1977: 186).

Third, Hume needs to hold that we can think about vice and virtue without actually having the relevant impressions – in which case we must do so by deploying the ideas of vice and virtue rather than the impressions – even if he holds that we cannot *pronounce* a person or action to be virtuous without having the corresponding impression. For otherwise we would not be able even to entertain the possibility that our moral judgements are mistaken, or wonder what the appropriate moral attitude in a particular case is. For example, I might judge that a certain politician is deplorably insincere and manipulative, and do so because of the moral sentiment I feel when I consider her actions. But I am still capable of considering the possibility that I have misjudged her: I can consider the possibility that she is a thoroughly virtuous person whose actions have not been presented in their best light by the media. Or I might, on meeting someone for the first time, form no moral view of her at all; but this does not stop me wondering whether or not she is considerate, selfish, generous, dishonest or whatever. Feeling no moral sentiment whatever towards her, I am not in a position to pronounce her to be any of these things; but I can perfectly well imagine that she might be.

A final disanalogy between the ethical and causal cases, and hence a reason to worry about whether the viability of a projectivist interpretation of Hume on ethics confers plausibility on a projectivist interpretation in the case of causation, comes from Kail:

[Hume's] 'projective' treatment of moral commitments is seen as virtu-
ally identical with [his] treatment of necessity commitments. There is
however a puzzling asymmetry, which to my knowledge has not been
commented on. In the case of necessity, as we have said, Hume's text is
littered with talk of hidden connections, and our ignorance of the
connecting principles, and yet in the moral case there is absolutely
nothing comparable to this – no talk of hidden moral properties or a
parallel confession of ignorance. For those who think that the two cases
are exactly parallel, we are owed a story about why there is this difference.

(Kail 2001: 36)

I shall argue in §7.2 and §7.3 that, if we want to avoid a sceptical realist interpretation of Hume, we need to read Hume's talk of hidden connections as doubly
hypothetical: he is supposing for the sake of the argument both that we can
successfully *think* about what I shall call 'real power' – a quality with which we
are utterly unacquainted and hence one that, it turns out, we cannot represent
by deploying the idea of necessary connection – and also that such real powers
actually exist, undetected by us. Supposing that this is what Hume is doing in the
case of causation, Kail's question is: why does Hume not engage in similarly
hypothetical talk about what we might call 'real values', real but undetectable
properties of vice and virtue, which our moral ideas might (mistakenly) be
thought to represent?

Well, in the case of real powers, Hume is addressing an existing and perhaps,
in the light of the Image of God doctrine, *prima facie* plausible position: the view
that the existence of the cause entails the existence of the effect, so that the
world is such that effects can in principle be inferred *a priori* from causes; it's just
that our limited cognitive powers render us (unlike God) unable to grasp that
nature. And – in §4 of the *Enquiry*, where most of the references to hidden
powers occur – he is showing that such a view does not help in explaining how
our inferences from causes to effects are actually generated. So there is a clear
reason for him to engage in hypothetical talk of real powers.

I suggest that there is simply no corresponding reason for Hume to engage in
hypothetical talk of real values. In the case of morals, Hume's central negative
argument is supposed to show that no matter of fact *whatsoever* could possibly
count as the 'object' of moral judgement, because what can be known through
reason 'can have no influence on conduct or behaviour':

The end of all moral speculations is to teach us our duty; and, by
proper representations of the deformity of vice and beauty of virtue,
beget correspondent habits, and engage us to avoid the one, and
embrace the other. But is this ever to be expected from inferences and
conclusions of the understanding, which of themselves have no hold of
the affections nor set in motion the active powers of men? They

155

discover truths: but where the truths which they discover are indifferent, and beget no desire or aversion, they can have no influence on conduct and behaviour. What is honourable, what is fair, what is becoming, what is noble, what is generous, takes possession of the heart, and animates us to embrace and maintain it. What is intelligible, what is evident, what is probable, what is true, procures only the cool assent of the understanding; and gratifying a speculative curiosity, puts an end to our researches.

(*E* 172)

It is thus the nature of matters of fact *in general* – the fact that they are the objects of reason and thus produce 'only the cool assent of the understanding' – that renders them incapable of being objects of moral judgement. Since real values, if they existed, would be matters of fact – they would be real, mind-independent features of people or actions – Hume's general argument rules out the possibility that our moral judgement – judgement that, of its nature, 'takes possession of the heart' and 'animates us' – might latch on to them.

The parallel argument would not work in the case of real powers, because there is nothing parallel in the nature of causal judgements *per se* which renders it impossible that those judgements should describe or purport to represent how things really stand in nature. Of course, Hume, *qua* projectivist, holds that it *is* impossible that those judgements should represent how things really stand in nature, but that is because the candidate objects of such judgements – real powers – lie beyond our cognitive reach. That causal judgements do not purport to represent genuine matters of fact cannot be straightforwardly ascertained by examining the nature and purpose of our ordinary causal talk and thought, whereas the fact that *moral* judgements do not purport to represent genuine matters of fact *can* be ascertained by examining the nature and purpose of our ordinary moral judgements: moral judgements produce motivation to act, and no belief in a matter of fact, just by itself, can do that.

Here's another way to put the point. In his discussion of causal reasoning, Hume starts out by arguing that we cannot detect any real powers, and so the inference from cause to effect cannot be explained by appealing to any observable, *a priori* inference-licensing features of the cause. But his job is not yet done, because one might respond that we can *infer* from past experience of constant conjunction that causes really do have a 'power of production' which renders them necessarily connected with their effects, and hence which licenses inference from causes to effects. In other words, unobservable real powers might explain what needs to be explained, even if observable real powers do not (because there are none). So Hume needs to – and does – respond to that objection, by showing that even if we *did* infer the existence of unobservable real powers, that would still not explain how we reason from causes to effects, because it would not explain how we come to believe that in the next case the observable properties of the cause will similarly signal the presence of the same power of production.

In Hume's discussion of morals, by contrast, whether the candidate objects of moral judgement, that is, real values, are detected or inferred – or even simply believed in no matter how we come to form those beliefs – makes no difference. It is the fact that real values would be objects of reason that makes them incapable of doing the job that needs to be done; there is no possibility that unobservable real values might explain what needs to be explained, even if observable ones don't (because there are none). The upshot of all this is that the disanalogy that Kail points out between Hume's treatment of causation and his treatment of morals is entirely compatible with a projectivist interpretation of both, because the difference can be explained by a disanalogy in the nature of what Hume is discussing. Moral judgements, by their very nature, produce a motive for action, and so cannot be objects of reason. Causal judgements lack this feature and so could, in principle, be objects of reason.

The claim I have been trying to establish is that *if* projectivism is a viable interpretative position in the ethical case, then it is also a viable interpretative position in the causal case. Admittedly, I have not given much by way of argument for the claim that, in the case of ethics, a projectivist interpretation is a viable option. But I think it is at least pretty clear that a projectivist interpretation does the best justice to Hume's claims that taste 'raises in a manner a new creation' (*E* 294). Insofar as there are parallels between Hume's treatment of the ethical case and his treatment of causation (as Stroud (2000) argues), we thus have at least some reason to think that the projectivist interpretation is a serious contender when it comes to Hume's conception of causation.

6.3 Causation and inference

Recall the Image of God doctrine introduced in §1.1. So far as causation is concerned, that doctrine has both metaphysical and epistemological consequences. The metaphysical consequence is roughly the claim that causal relations are, or are analogous to, entailment relations. The epistemological consequence is that, by grasping those relations, we can in principle gain *a priori* knowledge about the world; for example, penetration into the essence of a cause will deliver certain knowledge of what its effect will be. According to the Image of God doctrine, then, there is an intimate connection between the nature of causation, on the one hand, and the nature of *inference* (at least in ideal circumstances) concerning matters of fact, on the other. Causation is conceived as a relation such that grasp of its nature licenses inferences from one matter of fact to another. Or, to put it another way, *a priori* inference from causes to effects is possible because that inference mirrors the real, mind-independent relationship between causes and effects.

The Image of God doctrine thus, in a sense, derives the metaphysics of causation from the epistemology (or, at least, from the epistemology of causation that we would *like* to be true: we would *like* the inference from causes to effects to be *a priori*, and hence capable of generating certain knowledge). According to the projectivist interpretation, Hume has the same conception of the explanatory order: the story about what it *is* for one thing to cause another derives from the story about how it is that we infer one matter of fact from another. The difference between Hume and the upholders of the Image of God doctrine is that Hume rejects the Insight Ideal – the epistemological upshot of the doctrine – and replaces it with the claim that inferences from one matter of fact to another are due to the operation of an associative mechanism: they are a result of habit rather than the operation of the faculty of reason. The associative mechanism itself is, by definition, a *mental* mechanism: a mechanism by which one idea 'attracts' another as a result of custom or habit. So, unlike upholders of the Image of God doctrine, Hume cannot hold that there is any feature of the world that *corresponds* to the operation of that inferential mechanism. The world cannot literally operate in a way that mirrors the associative mechanism of causation: billiard balls do not act on one another out of custom or habit. So if we are to think of the world as somehow reflecting and justifying our inferential habits, that can only be because we project those habits on to the world. According to the Image of God doctrine, our inferential habits reflect pre-existing, mind-independent, inference-justifying relations. According to Hume *qua* projectivist, we impose our inferential habits on to the world. When we come to think of two events, c and e, as causally related, we take ourselves to be justified in inferring e from c, and we do so in virtue of our taking them to be so related. But this is only because it is that very inferential habit that we projected on to them in the first place, in coming to think of them as causally related.

I argued in §3.8 that Hume conceives of causal reasoning as reasoning from the cause, just by itself, to the effect, and pointed out that his own account of causal reasoning is in a sense very similar to the account according to which it proceeds by penetrating into the essence of the cause (c) and deducing the effect (e) from what is revealed by that penetration. On both accounts, then, causal inference just looks like this:

(CR1) (P1) c has occurred
       _____

       (C) e will occur

According to the penetration-into-essences view, (CR1) is a case of *causal* reasoning because it is only when e is the effect of c that the inference will be justified, since only then will c have an essence, penetration into which enables us to infer e. On Hume's view, by contrast, (CR1) is a case of *causal* reasoning because, thanks to the associative mechanism of causation, when we infer e from c we *also* come to think of c as cause and e as effect. On the projectivist interpretation, our so thinking of them is not a matter of our performing any further cognitive feat – our ascertaining that the truth conditions for 'Cs cause Es' are met, say; rather, it is simply a matter of our projecting the inference itself on to the events.

158

There is a parallel here between causation and entailment that might make this point clearer. For Hume, paradigm causal inference does *not* proceed by starting out with a causal claim as a premise; it does not proceed like this:

(CR2)   (P1)   *C*s cause *E*s.
        (P2)   *c* has occurred.

        (C)   *e* will occur.

Similarly for entailment. If I infer, say, 'P' from 'P&Q', the inference proceeds like this:

(E1)   (P1)   P&Q

      (C)   P.

and not like this:

(E2)   (P1)   'P&Q' entails 'P'.
      (P2)   P&Q

      (C)   P.

The fact that 'P&Q' entails 'P' is what makes the inference from the former to the latter a legitimate inference; but it does not make the inference legitimate by functioning as an additional premise. My grasping the fact that 'P&Q' entails 'P' just *is*, in a sense, my grasping the fact that (E1) constitutes a valid inference.

This, I claim, is a pretty close parallel to Hume's conception of *causal* reasoning. My thinking of *c* and *e* as cause and effect is not an additional premise, *belief* in which legitimizes the inference. Instead, my thinking of *c* and *e* as cause and effect just *is*, in a sense, my thinking of the inference from '*c* occurs' to '*e* will occur' as a legitimate inference: my thinking of *c* as a *reason* to believe *e*.

This conception of what it is to think of *c* as a cause of *e* also makes good sense of Hume's apparent indecision about whether to think of causation as a feature of the *cause* which licenses inference to the effect or whether to think of it as a *relation*. This indecision is manifested in his claim that 'the terms of *efficacy, agency, power, force, energy, necessity, connexion,* and *productive quality,* are all nearly synonimous' (*T* 157). A productive quality, for example, is a feature of the cause itself, while 'connexion' is a relation *between* the cause and the effect. Let's look at the analogy with entailment again. Entailment is a relation between two (or more) propositions, P_1 and P_2.[3] But when P_1 entails P_2 it does so in virtue of some feature of P_1, namely its content. P_1 has the property of licensing inference to P_2. Similarly, on the account I am proposing here, for the causal case: to judge that *c* is a cause of *e* is to think of *c* and *e* as causally *related*, but it is also to think of c as a *reason* to believe e – that is, to think of c as *licensing* inference to e (though not, of course, *a priori* inference).

There are, of course, important disanalogies between deduction and entailment, on the one hand, and causal reasoning and causation, on the other. First, the premises and conclusion of a valid argument – like (E1) – are not distinct ideas, whereas the premises and conclusion of an argument like (CR1) are distinct. Correspondingly, causation is a genuine relation for Hume, while entailment, strictly speaking, is not. Second, entailment holds between mental or linguistic items – ideas – whereas causation is a relation between events in the world. This is precisely where projection comes into the story: in thinking of c and e as causally related, we project the inferential relation between the *idea* of c and the *idea* of e on to c and e themselves.

Third, deduction is guaranteed to be truth-preserving, whereas causal reasoning is not. Still, as I argued in §3.8, Hume holds that it is the *reliability* of reasoning from causes to effects that provides it with its legitimacy. Thus, since our thinking of events as causes and effects is a projection of our inferential practices, our so thinking of them will likewise be justified by the reliability of doing so, that is, by the extent to which they track the regularities in nature.

It is at this point, I think, that universal constant conjunction ought to enter the story. I argued in §5.5 that there is no direct evidence that Hume takes universal constant conjunction to be part of the meaning of 'cause'. A projectivist interpretation allows him to resist – as he seems to resist – taking universal constant conjunction to be part of the meaning of 'cause' by locating the answerability of causal claims to universal constant conjunction in the normative constraints that govern our causal talk, that is, in the appropriateness of projecting our inferential practices on to the world. To think of c as a cause of e is to express one's commitment to taking c to be a *reason* to believe in e: it is to conceive of the inference from c to e as a *legitimate* inference. And the source of the fact that belief in c is a reason to believe in e is the reliability of the inference from the former to the latter; that is, in the constant conjunction of Cs and Es. But this is not to say that thinking of c as a cause of e is a matter of believing *that* Cs and Es are universally constantly conjoined.

In the case of representational language, roughly, the meaning of a sentence determines its truth conditions, by determining how exactly the sentence represents the world as being. Once we've settled the truth conditions, we can ask what the appropriate methods are for ascertaining that those conditions are actually met. In other words, standards for what counts as a good reason to believe or disbelieve a given claim are settled in the light of a conception of what it takes for that claim to be true. For projective language, things go rather differently. We start out with a sentiment or habit or attitude – some sort of active mental response to the world – on the one hand and the world itself on the other. Projective language arises from adopting what Price calls the 'objective mode of speech'; and the adoption of that mode of speech arises *because* we want to think of the relationship between the sentiment or habit or attitude and the world on to which that sentiment or habit or attitude is projected as being one that is susceptible to normative constraints. Truth comes in right at the end: the truth or falsity of a sentence depends on whether or not the sentiment or habit or attitude is appropriate to how things mind-independently are, where appropriateness is a matter of meeting whatever normative constraints are in play.

Hume himself offers something very close to this story in the case of aesthetics. In 'Of the standard of taste', he notes that 'no sentiment represents what is really in the object' (Hume 1757: 230), but denies that it follows that 'every individual ought to acquiesce in his own sentiment, without pretending to regulate those of others' (*ibid.*), and immediately proceeds to discuss the 'general rules of art' (Hume 1757: 232) which deliver 'a true standard of taste and sentiment'. This standard, he says allows us to 'derive an idea of the perfect beauty; in like manner as the appearance of objects in day-light, to the eye of a man in health, is denominated their true and real colour, even while colour is allowed to be merely a phantasm of the senses' (Hume 1757: 234).

In the case of causation, then, the meeting of the constant conjunction requirement can be seen as playing a role in the truth of causal claims not via the representational route, so that to say that *c* caused *e* is (in part) to say *that Cs are constantly conjoined with Es*, but via the normative-constraint route. And here's how the normative story might go. Like dogs, with which we share our most basic inductive habits, our sensory experience automatically generates expectations: I expect this slice of bread to satisfy my hunger, and so eat it, just as a dog expects the meaty-smelling stuff in its bowl to satisfy *its* hunger, and so eats it. Dogs' inductive habits don't get very much more sophisticated than this, but of course ours do. If we are hungry, we can do better than gaze optimistically at an empty bowl: we can open a tin of beans, fry an egg, or go to the shop and buy a loaf of bread. The ability to plan ahead in this way – and of course the ability to engage in scientific enquiry – requires that we extrapolate from particular expectations, generated by particular sensory input, to the general case. That is, we need to be able to extend our expectations to relevantly similar unobserved cases, whether past, future or counterfactual.

In basic, everyday cases, so long as our mental mechanisms are not faulty, extrapolation will come about automatically. The associative principle of causation applies not just to present impressions but also to ideas; so if, for example, the impression of a fried egg leads me to expect a pleasant taste sensation, then if I merely imagine a fried egg my thoughts ought naturally to be conveyed to the idea of a pleasant taste. In the context of scientific enquiry, the need to extend our expectations to unobserved cases is no less pressing. For example, scientific experiments need to be thought of as repeatable if they are to have any value at all: learning that putting the acid in the beaker caused the explosion is not much use unless one takes it for granted that the same experiment would have the same result if reproduced exactly.

Given that such extrapolation is a fundamental requirement of human enquiry, it is easy to see why constant conjunction should function as a normative constraint on causal claims. If the concept of causation, construed projectivistically, is to do any serious work – if the adoption of the objective mode of speech is to have any point at all – we need to think of particular causal claims as claims that ought to be retracted if further Cs turned out not to be followed by Es, or if the person making the claim turned out to have chanced upon an unrepresentative sample of Cs, and so on.

The upshot of all this is that Hume can hold that the truth of causal claims requires constant conjunction, while at the same time denying that constant conjunction is part of the representational *meaning* of 'cause'. The truth of causal claims is to be derived from the normative constraints on our causal talk rather than on their representational content. So, given that a story can be told about why constant conjunction should function as a normative constraint, there is no need for Hume to hold that causal claims *represent* causally related events as being such that the constant conjunction requirement is met.

I claimed in §5.5 that Hume regards both the principle 'same cause, same effect' and the claim that causes and effects are contiguous as established empirical hypotheses and not analytic truths about the meaning of 'cause'. If we think of Hume as a projectivist, we can characterize him as holding that the requirements of constant conjunction and contiguity are indeed empirical claims – claims that might turn out to be false, holding the actual meaning of 'cause' fixed – even though they *also* function as normative constraints on our causal judgements. In fact, however, they turn out to be empirical claims *about us* – about our habits of expectation and inference – and not, or at least not directly, empirical claims about the world.

There are two pieces of evidence for this. First, Hume claims that his 'rules by which to judge of causes and effects' are 'form'd on the nature of our understanding, and on our experience of its operations in the judgments we form concerning objects' (T 149). Second, Hume says that the principle of same cause, same effect is one that 'we derive from experience, and is the source of all our philosophical reasonings. For when by any clear experiment we have discover'd the causes or effects of any phaenomenon, we immediately extend our observation to every phaenomenon of the same kind' (T 173–4). Given that the rules are formed 'on the nature of our understanding', this second claim should, I think, be read as follows: the experience from which the principle derives is the experience *of* our extending our observation to every phenomenon of the same kind, on the basis of a clear experiment. In other words, the experience from which the principle derives is experience, not of how external objects behave, but 'our experience of [the understanding's] operations in the judgements we form concerning objects'.

Hume's rules, then, are normative constraints, but constraints which have an empirical source: our own dispositions to judge and predict. And it is their empirical source that explains why Hume is so unconcerned with *prima facie* possible cases of causation in the absence of contiguity or constant conjunction. I argued in §5.5 that if Hume is a naïve regularity theorist, it is puzzling that he ignores what are really pretty obvious *prima facie* counter-examples to his theory.

But, *qua* projectivist, Hume has no particular reason to be concerned, because he can happily agree that our normative standards might change if we lived in a world that behaved differently to how the world *in fact* behaves.

Consider the analogy with morals. According to a projectivist account, our ethical talk takes 'natural' features of people and their behaviour as input – what they do, what its consequences are, what their intentions were in doing it and so on – and projects our ethical attitudes on to them, in the sense that we express those attitudes of approval or disapproval in our ethical talk and thought. Now that, just by itself, constitutes a substantive philosophical theory. As such, of course, one would need to motivate it and to answer objections. But here is one thing that one would not have to do, in the sense that it would be wrong to accuse someone who fails to do it of having failed to give a complete philosoph-ical account of our ethical talk and thought. One would not have to run through all the possible things that moral agents might do, and make claims about what our ethical reactions to all those things would or should be. It is no objection to a projectivist account of ethical discourse to point out that no projectivist has told us how we would or ought to respond to the behaviour of wizards, or to people who can read our minds, or to alien beings with a radically different psychology. The merits or otherwise of projectivism in ethics do not depend on how or whether projectivists respond to those sorts of cases: it does not matter whether we have any inkling of what our ethical reactions in such cases would be.

Similarly, I claim, for the projectivist account of causation that I am proposing on Hume's behalf. Hume thinks that the world is, in fact, determin-istic, and that it is a world where causally related events are always either directly or, via a chain of contiguous events, indirectly spatio-temporally contiguous. But he is in no way obliged to tell us how he would react, or how any of us *should* react, if we were confronted with cases in which these conditions did not, or did not obviously, obtain.

Suppose, for example, we had at our disposal a well-established scientific theory which hypothesized that spatio-temporally separated events of kinds A and B are constantly conjoined, but which also hypothesized that there is no chain of inter-mediate events hooking them together. Would we regard the allegedly constantly conjoined events as causally connected? Perhaps so, and perhaps not.

We might regard them as causally connected but refuse to believe that there are no intermediate events hooking them together, and persist, perhaps fruitlessly, in searching for the missing link. Or we might be persuaded that there is no missing link and infer that they cannot be causally connected, and therefore suppose that the observed constant conjunction between As and Bs is purely accidental. In that case, we would not be prepared to 'extend our observation' to future cases: we would not expect the next A to be followed by a B. If we took one of those paths, everything would be as Hume says it in fact is: we would be refusing to extend our inferential habits to non-contiguous events. To put it another way, it would turn out that the associative mechanism of causation is pretty robust: it would turn out to dig its heels in, as it were, when confronted with problem cases.

On the other hand, we might eventually come to accept that the *A*s and the *B*s *are* causally connected: we might find ourselves naturally and instinctively inferring from one to the other, and/or we might accept that the scientific theory in question is a fruitful one to which we can find no sensible alternative. In that case, it would turn out that we were able to give up on contiguity: it would turn out that, while *in fact* our habits of expectation track only regularities that also meet the contiguity requirement, this turns out to be a relatively contingent feature of our psychology. It would turn out, in other words, that the associative mechanism is fairly malleable: it would turn out to be capable of modification in response to certain sorts of changes in our experience. And such modification would result in a shift in our normative standards, just as the ability to read minds might result in a shift in our ethical standards: a shift in whether or not we think it appropriate to blame someone for lying, say, and a corresponding shift in whether we judge lying to be wrong. In cases where we had a well-established hypothesis to the effect that non-contiguous kinds of event *A* and *B* are constantly conjoined, but where after careful investigation we could discern no further events hooking them together, we might think it reasonable to abandon the search and conclude that *A*s and *B*s are constantly conjoined but neither directly nor indirectly contiguous. We might, in other words, think it reasonable to judge that *A*s cause *B*s, but abandon the principle that causes are contiguous with their effects.

6.4 Causal and accidental regularities again

In §5.6 we saw that, *qua* naïve regularity theorist, Hume is not in a position to draw any distinction between causal and accidental regularities, since, according to the naïve regularity theory, 'all *A*s are followed by *B*s' and '*A*s cause *B*s' mean the same. I argued that those attempts to draw the distinction on Hume's behalf that are broadly sympathetic to the traditional interpretation in fact push Hume in the direction of projectivism, by attempting to locate the difference between lawlike and accidental regularities in differences in epistemic attitude.

The projectivist interpretation delivers a perfectly straightforward solution to the problem: 'all *A*s are followed by *B*s' and '*A*s cause *B*s' do not mean the same thing at all. For, first, the idea of necessary connection is part of the meaning of the latter but not the former and, second, 'all *A*s are followed by *B*s' is not even *part* of the meaning of '*A*s cause *B*s'.

There is, however, a related worry, raised by Stroud, concerning whether Hume can hold that we are capable of *believing* that there are any accidental regularities. Stroud claims that on Hume's view the 'repeated observation of similar phenomena precludes our thinking of them as occurring together merely coincidentally' (Stroud 1977: 93). He continues:

> Is this an accurate description of our thought about causality? This is to raise the question whether the 'data' actually are as Hume claims. Do we in fact think it is impossible for a recurring pattern of phenomena . . .

to continue for all time, but merely coincidentally? Hume's theory implies that any such pattern we observed would lead us to believe that the phenomena were causally connected, and so it would be impossible for us to see it as merely coincidental. We could never believe in 'historical accidents on the cosmic scale' (Kneale 1954: 229). But surely we can acknowledge such 'accidents' as at least a possibility. Of course, any correlation we found to hold for a long time under varied circumstances would lead us to suspect that there was a causal connection of some sort in the offing, but after repeated failure to find any connection mightn't we suspect that the correlation is merely accidental? On Hume's theory we could not. We would inevitably be led to believe that there is a causal connection.

(Stroud 1977: 93)

Beauchamp and Rosenberg's response to Stroud's objection is to say: 'It simply will not do to maintain, as Barry Stroud does, that Hume never makes the distinction [between accidental and lawlike generalizations] and could not have countenanced belief in accidental but universal regularities' (1981: 144). However, Beauchamp and Rosenberg's own account, discussed in §5.6, does not address Stroud's worry. They claim that *when* we regard a generalization as merely accidental, we will not regard its truth as a basis for prediction and counterfactual reasoning (see Beauchamp and Rosenberg 1981: 135). But Stroud's worry is that Hume's account of the genesis of causal judgement seems to preclude the possibility of our ever being in that situation. For if experienced constant conjunction is all that is required to generate the judgement that *A*s cause *B*s, we cannot regard *any* observed regularity as merely accidental: the associative mechanism of causation will operate and thereby compel us to regard it as a causal regularity.

Well, in fact Hume himself provides the beginning of an answer to Stroud's worry in his discussion of 'unphilosophical probability' (*T* 143–55). There, he says:

We shall afterwards take notice of some general rules, by which we ought to regulate our judgment concerning causes and effects; and these rules are form'd on the nature of our understanding, and on our experience of its operations in the judgments we form concerning objects. By them we learn to distinguish the accidental circumstances from the efficacious causes; and when we find that an effect can be produc'd without the concurrence of any particular circumstance, we conclude that that circumstance makes not a part of the efficacious cause, however frequently conjoin'd with it. But as this frequent conjunction necessarily makes it have some effect on the imagination, in spite of the opposite conclusion from general rules, the opposition of these two principles produces a contrariety in our thoughts, and causes us to ascribe the one inference to our judgment, and the other to our imagination.

(*T* 149)

Hume clearly holds, then, that our *judgements* 'concerning causes and effects' can come apart from what is delivered by the brute operation of the associative mechanism of causation; and this is what happens when we realize that an observed correlation is accidental rather than causal. Observed constant conjunction of *A*s and *B*s will automatically trigger the associative mechanism and induce me to think of *A*s as 'efficacious causes' of *B*s; but reflection on Hume's 'rules' might well lead me to think otherwise. For example, suppose that on each occasion that I have eaten a tomato in Mexico I have been ill afterwards – so ill, in fact, that I have developed a pathological aversion to Mexican tomatoes and am therefore confident that I will never eat another. But I also have good reason to believe that the illness was caused on each occasion by bacteria in the water in which the tomato was washed, and not by the tomato itself. So I have every reason to think that every Mexican tomato ever eaten by me is followed by illness, thanks to aversion that prevents me from eating any more. But I am perfectly capable of thinking of this as a merely accidental regularity; that is, I am perfectly capable of judging that the tomatoes themselves were merely 'accidental circumstances' rather than 'efficacious causes' of illness. Correspondingly, I am perfectly capable of judging my aversion to Mexican tomatoes to be irrational, based as it is on the unavoidable expectation of ensuing illness which the thought of a Mexican tomato induces in me.

From a projectivist perspective, the point here is that the norms that distinguish causal from accidental regularities just *are* the norms that distinguish between rational and irrational expectations. To put it in terms that are admittedly not Hume's, to think of the *A*s as merely accidental circumstances with respect to the *B*s is to refuse to endorse the inference which the associative mechanism compels us to draw: it is to regard the inference as irrational or ungrounded.[4]

Does all this answer Stroud's worry? Well, the example above is a special case of universal constant conjunction, because I stipulated that I have good reason to believe that I had observed all the *A*s, and this is what gives me good reason to think that *all A*s are followed by *B*s. But Stroud's worry seems to be that what Hume cannot, but should, allow is that we can think of an *ongoing* regularity – one we have no reason to think we've got to the end of – as accidental. And it appears that he is right to hold that Hume cannot allow that we can (or, at least, can rationally) think of an ongoing regularity as accidental. For Hume, for me to believe that a correlation between *A*s and *B*s will continue, I *have* to think of the *A*s as causes of *B*s rather than as accidental circumstances. For if I think of the *A*s merely as accidental circumstances, I will not regard the observation of an *A* as grounds for expecting a *B*, and so will not take myself to have any reason to believe that all *A*s – including future *A*s – will be *B*s.

It is unclear why this should count as an objection to Hume, however. To the extent that 'repeated failure to find any connection' between *A*s and *B*s will lead us to suspect that the correlation is merely accidental, presumably we ought to believe only that the *observed* correlation is accidental; we ought not to take ourselves to have any reason to think that the correlation will persist in the future. In other words, it seems entirely *right* to hold that we cannot rationally think of the *A*s and *B*s as accidentally correlated and yet *also* believe that the correlation is a universal one. But – *pace* Stroud – this is not to say that we cannot acknowledge 'historical accidents on the cosmic scale' as 'at least a possibility'. We can perfectly well imagine that there are cosmic accidents in general. But that is a different matter to believing that a particular correlation is such a cosmic accident. If we have reason to believe that there will be no more *A*s, we can perfectly well believe that it is an accident that all *A*s are *B*s; but if we have no reason to think that there will be no more *A*s, then we cannot believe that it is an accident that all *A*s are *B*s because we cannot (rationally) believe that all *A*s are *B*s at all.

6.5 What does the idea of necessary connection add?

I want now to address a different worry that Stroud raises (1977: 224–34), concerning the question of what our having the idea of necessary connection adds to our understanding of the world. He brings the worry out by considering how we differ from hypothetical beings whose minds work just like ours do except that they lack the impression – and hence the idea – of necessary connection. Let's call such beings 'connectionless beings'. Stroud notes that, since their minds operate according to just the same associative principles as ours do, connectionless beings would come to have just the same expectations, on the basis of past regularities and current experience, as we do: they too would infer, and be just as certain about it as we are, that the black will move on seeing the white make contact with it.

Connectionless beings, however, 'would presumably differ from us in never saying or believing that certain things *must* happen, or that two sorts of things come together *of necessity*' (Stroud 1977: 227). But Stroud's worry is that Hume is not in a position to think that this difference amounts to anything very significant:

> [I]it would seem that the notion of necessity does not serve to describe or refer to some objective feature of the world that we, but not they, have discovered. All their beliefs about the actual course of their experience would be the same as ours. And although our minds do differ from theirs in 'possessing' the idea of necessary connection, surely we are not actually describing or referring to that difference, or to anything else in our minds, when we use the word 'must' or attach the idea of necessity to something we believe. What then is the difference? According to the theory of ideas, we, but not they, are simply the beneficiaries of an additional mental item that forces itself into our minds on certain occasions, and we then go through the otherwise empty ritual of adding that unanalysable idea of necessary connection to some of our beliefs.
>
> (Stroud 1977: 227)

The worry, then, is that, according to Hume's theory of ideas, the having and deploying of the idea of necessary connection can be no more than a mere 'empty ritual'. The mere possession of a mental object – the 'having' of the idea of necessary connection – cannot explain the important role that thinking of the world in causal terms has in our judgement and reasoning. What 'needs to be understood before Hume's programme can succeed', Stroud says, is 'how it is possible for us to think about more than the actual course of events in the world, or what is involved in our accepting statements whose modality is stronger than "existence" or what is actually the case' (1977: 230).

Stroud sees this problem with the idea of necessary connection as part of a much wider problem whose root lies in the theory of ideas – in the view that the ability to think about the world, to deploy concepts, is merely a matter of the presence in the mind of a 'mental item'.[5] I shall not discuss whether or not Stroud is right about this in general; rather, I want to argue that, given a projectivist interpretation, the problem seems far less worrying – at least as far as the idea of necessary connection is concerned.

Note, first, that Stroud takes it for granted that, on Hume's view, connectionless beings' 'beliefs about the actual course of their experience would be the same as ours'. There is a sense in which this is true. Once we have been persuaded by Hume's arguments that there is no *sensory* impression of necessary connection (contrary to what we may ordinarily be inclined to think), our beliefs about the actual course of *sensory* experience will be the same as those of the connectionless beings. However, I argued in §4.3 that Hume takes the impression of necessary connection to 'infect' sensory experience, so that, once the habit of inferring *E*s from *C*s has been established, *C*s and *E*s will seem not 'entirely loose and separate' but causally connected. This already – and independently of the projectivist interpretation – establishes a big difference between us and the connectionless beings, for whom events will still seem loose and separate, even after the determination of the mind has been established.

Stroud also seems to think that it is relevant that, on Hume's view, 'the notion of necessity does not serve to describe or refer to some objective feature of the world that we, but not they [that is, connectionless beings], have discovered' (1977: 227). So, now, suppose that the notion of necessity *did* serve to describe or refer to genuine, mind-independent necessary connections which we 'discovered'. Suppose, in other words, that the view that Hume is attacking – the view that we detect genuine, mind-independent, *a priori* inference-licensing necessary connections between events – were correct. For current purposes, I'll call that view 'causal realism'. Stroud appears to think that if causal realism were true there would be no problem.

Why might this be? Well, Stroud seems to demand two related things of an adequate account of the 'having' of the idea of necessary connection. First, it must explain how we are able to think of the world as being such that something *must* happen, or that one event happens *because* another event happens, and so on. And, second, it must explain how we are able to think about more than what *actually* happens: how we are able to 'go beyond beliefs about the course of all actual events, past, present and future' (Stroud 1977: 229), which is what we do when we engage in counterfactual reasoning. We can see how causal realism succeeds on both counts. It succeeds on the first count because, on that view, our causal thought and experience unproblematically *represent* the world as being such that, given one event, another *must* happen, or such that one event happens *because* another happens. And it succeeds on the second count because if we are capable of believing that As and Bs are necessarily connected, then presumably we are also perfectly capable of believing that, had an A occurred, it would have been necessarily connected to a B – and hence believing that if an A had occurred a B would have occurred.

In fact, we can add a third requirement on an adequate account of the having of the idea of necessary connection – one that lies at the heart of Hume's interest in causation. It must explain how an impression of, or a belief in, one matter of fact can be a *good reason* to believe some other matter of fact. That is, the idea of necessary connection must be such that it allows us to conceive of our inferences from causes to effects as *rational* inferences. Again, causal realism satisfies this requirement: if our sensory experience reveals an event – the cause – to be such that another event – the effect – is *guaranteed* to follow, then of course our having of the idea of necessary connection explains why an impression of the cause constitutes a good reason to believe that the effect will follow. Indeed, if we think of the issue in terms of the Image of God doctrine, it is the whole *point* of causal realism that it satisfies this requirement: the whole point of holding that the world is a world of detectable, *a priori* inference-licensing necessary connections is precisely that their detection licenses *a priori* inference.

So causal realism satisfies the three requirements for an adequate theory of what is involved in having the idea of necessary connection. What about Hume's own view? Is Stroud right to say that that view *fails* to satisfy the requirements? Well, of course there are very large differences between Hume's view, *qua* projectivist, and the causal realist view he is attacking. *Qua* projectivist, Hume rejects the epistemological thesis that inference from causes to effects is *a priori* inference, and he rejects the corresponding metaphysical thesis that necessary connection is the relation, or a feature of the cause, that makes such *a priori* inference possible. He also rejects the semantic thesis that our thinking of events as causally or necessarily connected is a matter of *representing* them as standing in such a relation. Despite these differences, however, there is a close connection between causal realism and the projectivist view I am attributing to Hume; for, according to both views, our deployment of the idea of necessary connection is inextricably linked with our conceiving of causes as *grounds* for our expectations. Our having the idea of necessary connection just *is* a matter of our conceiving of the world as a world of causal relations: as a world whose causal structure is revealed by and serves to justify our inductive inferences.

Of course, the major difference between causal realism and projectivism is that on the projectivist view causal reasoning only 'reveals' the causal structure of the world because that causal structure is itself a projection of our inferential habits. But this (from a projectivist perspective) does not make our conception of the world as causally structured any less central to our conception of our inferential habits as rationally constrained by the world. Given all this, projectivism seems to me to meet the three requirements just as well as causal realism does; the fact that, on the projectivist view, our thinking of events as causally or necessarily connected is a matter of projection rather than representation does not make the having of the idea of necessary connection any more of an 'empty ritual' than it is on the causal realist view.

What about the connectionless beings? Does the projectivist interpretation provide a conception of what the having of the idea of necessary connection amounts to which makes us importantly different to connectionless beings? Is there an important difference between being able to think or say 'the black *must* move' and being able to say only 'the black *will* move'? I think so. For, in saying or thinking that the black *must* move, we conceive of ourselves of having good *reasons* for thinking that the black will move. In his discussion of Hume on inductive inference, Stroud says: 'To say that the murderer *must* have only four toes on the left foot is to indicate that what you already know is good or conclusive reason to believe that about the murderer, and not just that he does have only four toes on the left foot' (1977: 63). On the projectivist interpretation, the causal case – one's thinking that the black *must* move – is just the same. Indeed, Stroud's case *is* a causal case – at least for Hume, given that he holds that *all* reasoning concerning matters of fact and existence is causal reasoning. Our having good or conclusive reason to believe that the murderer has only four toes on the left foot, and our consequently coming to hold that the murderer *must* have only four toes on the left foot, is a matter of reasoning from effects to causes. The inference from crime-scene evidence – footprints in the sand, say – to facts about the murderer's anatomy just *is* a matter of thinking of the footprints as effects, and drawing a conclusion about what caused them. In other words, Hume would, I think, deny that there is any special epistemic, as opposed to causal, sense of 'must' at work in the claim that the murderer must have only four toes on the left foot: connectionless beings would be no more able to think or say that the murderer must have four toes than they are able to think or say that the black ball must move.

It does not follow from any of this that we are in a *better* position than are the connectionless beings if our aim is to track the regularities in nature – that is, to make, and have confidence in, predictions that turn out to be true. As Stroud notes, it is 'implausible to suggest that [connectionless beings] would differ in being less *certain* than we are about, say, billiard balls, falling bodies or death. If their minds worked according to the [associative principle of causation], there is no reason to suppose that less force and vivacity, and therefore less certainty, would be transmitted from impression to idea in their case than in ours' (Stroud 1977: 227). And of course connectionless beings can 'indicate' that they have good reason to believe that the murderer has four toes on the left foot by saying so, rather than saying (as they cannot, because they lack the idea of necessary connection) that the murderer *must* have four toes on the left foot. On the other hand, it is no part of Hume's thesis that we are in a better position than connectionless beings; it is no part of his thesis that we, armed as we are with the idea of necessary connection, will be better able to get around in the world, or will be better scientists, or whatever, than connectionless beings. Because we project our habits of expectation on to the world and they do not, we think of reasoning concerning matters of fact as *causal* reasoning – as reasoning from causes to effects and vice versa – while they do not. But there is a sense in which it is the having of the habit, and one's thinking of the habit as legitimate or justified, that is important, and not the ability to project the habit on to the world in such a way that one gets to think of the world as a world of causes and effects.

Having said that much, there is still a sense in which Hume can hold that we are better off than our connectionless counterparts. Connectionless beings have the associative mechanism of causation (though of course they would not call it that). That mechanism will generate just the same expectations as it does in us, and will track nature's regularities just as successfully. But, because the impression of necessary connection arises from the operation of the mechanism, we can track the operation of the mechanism much more easily than they can; and we will therefore find it much easier to conceive of the inferences generated by the operation of the mechanism as rational.

To see why, consider what is needed in order for connectionless beings to conceive of the inferences generated by the associative mechanism of causation as rational. The mechanism will generate expectations, given observed constant conjunction and a present impression as input, just as ours does. Connectionless beings will be able to tell that there is such an associative mechanism, because they will be in a position to notice that sometimes an expectation will naturally arise thanks to their having previously observed the relevant constant conjunction, and so they will come to realize that an associative mechanism, with experienced constant conjunction of As and Bs and a present impression of an A as input, generates belief that a B will occur. And they will be able to consider the expectations generated by the associative mechanism – as opposed to those generated by superstition or education – as justified, just as we are. So far, so good. But none of this will be *obvious* to connectionless beings. To them, all events really will seem entirely loose and separate; and a given expectation – that the black will move, say – will simply appear in the mind *as* an expectation; it will not, as it were, wear its genesis in the associative mechanism on its sleeve. In order to think of a given expectation that a connectionless being finds herself with as rational, she will have to consciously think about how that expectation arose – about whether it was generated by the associative mechanism or whether it is due to some other, less reliable mechanism: education, say.

We, on the other hand, thanks to the impression of necessary connection, do not have to go through any such laborious procedure. When *we* come to expect that the black will move, that expectation *does* wear its genesis on its sleeve, for it is accompanied by a phenomenology that is lacking in cases where expectation is generated by, say, education. It is that phenomenology, and the corresponding projectivist semantics, that allows us automatically and legitimately to think of ourselves as rationally responding to a causally structured world, rather than to a world of loose and separate events.

Here is another way to put the point. I argued in §3.6 that, for Hume, basic causal reasoning is simply reasoning from cause to effect: it is not *inductive* reasoning, that is, reasoning from observed constant conjunction. Given this, we can engage in causal reasoning even when we cannot consciously remember the experienced constant conjunction which triggers the associative mechanism. As Hume says, 'past experience . . . may operate on our mind in such an insensible manner as never to be taken notice of, and may even in some measure be unknown to us' (T 104). In such cases, we are nonetheless able to think of the inference from c to e as rational, because we will automatically think of c and e as cause and effect. Connectionless beings are not so lucky. When their past experience operates in 'an insensible manner' they will lack any grounds for thinking that the expectation they actually acquire is any more reasonable than any other expectation, since for all they know they might have acquired it thanks to some unjust belief-forming mechanism. Their expectation will in fact be in harmony with the course of nature, but they have no way of telling that this is so. Connectionless beings, then, *must*, if they are to conceive of their inferences as rational, employ genuinely inductive reasoning: they must consciously base their expectations on observed past constant conjunction. The projectivist interpretation thus not only does justice to the thought that the concept of causation makes a genuine difference to us; it also allows Hume to hold that we are in a better position than our connectionless counterparts.

Consider how things are with dogs. Dogs' expectations, according to Hume, are generated by the same associative mechanism as ours. But dogs, unlike us, are not capable of caring about *how* their expectations are generated; they are not capable of conceiving of one expectation as more or less rational than another. Dogs thus have no use for an impression of necessary connection; for them, such an impression would be (or perhaps is) merely a 'feeling' they get when they expect *walk soon* or *dinner now*. Connectionless beings, unlike dogs, *are* capable of caring about how their expectations are generated, and they are capable of conceiving one expectation as more or less rational than another. But their ability to do so is hampered by their lack of an impression, and hence an idea, of necessary connection. If they had such an impression they would be able to think of themselves as reasoning from causes to effects – rather than succumbing to superstition, say – without having consciously to consult past experience in order to work out what generated their expectation on a given occasion. We, unlike connectionless beings, can do just that.

7

SCEPTICAL REALISM

The claim that it is incoherent, or at best highly undesirable, to think that the world contains natural necessity, powers, essences, irreducible dispositions and the like went pretty much uncontested amongst analytic philosophers for quite a long period in the twentieth century. Perhaps that is why the sceptical realist interpretation of Hume on causation offered in Norman Kemp Smith's *The Philosophy of David Hume* (1941) was for a long time mostly either quickly dispatched (see, for example, Robinson 1962: 168–9) or else ignored completely. Even Stroud, who acknowledges a debt to Kemp Smith and praises him for identifying 'Hume's philosophical naturalism' (Stroud 1977: x–xi), ignores the realist element in Kemp Smith's interpretation: the claim that Hume 'is convinced that [causal agency] is a form of *connexion*, and further that it is a connexion which is *necessary*, and that it is this *necessity* which is its essential differentia' (Kemp Smith 1941: 369).

Theories of causation that seek to do justice to the mantra 'no necessary connections between distinct existences' have been falling out of favour in recent years, however, thanks to the efforts of Harré and Madden (1975), Michael Tooley (1977), David Armstrong (1983; Heathcote and Armstrong 1991), C.B. Martin (1993), Brian Ellis (2001, 2002) and others. This change in the philosophical climate has been accompanied by, and is perhaps partially responsible for, an increase in interest in the sceptical realist interpretation of Hume. (See, for example, Wright 1983; Craig 1987: chs 1 and 2; Strawson 1989; Read and Richman 2000; Buckle 2001; Kail 2001.)

According to sceptical realists – by which I mean those who attribute a sceptical realist position to Hume – Hume thinks that causation consists in what I shall call 'real powers'. Real powers are thoroughly mind-independent and are more than mere regular association. They are 'secret', and Hume's definitions are 'imperfect', because we cannot grasp their nature, and we cannot grasp their nature because that nature is not revealed to us in sensory experience. But we believe in it and refer to it nonetheless. 'Sceptical realism' is thus so-called because Hume is a realist about causation – he believes in real powers – but is also sceptical about them, in the sense that he holds that we cannot know or even conceive of their true nature.[1]

In §7.1 I show how a sceptical realist interpretation of Hume on causation can be generated by drawing a parallel between what he says about belief in the external world and what he thinks about causation. In §7.2 I defend non-sceptical realist interpretations against the charge that they are inconsistent with what Hume says about secret powers in his discussion, in the early stages of both the *Treatise* and the *Enquiry*, of causal reasoning; and in §7.3 I do the same for what he says in the *Enquiry* about the imperfection of his definitions and about occasionalism. These pieces of textual evidence, taken in isolation, therefore do not count decisively in favour of the sceptical realist interpretation.

In §7.4 I argue that there are in fact (at least) three versions of 'the' sceptical realist interpretation: Wright (1983, 2000), Strawson (1989, 2000) and Buckle (2001) attribute three different, and in some respects competing, conceptions of the nature of real power to Hume. In §7.5 I argue that one central aspect of Strawson's version of sceptical realism is in tension with the claim – which I take to be a fundamental requirement of any sceptical realist interpretation – that belief in real powers is a natural belief. The problem here is that Strawson takes Hume to be a subjectivist about necessity. If belief in real powers is to be a natural belief, it seems that Hume must hold that the associative mechanism of causation is responsible for our acquiring it, and so the belief in question must be one that involves deploying the idea of necessary connection. In §7.6 I argue that one cannot hold that Hume believes in real powers thanks to any philosophical argument – a position that is suggested by both Strawson and Craig. In §7.7 I return to the issues that divide the different versions of sceptical realism, and argue that these internal differences matter, in the sense that the issue of what general reasons there are to think that Hume is a sceptical realist depends on which kind of sceptical realist we take him to be.

Finally, and rather inconclusively, I begin §7.8 by giving some general reasons to think that the case for a sceptical realist interpretation of Hume on causation is not, as things currently stand, compelling. I end by arguing that the major obstacle to deciding which interpretation (out of the plausible candidates) is the *right* interpretation of Hume – an obstacle that I can see no decisive way to overcome – is that the *Treatise* and the first *Enquiry appear* to express different views: projectivism and sceptical realism, respectively. So either Hume expressed himself very badly in one or other of the works or he changed his mind. Unfortunately, neither option is especially appealing. Following Craig, I tentatively suggest that Hume was not sufficiently interested in providing a positive account of the semantics of 'cause' or the metaphysics of causation to commit himself decisively to one view rather than the other. After all, despite their obvious differences, the projectivist interpretation and the sceptical realist interpretation – at least Wright's version of it – agree about Hume's attitude towards the Insight Ideal, about his account of the genesis of causal judgements, about the importance that such judgements have for us, and about their legitimacy. If those are the issues with which Hume was most concerned, he had no need to be terribly concerned with the semantic and metaphysical issues that divide the two interpretations.

7.1 Ideas, representation and the external world

Hume's relationship with the external world is an uneasy one. His whole project starts, as it were, from the inside. He is interested in how the mind works: how we get to have the beliefs we do, how we infer one thing from another, and so on. And, being an empiricist, he holds that the source of all our ideas is impressions. But what is the relationship between our impressions and the external world itself – for example between my impression of a tree and the tree itself? Hume does not want to take Locke's route and claim that (some of) our impressions *resemble* mind-independent objects – for how could we possibly establish that an impression resembles something that, by definition, is not available for inspection? My only access to the tree is via my impression of it, so there is no possibility of comparing the two and seeing that the former resembles the latter. However, Hume does not follow Berkeley to the conclusion that everything is mental: that there are perceptions and nothing else.

So, on the one hand, Hume, unlike Berkeley, clearly thinks that belief in mind-independent reality is possible; indeed, as we shall see, he thinks it is practically unavoidable. But the mere possibility of such a belief seems to be in serious tension with his own official theory of ideas. As Hume puts the matter, 'since nothing is ever present to the mind but perceptions, and since all ideas are deriv'd from something antecedently present to the mind; it follows, that 'tis impossible for us so much as to conceive or form an idea of any thing specifically different from ideas and impressions' (*T* 67). But if we cannot so much as form the idea of trees considered as fully mind-independent objects, as opposed to trees-as-mediated-by-my-impressions, how is belief in such things possible, given that beliefs, for Hume, are merely 'lively' ideas?

That is not the only problem with belief in mind-independent reality. Hume says that beliefs about the external world that are not beliefs about what is immediately given in sensation must arise from the relation of cause and effect. But there is no possibility of the belief in objects 'specifically different' from impressions arising from this source – for we have no experience of constant conjunction between how things mind-independently are, on the one hand, and our impressions, on the other. So Hume appears to have two problems: first, he cannot explain how we can so much as form an *idea* of mind-independent reality and, second, supposing that we could somehow at least coherently entertain the possibility of such a reality existing, he cannot explain how we could *believe* that it does.

If we set the traditional and projectivist interpretations aside and instead start out with the assumption that Hume does believe in what I have been calling 'real powers', he faces two problems with respect to those real powers that are similar to those he faces with respect to the external world. He has shown that the idea of necessary connection is derived from an impression of reflection, so real powers cannot be *detected* by sensation. But, in that case, how can we so much as consider the possibility that real powers really exist in nature? We do not appear to have any idea whose content could latch on – via its impression-source – to any such powers. That is the first problem. The second problem is this. Grant that somehow an idea of real powers is possible. What would be the source of the *belief* that such powers exist? An immediate sceptical problem presents itself: if our causal talk responds only to regularities, as he claims, what possible reason could we have for believing that there are real powers which underlie those regularities? Reasoning from effects to causes cannot deliver belief in real power any more than it can deliver belief in mind-independent objects that cause our impressions, since there is no *experienced* constant conjunction between the existence of a regularity on the one hand and the existence of real powers underlying them on the other, and so the associative mechanism of causation lacks the input required in order for it to operate.[2]

The sceptical realist interpretation of Hume on causation can be seen as taking solutions to the two problems which Hume faces with respect to the external world and applying those solutions to the case of causation too. Let's start with the second problem. Grant that we can have some sort of idea of mind-independent reality. How, for Hume, can that idea come to have the status of belief? The solution is to appeal to what Norman Kemp Smith calls Hume's 'theory of natural belief', natural belief being 'due to the ultimate instincts or propensities which constitute human nature' (Kemp Smith 1941: 86). In other words, natural belief is a product of the imagination. Belief in the existence of the external world is one such belief: it is ' "inevitable", "indispensable", and . . . thus removed beyond the reach of our sceptical doubts' (Kemp Smith 1941: 87). As Hume puts it:

> Thus the sceptic still continues to reason and believe, even tho' he asserts, that he cannot defend his reason by reason; and by the same rule he must assent to the principle concerning the existence of body, tho' he cannot pretend by any arguments of philosophy to maintain its veracity. Nature has not left this to his choice, and has doubtless esteem'd it an affair of too great importance to be trusted to our uncertain reasonings and speculations.
>
> (*T* 187)

Similarly for causation: according to sceptical realists, Hume holds that belief in real causal powers is psychologically mandatory, both in the sense of being inevitable – we cannot help but have it – and in the sense of being indispensable: we would fare very badly without it. Scepticism with respect to real powers thus shares the fate of scepticism with respect to the external world: philosophical argument cannot prove the sceptic wrong, but, despite her avowed sceptical position, she will continue to reason about and believe in real powers, just like the rest of us.

What about the first problem: how, for Hume, is it possible for us to have so much as an *idea* of a mind-independent external world? The sceptical realist solution is to appeal to the distinction which Hume sometimes makes between what we can 'suppose' and what we can 'conceive'. The idea, roughly, is that we can *suppose* something to be the case (the existence of mind-independent reality, for example) even though we cannot fully *conceive* of what it is we are thereby supposing. The best we can get is what Hume calls a 'relative' idea:

> The farthest we can go towards a conception of external objects, when suppos'd *specifically* different from our perceptions, is to form a *relative* idea of them, without pretending to *comprehend* the related objects.
>
> (*T* 68)

As Strawson glosses Hume's claim: 'We cannot "comprehend" external objects in any way, on the terms of the theory of ideas: that is (considering the etymology of 'comprehend'), we cannot in any way encompassingly take hold of their real nature in thought. We cannot form any *positively contentful conception* of their nature' (Strawson 1989: 50). Nonetheless, according to Hume, the fact that we can form a relative idea of mind-independent reality means that we are able to *refer* to it: we can talk *about* it, even though we must recognize – once we recognize that mind-independent reality is not made up of impressions – that its nature is utterly ungraspable. Similarly for the idea of causation. Even though we cannot 'comprehend' real powers, we can still refer to and talk about them, even though we must recognize – once we recognize that we have no sensory impression of necessary connection – that their nature is utterly ungraspable.

Sceptical realism is thus so called because, *qua* sceptical realist, Hume believes in – indeed, thinks that we are psychologically compelled to believe in – both the external world and real powers. Hence he is a realist. But he is a sceptic in the sense that he thinks that in both cases the true nature of *what* we believe in – considered as something independent of our ideas – is ungraspable by the human mind. We cannot penetrate into essences – of matter, or of real powers – but we are nonetheless compelled to believe that they exist.

It is important to recognize that belief in mind-independent reality here is not supposed to be, as it were, an additional ontological commitment over and above our ordinary beliefs in tables, chairs, cats and dogs. Hume's picture here is not that of a kind of Berkeleian phenomenalism, so that our talk of cats and dogs is *really* just talk about perceptions, together with a Kantian belief in an unknowable noumenal mind-independent reality. For Hume, thanks to the operation of the imagination we ordinarily – and mistakenly – assume that external objects *are* impressions of sensation: 'the vulgar confound perceptions and objects, and attribute a distinct continu'd existence to the very things they feel and see' (*T* 193). But he is not recommending that we correct the mistake by holding that we can *really* only legitimately think and talk about the very things we feel and see – that is, sensory impressions – but are nonetheless compelled to believe in something unspecific lying behind those impressions. Rather, as John Wright argues (1983: ch. 3), Hume is recommending a version of indirect realism: our ideas and impressions *represent* mind-independent reality, and thus represent that reality as a world of mind-independent chairs, tables, cats and dogs. But those ideas are *inadequate* ideas of what they represent. When we attempt to think about what it is that our ideas represent independently of the ideas themselves – when we attempt to conceive external objects *qua* things that are 'specifically different to' our ideas – we fail, for of course we can only really intelligibly think about them by deploying the very ideas to which we are supposing them specifically different.

How might this conception of our ability to represent external objects despite the fact that we form only a 'relative' idea of them 'when suppos'd *specifically* different from our perceptions' be transposed to the causal case? Well, the general idea is that the two cases are more or less straightforwardly analogous. We cannot grasp the true nature of real powers, but we can nonetheless 'suppose' that they exist: we can form a 'relative' idea of them (see, for example, Strawson 1989: 49–58; 2000: 33–43; Buckle 2001: 202–8). Our idea of causation is an inadequate idea of what it represents, and we know that this is so because the idea of causation is not derived from any impression of real power.

In fact, different sceptical realists take different views about exactly how the story goes in the case of causation. Wright holds that it is the idea of necessary connection that is an inadequate idea of what it represents:

> [T]he supposition of causal necessity is no less 'irresistible' than what Hume calls 'the customary transition from causes to effects, and from effects to causes' (*T* 225). In fact, both are the results of exactly the same mechanism (custom), and are in themselves not essentially different ... For Hume, the belief in power or objective necessary connection is inextricably bound up with the inference of the mind (cf. *E* 37).
>
> (Wright 2000: 95)

So Wright holds that belief in real powers is belief in 'objective necessary connection'; but the true *nature* of objective necessary connection eludes us because the origin of the idea of necessary connection is an impression of reflection rather than sensation. Buckle also holds that the idea of necessary connection 'is manifestly inadequate to the reality for which it stands' (2001: 205), although, unlike Wright, he does not explicitly claim that what we thereby believe in is 'objective necessary connection'.

By contrast to both Wright and Buckle, Strawson holds that Hume is a subjectivist about necessity. Our idea of necessary connection does not represent how things are in nature at all – 'all necessities whatever are only in the mind' (Strawson 1989: 157) – but our *causal* talk nonetheless refers to real powers: to something of which we have only a 'relative' idea. I have more to say about the differences between different sceptical realist positions in §7.4.

According to sceptical realists, then, Hume does not abandon the Copy Principle; he really does hold that all our ideas are copied from impressions. However, contrary to the characterization offered in §5.1, he does not deploy

that principle in order to reach any conclusion to the effect that the idea of necessary connection (or, in Strawson's case, causation) cannot represent the world as
having a quality that, in fact, it could not possess. Instead, the idea represents the
world in a way that it in fact is – as a world of real powers – but does so only
inadequately: it does not and cannot capture the *nature* of what it represents.

The issue concerning the importance for Hume of 'relative' ideas and the
distinction between what can be 'conceived' and what can be 'supposed' is, of
course, a matter of dispute – not just in the case of causation, but in general (see,
for instance, Blackburn 2000: 101–3; Flage 2000). However, Hume is undoubt-
edly a realist about the external world – at least when he is dining, playing
backgammon, conversing and being merry with his friends rather than sitting in
his study and heating up his brain by worrying about sceptical arguments (*T*
268–9). And it therefore seems that he *must* have a sceptical realist view about the
external world, and must therefore hold that we can only form a 'relative' idea of
external objects when considered 'specifically different' from our perceptions.

However, while a sceptical realist interpretation of Hume on the external
world obviously puts a sceptical realist interpretation of Hume on causation on
the agenda, it does not, just by itself, force us to accept it, for it does not compel
Hume to think that *all* our ideas are inadequate representations of mind-
independent features of reality. As we saw in Chapter 6, Hume very clearly does
not think that beauty, vice and virtue are features of mind-independent reality,
and hence does not think that our *ideas* of vice and virtue are inadequate *representations* of mind-independent reality. So it might be that Hume takes (at least
some) ideas that derive from *sensory* impressions to be inadequate representations
of mind-independent reality but takes ideas that derive from sentiment or
impressions of reflection – ideas whose source is internal rather than external –
to be mere projections on to, as opposed to inadequate representations of, the
external world. Wright says:

> It is clear then that at least in his discussion of external existence, Hume
> argues that we are not limited in our beliefs about objects to what is
> based on our legitimate impression-derived ideas. The same theme is to
> be found in his discussion of space and time in Part 2, Book I of the
> *Treatise* [see Wright 1983: 100–7]. Why then should there be an excep-
> tion in the case of Hume's discussion of causality?
>
> (Wright 2000: 90)

But we might equally well point out that in his discussion of morals Hume
argues that moral judgements cannot be inadequate representations of qualities
of objects. Why, then, should he take a different view when it comes to causation, given that both causal and moral pronouncements are a result of the
projection of something internal to the mind?

Accepting something like a sceptical realist interpretation of Hume's attitude
to belief about the external world therefore does not decisively resolve the issue

concerning causation in favour of sceptical realism. But it should certainly give us pause for thought. If Hume holds, as he appears to, that external reality in general is something whose ultimate nature is fundamentally beyond our ken and yet is something whose existence we cannot but believe in, why should he not take it for granted that real powers are simply a part of that external reality? After all, the question of whether causal powers might not be fundamental constituents of the world – whether the world might be a world of mere regularity – is a question philosophers have taken seriously largely because Hume's arguments have routinely been taken to show that there is no more to the world than regularity. So to assume that that question is one that Hume himself seriously entertains, because it seems a natural question for *us* to ask, is to put the cart before the horse.

Moreover, recall that, so far as causation is concerned, Hume's primary interest is in refuting the Insight Ideal: the claim that we can know the causal structure of the world *a priori*. The claim that our causal talk is talk about real powers does not in the least undermine Hume's refutation of the Insight Ideal, for it is the conclusion that we cannot penetrate into the essences of objects, and so cannot discern their causal powers in a way that would license *a priori* inference from causes to effects, which refutes the Insight Ideal. The claim that we nonetheless continue to believe that objects *have* real powers is of course fully consistent with that conclusion.

7.2 Real powers in Hume's discussion of causal reasoning

One major argument in favour of the sceptical realist interpretation – pursued at length by Strawson (1989) in particular – is that Hume frequently uses expressions like 'secret power' and 'inviolable connexion' in a way that appears to be inconsistent with the claim that he does not believe that there is any more to causation in the objects than regularity. Here are some examples:

> [T]he ultimate force and efficacy of nature is perfectly unknown to us, and . . . 'tis in vain that we search for it in all the known qualities of matter.
>
> (*T* 159)

> [N]ature has kept us at a great distance from all her secrets, and has afforded us only the knowledge of a few superficial qualities of objects; while she conceals from us those powers and principles on which the influence of these objects entirely depends.
>
> (*E* 32–3)

> [W]e are ignorant of those powers and forces, on which [the] regular course and succession of objects totally depends.
>
> (*E* 55)

These and other passages suggest that Hume holds that there *is* such a thing as 'ultimate force and efficacy' but that we cannot know anything about its nature.

Moreover, this characterization of Hume's view fits well with his insistence, in §7 of the *Enquiry*, that his discussion of the impression-source of the idea of necessary connection reveals 'the surprising ignorance and weakness of the understanding' (*E* 76). He continues:

> For surely, if there be any relation among objects which it imports to us to know perfectly, it is that of cause and effect. On this are founded all our reasonings concerning maters of fact or existence. By means of it alone we attain any assurance concerning objects which are removed from the present testimony of our memory and senses. The only immediate utility of all sciences, is to teach us, how to control and regulate future events by their causes. Our thoughts and enquiries are, therefore, every moment, employed about this relation: Yet so imperfect are the ideas which we form concerning it, that it is impossible to give any just definition of cause, except what is drawn from something extraneous and foreign to it.
>
> (*E* 76)

And, having given his two definitions, he says:

> But though both these definitions be drawn from circumstances foreign to the cause, we cannot remedy this inconvenience, or attain any more perfect definition, which may point out that circumstance in the cause, which gives it a connexion with its effect. We have no idea of this connexion, nor even any distinct notion what it is we desire to know, when we endeavour at a conception of it.
>
> (*E* 77)

What Hume seems to be claiming here is that there *is* a mind-independent relation between causes and effects, and that this relation is what we refer to in our causal thought and talk. But, because of the 'ignorance and weakness of the understanding', we cannot form an adequate idea of that relation; all we can form adequate ideas of – constant conjunction, the felt transition of the mind, and so on – are elements that are 'extraneous and foreign' to it.

Sceptical realists take these two elements of the text to fit neatly together: Hume's talk of secret powers and forces elsewhere in the *Treatise* and the *Enquiry* is talk about *causation* – the very relation he provides 'imperfect' definitions of in §7 of the *Enquiry*. Defenders of the traditional and projectivist interpretations, by contrast, appear to need to explain away the relevant passages. Can this be done? In this section I discuss two strategies for dealing with the apparently recalcitrant passages that appear in Hume's discussion of causal reasoning in the earlier stages of the *Treatise* and the *Enquiry*. In §7.3 I turn to the realist-sounding passages in his discussion of the idea of necessary connection.

Two very different strategies for dealing with the apparently recalcitrant passages have been proposed. The first strategy – favoured by Kenneth Winkler (2000) and, apparently, Blackburn (2000) – is to interpret the relevant assertions as simply a part of the first-order causal talk which Hume endorses. According to Winkler, 'the unknown powers and forces of *E* 55 may be nothing more than unknown objects, as his definitions of "cause" themselves suggest' (2000: 56). Winkler is here thinking of Hume as a regularity theorist and claiming that Hume's realist-sounding assertions earlier in the *Enquiry* (and, less frequently, in the *Treatise*) should be 'retrospectively reinterpreted' (2000: 54) in the light of the definitions of causation he will later provide. In other words, Hume (sensibly) holds that many causes and powers are unknown, in the sense that we do not know, for example, what the immediate physiological causes of our bodily movements are. So he can perfectly well talk about – and believe in – 'secret powers' and mean no more than that there are some constant conjunctions (for example constant conjunctions between the behaviour of nerves and muscles on the one hand and bodily movements on the other) which we cannot observe.

Blackburn agrees that Hume's realist-sounding claims are to be taken at face value, as assertions that are simply part of the causal talk that he endorses. For Blackburn, however, no retrospective reinterpretation is necessary, since on the projectivist interpretation Hume is not – in his two definitions or anywhere else – claiming that our ordinary concept of causation needs to be revised. So to think that Hume's talk of inviolable connections and the like is intended to be construed as talk about real powers would be just as much of a mistake as it is to think that his moral pronouncements should be construed as talk about mind-independent moral properties:

> [I]t is simply no good citing one more time the places where Hume shows sympathy with unknown causes, hidden springs and principles, the propriety of thinking of matter as containing within itself the power to initiate motion, and so on. . . . This is like staring at passages where he says, for instance, that ingratitude is horrid, and claiming him for moral realism.
>
> (Blackburn 2000: 110–11)

The second strategy is to claim that to take the relevant passages to commit Hume to the existence of real powers or forces is to commit a fallacy: what Anne Jaap Jacobson calls the 'Bishop Sheen Fallacy'. Here is an example: 'atheists maintain that we have no knowledge of God; therefore atheists believe that God exists' (Jacobson 2000: 163).) According to Jacobson, an 'assertion of the form, "We are ignorant of the *X*" tells us at most that the context of discourse is one in which some people are prepared to use the term referentially' (*ibid.*). On Jacobson's view, then, Hume's apparent avowals of belief in real powers, when he says things such as 'the ultimate force and efficacy of nature is perfectly unknown to us' (*T* 159), are not to be interpreted in line with one's favoured (projectivist or traditional) interpretation, as Winkler and Blackburn claim. Rather, we really should take Hume to be talking hypothetically about something ungraspable that lies behind the regularities.

Winkler and Blackburn thus take Hume's apparent avowals of belief in real powers to be genuine avowals of belief, but not belief in real powers. Jacobson, on the other hand, takes them to be claims about real powers, but not avowals of belief: while Hume *sounds* as though he is taking the existence of real powers for granted, and hence sounds as though he genuinely believes in them, he is really just taking their existence for granted for the sake of the argument. I shall argue that Winkler's and Blackburn's approach is considerably less promising than Jacobson's.

Winkler and Blackburn are, of course, right that being a regularity theorist or a projectivist about causation would not rob Hume of the right to talk of secret powers, hidden springs and so on. On neither interpretation does Hume claim that there is anything illegitimate in our engaging in talk of powers, force, energy, connection and so on; he simply has a view about what we mean (or what we ought to mean, if we characterize him as a conceptual revisionist) when we do so. And of course many of nature's regularities are unknown and, given our limited observational capacities, quite possibly unknowable. Even so, there are two problems with Winkler's and Blackburn's strategy.

The first problem, raised by Wright (2000), is that most of the claims of Hume's which we are supposed to read according to our favoured interpretation seem to allude to powers that are 'secret' in the sense of being beyond our comprehension. Here is an example Hume gives of the 'powers and principles on which the influence of . . . objects entirely depends' which nature 'conceals from us' (*E* 33):

> [A]s to that wonderful force or power, which would carry on a moving body for ever in a continued change of place, and which bodies never lose but by communicating it to others; of this we cannot form the most distant conception.
>
> (*E* 33)

Winkler's and Blackburn's strategy fails to capture the thought that such 'secret powers' are such that 'we cannot form the most distant conception' of them. As Wright says, '[o]ur ignorance of unknown powers is . . . characterized [by Hume] as a certain lack of understanding' (2000: 93). *Qua* hidden regularities, however, nature's powers and forces are not incomprehensible at all. Indeed, in the case of a body's continuing to move for ever unless it is interfered with in some way, there *isn't* even a hidden regularity. Similarly, *qua* projection of our inferential habits, nature's powers and forces are no more incomprehensible than is the nature of beauty or ingratitude. We are perfectly well acquainted with our own sentiments, and once we realize that the projection of these sentiments constitutes the content of our moral and aesthetic talk there is nothing essentially ungraspable about the nature of moral and aesthetic properties. Similarly, on the projectivist interpretation, there is nothing about causation that is ungraspable by us.

The second problem concerns Hume's argumentative strategy in the passages where the density of references to secret powers and so on is at its highest: in §4 of the *Enquiry* and in the corresponding part of the *Treatise*, where he is arguing that appeal to secret 'powers of production' cannot deliver an account of causal reasoning according to which we infer effects from causes *a priori*. In these passages – so I argued in §3.6 – Hume is addressing the possibility that experience of past constant conjunction can somehow deliver what experience of a single event cannot: knowledge that a given event *c* has a secret nature in virtue of which it is guaranteed to produce event *e*. It is hard to see how, in this context, 'secret nature' could be read according to the traditional or projectivist interpretation. The guarantee that *c*'s secret nature provides, on the view Hume is discussing, is the kind that is supposed to license *a priori* inference to *e*; but on neither the projectivist nor the traditional interpretation do causal features that are hidden from our view constitute features that could in principle license *a priori* inference from causes to effects.

Jacobson's strategy, by contrast, certainly makes excellent sense of the passages in this part of the *Treatise*. By this stage, Hume has already taken himself to establish that there can be no *a priori* inference from causes to effects – that is, he has established this without considering the possibility that such inference proceeds via appeal to secret powers. The attempt to ground the inference in secret powers comes as a kind of afterthought. 'Shou'd any one think to elide this argument', Hume says, 'I can only desire, that this reasoning may be produc'd, in order to be exposed to our examination' (*T* 90); and he then proceeds to lay out, and quickly dispatch, the attempt to ground the inference in secret powers. Before doing so, he says:

> 'Twere easy for me to shew the weakness of this reasoning [reasoning that attempts to establish that appeal to secret powers can deliver *a priori* inference from causes to effects] . . . were it proper to anticipate what I shall have occasion to remark afterwards concerning the idea we form of *power* or *efficacy*. . . . It shall therefore be allow'd for a moment, that the production of one object by another in any one instance implies a power; and that this power is connected with its effect.
>
> (*T* 90–1)

All this fits very well with Jacobson's interpretation. Hume here seems to be 'allowing' for the sake of the argument something that he will later deny: that we can successfully use the term 'power' to refer to what I have called 'real power' – something whose presence, if we could know about it, would license *a priori* inference from causes to effects. And he is also 'allowing' that the existence of such a real power is 'implied' by the production of one object by another – and hence that such a power *can* be known to exist. There is nothing in any of this to suggest that Hume really *believes* in such a thing. Nor – *pace* Winkler – is there any suggestion that we should retrospectively reinterpret what he says. On the contrary: he is asking us to suppose that the 'idea we form of *power* or *efficacy*' is not the idea that, as it turns out, we *actually* have, namely the idea arising from the felt transition of the mind; he is asking us to suppose that the idea of power really refers to *real* power.

In the *Enquiry*, however, Hume's whole discussion of 'the foundation of all conclusions from experience' (*E* 32) is framed in terms of secret powers: Hume *starts* with the observation that nature 'conceals from us those powers and principles on which the influence of these objects entirely depends' (*E* 33), and nowhere says that he is merely 'allowing' that there are such powers and principles for the sake of the argument. This difference of approach makes Jacobson's interpretation appear rather more strained when it comes to the *Enquiry*. I shall argue, however, that there is no real tension here.

A footnote, added to this part of the discussion by Hume in the 1750 edition, is relevant to the viability of Jacobson's interpretation as applied to the *Enquiry*. Having asserted our 'ignorance of natural powers' in the main text, Hume says in the footnote: 'The word, Power, is here used in a loose and popular sense. The more accurate explication of it would give additional evidence to this argument. See Sect. 7 ["Of the idea of necessary connexion"]' (*E* 33n.). Winkler argues that, given that in §7 Hume shows the origin of the idea of power to be the felt determination of the mind, he is here clearly stating that his pervasive use of expressions like 'secret powers' in §4 should be retrospectively reinterpreted (2000: 54–5). However – assuming that the 'more accurate explication' Hume has in mind is his identification of the source of the idea of necessary connection – it seems to me that it is more plausible to take Hume to be allowing for the sake of the argument that we can successfully use the term 'power' to refer to *real* power: the 'loose and popular sense' of 'power' is the sense which, later in the *Enquiry*, he shows to be defective.

The footnote is contentious, however, because it is unclear what exactly Hume's reference to §7 is supposed to point to. Wright claims that the reference in the quoted footnote 'is almost certainly to a note which Hume added in the same [1750] edition, in which he insists that "the idea of *power* is relative as much as that of *cause*" (*E* 77n.)' (2000: 92), so that Hume's point in the disputed footnote is to 'show that the power is unknown to us' (*ibid.*). But Wright's claim can of course be denied: Hume might just as easily be reintroducing the caveat that he provides at the same stage of the *Treatise*, quoted earlier, wherein he 'allows' that 'the production of one object by another in any one instance implies a power; and that this power is connected with its effect' (*T* 91).

Strawson notes that Hume's argument in §4 of the *Enquiry* 'appeals essentially to Causation – to an essentially non-Regularity-theory notion of causation'

(1989: 183). But if Hume is doing the same thing here as he is doing at the corresponding point in the *Treatise*, then he 'appeals' to real powers only in the sense of assuming their existence for the sake of the argument. And of course this would be a perfectly sensible strategy for Hume, *qua* regularity theorist or projectivist, to adopt. He does not need to appeal to his own, controversial, view of causation in order to show that belief about matters of fact cannot come about through *a priori* reasoning; he can make that argument while conceding to his opponent the view that there are real (but secret) powers. And so he makes that concession, thereby ensuring that the argument must be accepted even by those who reject his positive view. Indeed, Hume has no choice but to proceed in the way he does. His own, positive account of causation depends on the claim that the idea of necessary connection derives from the operation of the associative mechanism of causation, and in order to establish this he *first* needs to show that it is that mechanism, and not *a priori* inference, that generates our expectations.

The upshot so far is that Hume's apparent avowals of belief in secret powers in §4 of the *Enquiry* and the corresponding passages in the *Treatise* do not provide a decisive argument against the traditional or projectivist interpretations and in favour of sceptical realism. But we now need to return to what Hume says in §7 of the *Enquiry*, which I think is harder to read in regularity theory or projectivist spirit.

7.3 Real powers in Hume's discussion of the idea of necessary connection

There are two passages in §7 of the *Enquiry* ('Of the idea of necessary connexion') that cause more serious trouble for the traditional and projectivist interpretations: Hume's argument against occasionalism (*E* 70–3) and his comments on the two definitions (*E* 76–7). I shall take these in reverse order.

First, then, the two definitions. Hume says:

> And what stronger instance can be produced of the surprising igno-
> rance and weakness of the understanding than the present? For surely,
> if there be any relation among objects which it imports to us to know
> perfectly, it is that of cause and effect. . . . Yet, so imperfect are the ideas
> which we form concerning it, that it is impossible to give any just defini-
> tion of cause, except what is drawn from something extraneous and
> foreign to it.
>
> (*E* 76)

And after giving the two definitions, he says:

> But though both these definitions be drawn from circumstances foreign
> to the cause, we cannot remedy this inconvenience, or attain any more

perfect definition, which may point out that circumstance in the cause, which gives it a connexion with its effect. We have no idea of this connexion, nor even any distinct notion what it is we desire to know, when we endeavour at a conception of it.

(*E* 77)

The problem is that here Hume really does appear to be expressing belief in real power; moreover, he appears to be claiming that real power is what causation is: 'so imperfect are the ideas which we form concerning [the relation of cause and effect] that it is impossible to give any just definition of cause, except what is drawn from something extraneous and foreign to it' (*E* 76); 'we cannot . . . attain any more perfect definition, which may point out that circumstance in the cause, which gives it a connexion with its effect' (*E* 77). Here there is no possibility of adopting Winkler's and Blackburn's strategy, so that we read 'that circumstance in the cause, which gives it a connexion with its effect' in the light of the traditional or the projectivist interpretation. For, according to both interpretations, Hume does not believe that there *is* any such unknowable circumstance: there 'may' be qualities with which we are 'utterly unacquainted' (*T* 168), but Hume does not and cannot *believe* that there *are* such qualities, let alone believe that there are unknowable relations between causes and effects. Nor, it seems, can we adopt Jacobson's strategy; Hume does not here appear to be merely supposing for the sake of the argument that there is such a 'circumstance in the cause'.

Do we now have a decisive reason to favour the sceptical realist interpretation? Not necessarily. Part of the difficulty in answering the question comes from the fact that what Hume says at this stage of the *Enquiry* is so very different from what he says at the corresponding stage of the *Treatise* (see §4.4). I argued in §5.2 and §6.1 that we can interpret Hume's talk of 'unknown qualities' in the *Treatise* as claiming that unknown qualities might well exist – and we can (rather misleadingly) give the arbitrary names 'efficacy' or 'power' to them if we like – but our *causal* talk and thought cannot latch on to any such thing.

Can we apply the same line of thought to this part of the *Enquiry*? Winkler does:

> Strawson . . . argues that the standard view has no way of making sense of Hume's belief (*E* 76) that his definitions of cause display our ignorance and weakness.
>
> It never occurs to Strawson that Hume's scepticism may consist in a *refusal to affirm* the existence of real powers. This enables the standard view to make very good sense of Hume's observation that his definitions display our weakness. His point is that we cannot manage to think that events are connected in anything more than thought. We try, but fail, to conceive of a real connection. A certain *conception* is unavailable to us – a conception we in some sense endeavour to have (*E* 77).[3]
>
> (Winkler 2000: 67)

Winkler's proposal succeeds, I think, in making sense of Hume's claim to have uncovered the 'surprising ignorance and weakness of the understanding'. As I said in §5.2, the traditional interpretation is often taken to credit Hume with the view that there is not, and could not be, anything over and above regularity – that is, there could not be any real powers – in nature. In other words, the traditional interpretation is often taken to credit Hume with the view that the limits of what can be thought determine the limits of what there is. If this were what Hume thought, then we would not be able to make sense of his claim to have shown the ignorance and weakness of the understanding. Part of Winkler's point is that the traditional interpretation is not committed to this claim; indeed, Hume himself says as much in the *Treatise* when he says that he is 'ready to allow, that there may be several qualities . . . with which we are utterly unacquainted'. That this is so does indeed demonstrate the ignorance and weakness of the understanding: that with which we are utterly unacquainted lies beyond our cognitive grip, and we therefore cannot begin to make any substantive claims whatsoever about its nature, because we cannot genuinely conceive of what it could be like.

So far, so good. What about Hume's complaint that his definitions are 'drawn from circumstances foreign to the cause', and that 'we cannot remedy this inconvenience, or attain any more perfect definition, which may point out that circumstance in the cause, which gives it a connection with its effect' (*E* 77)? Well, to start with, we need to get clear on what it is that Hume is claiming to be extraneous and foreign to what. We know what it is that's extraneous and foreign: constant conjunction (first definition) and the conveyance of thought (second definition). But what are they foreign *to*? Strawson has this to say:

> These two definitions are held to be imperfect (as is our idea of causation, which they in effect capture) because they cannot representationally encompass causation or power 'as it is in itself', but can define it only by reference to what is 'extraneous and foreign' to it.
>
> (Strawson 1989: 208)

On Strawson's reading, then, it is causation itself to which constant conjunction and the felt determination of the mind are foreign. Buckle (2001: 207–8) and Wright (2000: 91) make the same claim. If that is right, then Hume seems here to be straightforwardly committing himself to the claim that there is more to causation than mere constant conjunction or the felt determination of the mind. But such a reading is not obligatory. Hume says that he is giving a 'definition of *cause*' (*E* 76; my italics), but then defines '*a* cause to be . . . ' (*ibid*.; my italics). And the second time he makes the 'circumstances foreign to the cause' claim (*E* 77), it is circumstances foreign to *the* cause, not circumstances foreign to the causal relation itself. It is therefore not unreasonable to hold that it is *the* cause – that is, the object or event that we designate as the cause of some other event – to which constant conjunction and the felt determination of the mind are being claimed to be extraneous and foreign. And of course they *are* extraneous and foreign to *the* cause, even if Hume thinks that causation itself amounts to no more than constant conjunction or the felt determination of the mind. That past collisions of one ball with another have been followed by the movement of the second ball, and that this particular collision conveys my thought to the movement of the second, are both extraneous and foreign to the collision – the *event* that is the cause – itself. So we need not attribute to Hume any commitment to the claim that *causation* is something over and above mere regularity, or something over and above the projection of our habits of inference. We only need to attribute to him the claim that the circumstances in virtue of which one event, *c*, is a cause of another event, *e*, are not circumstances that reside wholly in the nature of *c*. Something else is required as well: the constant conjunction of *C*s and *E*s, and/or the felt transition of the mind.

This leaves us with the claim that 'we cannot . . . attain any more perfect definition, which may point out the circumstance in the cause, which gives it a connexion with its effect' (*E* 77) – a claim which appears to commit Hume to thinking that there is such a 'circumstance'. I take it that Winkler's suggestion – and I think this is the best that can be done – is that we should read Hume's claim as something like this: we cannot attain any more perfect definition which may point out the circumstance in the cause which gives it a connection with its effect – *if there is one* (and we do not even have the slightest conception of what it would be for there to be one). The idea here would be that Hume is not claiming that there is such a thing as real power, which we can only imperfectly define. Rather, he is claiming that we would perhaps *like* to be able to identify some 'circumstance in the cause, which gives it a connexion with its effect'; but, since we cannot, we will have to make do with something we *can* identify. Causation turns out not to be what we might have hoped it would be, and so the definitions are imperfect in the sense that our hopes cannot be satisfied.

Of course, I argued in §4.6 that Hume's 'definitions' should not be thought of as *definitions* at all: they merely specify the conditions under which we come to think of two events as causally related. The claim just made about Hume's 'extraneous and foreign' comment can be transposed to fit this conception of the two definitions: we would like to identify some circumstance in the cause itself in virtue of which we in fact come to think of it *as* a cause of some other event. But we cannot do this. What enables us to think of it as the cause is something extraneous and foreign to it: past constant conjunction in the case where we compare two arbitrary ideas (causation as a philosophical relation), and the felt determination of the mind in the case where the associative mechanism of causation is operating (causation as a natural relation).

That's the first passage in §7 of the *Enquiry* that might be thought to make trouble for a traditional or projectivist interpretation. The second, which is harder to reconcile with those interpretations, is Hume's argument against occasionalism. Occasionalism is the thesis that God's will is the immediate cause of everything that happens in the universe. The events that we ordinarily think of as causes are in fact merely 'occasions': they are regularly associated with effects, but are not real causes of those effects. As Hume puts it:

> [Occasionalists] pretend that those objects which are commonly denominated *causes*, are in reality nothing but *occasions*; and that the true and direct principle of every effect is not any power or force in nature, but a volition of the Supreme Being, who wills that such particular objects should for ever be conjoined with each other. Instead of saying that one billiard-ball moves another with a force which it has derived from the author of nature, it is the Deity himself, they say, who, by a particular volition, moves the second ball.
>
> (*E* 70)

The argument for occasionalism starts from the premise that we cannot comprehend any connection between the events we ordinarily think of as causes and their effects. Occasionalists conclude from this that those events are not really causally related, and so, since nothing that occurs in the universe is caused by any preceding event but must nonetheless have a cause, all events must be caused by the will of God.

Part of Hume's response to this argument is, in effect, to accuse the occasionalist of double standards. As he puts it in the *Treatise*:

> [I]f every idea be deriv'd from an impression, the idea of a deity proceeds from the same origin; and if no impression, either of sensation or reflection, implies any force or efficacy, 'tis equally impossible to discover or even imagine any such active principle in the deity. Since these philosophers, therefore, have concluded, that matter cannot be endow'd with any efficacious principle, because 'tis impossible to discover in it such a principle; the same course of reasoning shou'd determine them to exclude it from the supreme being.
>
> (*T* 160)

This conclusion, he says, can be avoided 'by concluding from the very first, that they have no adequate idea of power or efficacy in any object; since neither in body nor spirit, neither in superior nor inferior natures, are they able to discover one single instance of it' (*ibid.*). Clearly, since Hume thinks that events really are causes of other events, and not mere occasions, he is claiming that the lack of an 'adequate idea of power or efficacy', conceived as *real* power, does not entail that no event ever causes any other event.

But there are two ways in which Hume might be intending this claim to be read. He might be making the point that the occasionalists have a mistaken conception of what it is for one thing to cause another – a conception that presupposes that causation, if it exists at all, must be real power. The fact that we have no 'adequate idea' of power, conceived as *real* power, shows that we cannot legitimately expect our causal claims to be answerable to any such thing. This reading seems plausible in the light of the fact that Hume says, '*if* no impression, either of sensation *or reflection*, implies any force or efficacy . . . ' (*ibid.*; my italics). For, on Hume's own view, there *is* an idea of force or efficacy that derives from an impression – an impression of reflection. So it looks as though Hume is looking to avoid the conclusion that there is no causation anywhere in the universe by denying the occasionalists' premise that no impression of sensation *or reflection* implies any force or efficacy.

This reading of Hume's argument is, of course, friendliest to the projectivist interpretation. But another reading is possible. Hume begins his discussion of occasionalism in the *Treatise* with the observation that 'the *Cartesians* in particular, having establish'd it as a principle, that we are perfectly acquainted with the essence of matter, have very naturally inferr'd, that it is endow'd with no efficacy, and that 'tis impossible for it of itself to communicate motion, or produce any of those effects, which we ascribe to it' (*T* 159). So we could instead read Hume as denying the occasionalists' assumption that we are 'perfectly acquainted with the essence of matter', and hence denying that the absence of an 'adequate idea' of real power is any reason to suppose that real power does not exist.

This second reading of Hume's argument is, of course, friendliest to the sceptical realist interpretation. But it does not fit well with the overall thrust of this part of the *Treatise*. After all, just two pages later, Hume says:

> [W]hen we talk of any being . . . as endow'd with a power or force, proportion'd to any effect; when we speak of a necessary connexion betwixt objects, and suppose, that this connexion depends upon an efficacy or energy, with which any of these objects are endow'd; in all these expressions, *so apply'd*, we have really no distinct meaning, and make use only of common words, without clear and determinate ideas. But . . . 'tis more probable, that these expressions do here lose their true meaning by being *wrong apply'd*, than that they never have any meaning.
> (*T* 162)

This passage fits much better with the former conception of Hume's objection to occasionalism described earlier in this section: the occasionalists' mistake is to wrongly apply the notions of power and force – that is, to suppose that those ideas are intended to refer to real, mind-independent features with which objects are 'endowed'.

On the other hand, the second reading of Hume's objection fits considerably better with his discussion of occasionalism in the *Enquiry* than does the first. In the *Enquiry*, Hume puts his objection to the argument that is supposed to lead to occasionalism like this:

> I cannot perceive any force in the arguments on which this theory is founded. We are ignorant, it is true, of the manner in which bodies

191

operate on each other: Their force or energy is entirely incomprehensible. But are we not equally ignorant of the manner or force by which a mind, even the supreme mind, operates either on itself or on body? . . . Were our ignorance, therefore, a good reason for rejecting any thing, we should be led into that principle of denying all energy in the Supreme Being as much as in the grossest matter. We surely comprehend as little the operations of one as of the other. Is it more difficult to conceive that motion may arise from impulse than that it may arise from volition? All we know is our profound ignorance in both cases.

(*E* 72–3)

Here, Hume appears to be categorically denying the claim that 'our ignorance' is 'a good reason for rejecting any thing', and, in particular, denying that our ignorance of the nature of 'force or energy' – that is, of the nature of real power – is any reason for thinking that there *is* no real power.

Can we read what Hume says here in a way that is consistent with the traditional and projectivist interpretations? Perhaps we can – at a push. Sceptical realists claim that Hume is rejecting the principle that ignorance is 'a good reason for rejecting any thing', and hence rejecting a principle that, *qua* regularity theorist or projectivist, he allegedly needs to endorse: we are ignorant of real powers and hence have good reason to think that none exist, and so there *are* no real powers and our causal talk cannot be talk *about* real powers. But, as I argued in §5.2 and §6.1, *qua* regularity theorist or projectivist, Hume does not in fact need to endorse that principle. He can be agnostic about whether or not there are any real powers (there may be qualities with which we are utterly unacquainted) and still reach the conclusion that our causal talk is not talk *about* real powers: our lack of cognitive grip on real powers puts them (if they exist) beyond the reach of our thought. So we *can* see Hume here as saying that we are ignorant of force or energy in objects, *if there is such a thing*. That is, he is here using 'force' and 'energy' in a way in which he ultimately claims they should not be used – to (purportedly) refer to real powers – and showing that, granting for the sake of the argument the legitimacy of so using those expressions, we are likewise ignorant of the 'energy' of the Supreme Being.

What I hope to have established in this section and in §7.2 is that one *can* read Hume's apparent avowals of belief in real powers, in both the *Treatise* and the *Enquiry*, in a way that does not commit him to sceptical realism. But, of course, the fact that we *can* explain away the apparent avowals of belief in real powers and thus see Hume as a regularity theorist or a projectivist does not entail that we *should* so see him – any more than the fact that we can take the apparent avowals to be genuine avowals of belief in real powers entails that we should see Hume as a sceptical realist. However, it does seem that the most natural reading of those apparent avowals in the *Enquiry* is the sceptical realist reading, while the most natural reading of them in the *Treatise* is as concessions made for the sake of the argument. In each case, we *can* take our favoured interpretation and read it into what Hume says in the work which seems not to fit that interpretation very well; but we need a general reason to prefer one interpretation to the other, or a more general reason to think that one work rather than the other best expresses Hume's view. I return to this issue in §7.8.

7.4 Varieties of sceptical realism

According to sceptical realism, Hume believes in real powers. But what exactly is it that he thereby takes himself to believe in? One might think that this is a bad question to ask; after all, don't sceptical realists all agree that this whatever-it-is is something of which we lack any positive conception? However, in fact, Hume himself, *qua* sceptical realist, appears to offer different conceptions of real power in various places; and, correspondingly, sceptical realists attribute to Hume a variety of different views concerning the nature of real powers.

Both Wright and Buckle stress Hume's admiration of, and debt to, Newton and claim that Hume's project, his 'science of man', enshrines a Newtonian position not only in a methodological sense but also in a metaphysical sense. That is to say, Hume's approach takes for granted not only the method of observation and experiment which, in Newton's hands, had achieved such spectacular success, but also the existence of real powers; and the existence of such real powers is taken by Hume to be not only a part of Newton's own worldview, but something that is crucial to the success of that worldview.[4] Thus Wright, in the context of noting Hume's approval of Newton's 'recourse to an ethereal active fluid to explain his universal attraction' (*E* 73*n.*), says:

> Unlike Berkeley, Hume believes that there is more to science than the discovery of general laws of nature [that is, regularities under which phenomena are subsumed]. He clearly accepts the existence of real physical force and believes that science makes progress by postulating such forces *as* physical. In order to understand Hume's own philosophical views on causation one must recognize that he did not question the existence of real forces in nature any more than he questioned the existence of independent external objects themselves. Hume held that the existence of these things must be taken 'for granted in all our reasonings'.
>
> (Wright 1983: 146–7)

Buckle's view is, I think, roughly similar. Buckle stresses Hume's commitment to the view that the world is basically mechanistic.[5] It is a world of matter in motion: of particles bashing into each other and thereby imparting motion to one another; and of forces which also impart motion, as when gravity makes a mug crash to the floor when one drops it. Hume applies this mechanistic worldview to the mind itself, so that, for example, one idea introduces another by means of 'a kind of ATTRACTION, which in the mental world will be found to have as extraordinary effects as in the natural, and to show itself in as many and as various forms' (*T* 12–13).

Given Wright's claim that Hume 'accepts the existence of real force' and Buckle's stress on Hume's commitment to 'mechanisms', one might expect them to conceive of the real powers Hume believes in to be something like *forces*: the 'kind of attraction' which 'shows itself' in both the mental and the natural worlds, as with the associative principles of the imagination and, for example, 'that wonderful force or power, which would carry on a moving body for ever in a continued change of place, and which bodies never lose but by communicating it to others' (*E* 33). It is easy to see how one might conceive of forces as something over and above mere regularity; for example, when a small piece of iron moves towards a magnet, it is natural to think that there is more going on than meets the eye. That is, it is natural to think that the force exerted on the iron by the magnet is not *just* a matter of the observed fact that the former moves towards the latter, or indeed that similar movements occur in similar circumstances.

Conceived as forces, real powers would thus be something over and above mere regularity. But in fact both Wright and Buckle have something else in mind when they attribute belief in real powers to Hume: they both attribute to him the view that it is hidden *natures* or *essences* that Hume believes in. For Buckle, this belief is one that Hume has taken straight from Newton. Here, for example, is Newton complaining about the Aristotelians' claims to have discovered the 'occult' qualities of things, and claiming that his own laws of motion and principle of gravity are, as they should be, restricted to describing the observable phenomena. The truth of those laws, he says, appear to us

> by Phaenomena, though their Causes be not yet discover'd. For these are manifest Qualities, and their Causes only are occult. And the *Aristotelians* gave the Name of occult Qualities, not to manifest Qualities, but to such Qualities only as they supposed to lie hid in Bodies, and to be the unknown Causes of manifest Effects. . . . Such occult Qualities put a stop to the Improvement of natural Philosophy.
>
> (Newton 1730: 401)

As Buckle paraphrases Newton's complaint, the Aristotelians 'lay claim to knowledge of the underlying causes of natural processes. This "put a stop to the Improvement of natural Philosophy" because there is in fact no access to such ultimate principles' (Buckle 2001: 87) – but to deny knowledge of such underlying causes is not, of course, to say that they do not exist. Hume's belief in real powers, on Buckle's view, is, like Newton's, a belief in such underlying causes whose nature cannot be grasped by us:

> What is clear . . . is that mechanical philosophy holds that there is a real world independent of us, a world of matter in motion. This world

works in the specific way that it does because of the different mechanisms that make each thing what it is, and so the different mechanisms
constitute the distinguishing powers of different objects. Thus the
power of the clock to keep time, or of the pulley to lift weights, is
constituted by their different mechanisms. The mechanical model of
the world proposes the same type of explanation for the natural powers
of objects, whether the power of bread to nourish, or of rhubarb to
purge, or of opium to induce sleep: powers are at bottom mechanisms.
Since the mechanisms are inaccessible to perceivers like us, the powers
of the objects must remain hidden: all that we can observe are their
effects in the world, including their effects on us.

(Buckle 2001: 193–4)

The conception of real powers which Buckle attributes to Hume is thus, in a
sense, a fairly unspecific one: objects have underlying natures – mechanisms –
which make them the objects that they are, and also endow them with their
causal powers; but we really cannot say anything more specific about the nature
of those mechanisms or powers because they are inaccessible to us.

Wright, by contrast, attributes a very specific view to Hume about the nature
of real powers. Wright says that 'our recognition that Hume accepted real forces
should not make us forget that he retained an ideal of knowledge of true causes
which was derived from the Cartesians' and that Hume 'tends to think of the
unknown ontological causation' in terms of his 'own modified Cartesian criterion of knowledge of causation' (Wright 1983: 147). That criterion is, in effect,
that claim that the 'true manner of conceiving a particular power in a particular
body' is to 'conceive the connexion betwixt cause and effect' in such a way that
we should 'be able to pronounce, from a simple view of the one, that it must be
follow'd or preceded by the other' (*T* 161; quoted in Wright 1983: 140). Wright
thus attributes to Hume the view that real powers are *a priori* inference-licensing,
or AP, properties.

Of course, Hume argues that there are no AP properties whose nature we
can grasp; and that argument, as we saw in Chapter 3, rests on the distinctness
of our *ideas* of the cause and the effect. The distinctness and hence separability
of the idea of the cause and the idea of the effect show that we cannot discern
any AP property in the cause – since if we could discern such a property we
would no more be able to imagine the cause without the effect than we can
imagine a particular tomato's being red-and-round without thereby imagining it
to be red. But, according to Wright, Hume nonetheless maintains that AP properties exist and are what we refer to in our causal talk.

Recall Hume's argument against occasionalism, discussed in §7.3. The
occasionalists argue that (a) since we cannot perceive any connection between
events we ordinarily think of as causes and effects there *is* no connection
between those events, and so (b) all effects are really caused directly by God. On
a sceptical realist reading of Hume's argument, he objects to the first part of the

195

argument, (a): ignorance of real powers provides no grounds for positively asserting that they do not exist. As Wright notes, the inference drawn by the occasionalists in (a) is analogous to a familiar move made by Descartes in the Sixth Meditation: Descartes argues that there is a 'real distinction' between mind and body on the grounds that we can imagine one without the other. In other words, the separability, and hence distinctness, of our *ideas* of mind and body is supposed to entail the distinctness of the mind and the body themselves. One can cast the occasionalists' argument in the same light: the separability, and hence distinctness, of the ideas of the (alleged) cause and effect demonstrates the distinctness of the (alleged) cause and effect themselves; and so, given the Cartesian criterion, demonstrates that there can be no necessary connection between them.[6]

The point here is that to think of real powers as AP properties just *is* to think of causes and effects as not really distinct from one another. Our *ideas* of causes and effects are distinct, and so we cannot infer effects from causes *a priori*. But our ideas of causes and effects are inadequate: they do not reveal the true nature of the events themselves. If, *per impossibile* given our nature, the true nature of the cause itself could be revealed by perception, so that our idea of the cause were adequate to the reality it represented, the idea of the cause would not be distinct from the idea of the effect and we would be able to infer the existence of the effect *a priori*. As we saw in Chapter 3, if the relation between cause and effect is to be quasi-logical, then they must not be genuinely logically distinct. Wright explicitly embraces this view – 'the view that there is no absolute distinction between the particular objects of our ideas of cause and effect' (1983: 160) – on Hume's behalf.

Wright notes that Hume 'attempts to develop the idea of necessity' in Part IX of the *Dialogues Concerning Natural Religion* (1779) and that the 'idea of an ontological necessary connection in finite objects is seriously considered by both characters who are generally considered as candidates for Hume's own views – namely, Cleanthes and Philo' (Wright 1983: 147). There, Philo

claims that if we could 'penetrate into the intimate nature of bodies, we should clearly see why it was absolutely impossible' that the universe could be structured in any other way than the way it is actually structured. He likens the knowledge which we should then have to the knowledge possessed by a 'skilful algebraist' who can discover why, of necessity, the sum of the digits of the products of 9 is equal to 9 or some lesser product of 9. 'To a superficial observer, so wonderful a regularity may be admired as the effect either of chance or design' [Hume (1779: 235)]. The algebraist penetrates into the nature of number and shows the necessity of the regularity. But in the case of the external world we are all such superficial observers. We lack the knowledge of the nature of matter that the algebraist has of the nature of number. Nevertheless Philo [and hence Hume] clearly expresses his belief in the possibility of such an inherent necessary principle in the nature of matter itself.

(Wright 1983: 149–50)

But Wright goes on to attribute to Hume the stronger view that an 'inherent necessary principle in the nature of matter' is not merely possible, but actual:

Thus we see that Hume attempts some description of the necessity of which we would be aware *if* our ideas were adequate representations of reality. This gives us some notion of the necessary connection which he, like his rationalist predecessors, identifies with the power or force of the cause. Hume suggests that this necessity is inherent in nature itself. Yet, according to him, the necessity is entirely inconceivable by us. For, as we learn from our metaphysical reasonings, our actual ideas are distinct and separable.

(Wright 1983: 150)

The conception of real powers that Strawson attributes to Hume is different again. While Wright holds that Hume believes in objective necessary connections, Strawson holds that Hume is a 'global subjectivist' about necessity: 'all necessities whatever are only in the mind. Really, necessity is just a feeling we have about certain things – about 2 + 2 = 4, and about what this billiard ball does to that one, and about the sum of the angles of a triangle' (Strawson 1989: 157). There is certainly some textual evidence which points Hume in this direction. In particular, he says:

Thus as the necessity, which makes two times two equal to four, or three angles of a triangle equal to two right ones, lies only in the act of the understanding, by which we consider and compare these ideas; in like manner the necessity or power, which unites causes and effects, lies in the determination of the mind to pass from one to the other.

(*T* 166)

But, Strawson continues:

No sooner has Hume made this strong, globally subjectivist claim about necessity in general than one sees that he now badly needs to differentiate the two things he has equated in the particular case of his discussion of causation: he needs to differentiate *necessity*, understood in the strong, subjectivist way as something that is inevitably 'only in the mind', from 'the principle, on which [the] mutual influence of bodies depends', the 'ultimate connexion' between objects – i.e. from Causation or *causal power*.

(Strawson 1989: 158)

So according to Strawson's Hume, what I am calling 'real power', and what Strawson usually calls 'Causation', cannot *be* objective necessary connection, since necessary connection, on Hume's view, resides in the mind. What, then, *is* real power? For Strawson, real power is, as Hume puts it, that upon which the 'regular course and succession of objects totally depends' (*E* 55); or, in Strawson's words, 'whatever it is about the universe (or matter) which is that in virtue of which it is regular' (1989: 126). The essence of real power, for Strawson's Hume, is that it generates the regularities we observe; and so to make a causal claim is to refer not to the regularities themselves or to the transition of the mind, but to that which underlies and is responsible for the regularities.

It seems, then, that Strawson and Wright disagree quite dramatically about the nature of real powers: for Wright, Hume believes in objective necessary connections, while, for Strawson, Hume holds that there can be no objective *necessary* connections, since all necessity is subjective. But in fact the issue is rather less clear cut. Strawson points out that Hume sometimes has a tendency to 'equate' necessity and Causation, as when he says that 'the terms of *efficacy, agency, power, force, energy, necessity, connexion,* and *productive quality,* are all nearly synonymous' (*T* 157). Strawson holds that this tendency leads to Hume's being 'in part *confused* in what he is saying about causation' (1989: 157): he needs to distinguish between Causation (that is, real power), which is an objective, mind-independent feature of the world, and necessity, which is subjective – it is inevitably 'all in the mind'. Strawson goes on to say:

> The complex of ideas is dense here. But perhaps the key reason why Hume accepts the equation of Causation and necessity is his unquestioned belief that Causation has the AP property – so that knowledge of it must make possible inferences which have the same certainty or *necessity* as mathematical or geometrical inferences. It must be remembered that it would be natural for Hume to take the equation for granted, as being simply built into the conception of causation which he found in circulation at the time, and which he undertook to criticize.
>
> (Strawson 1989: 158–9)

Strawson's claim here seems to be this: Hume categorically believes that Causation has the AP property ('categorically' in the sense that this is not part of what he is confused about). But, since knowledge of AP properties would make possible inferences that are certain – that is, inferences that are necessary in the subjective sense – he has a tendency to run together the two things he needs to keep apart, namely Causation (real power) and necessity.

One might think that Hume cannot coherently hold the view just ascribed to him on Strawson's behalf: how can he believe in AP properties *and* believe that all necessity is subjective? Well, perhaps the answer is something like this: 'necessity' just means 'certainty'. And so to say that something in the world is such that knowledge of it *would* generate certainty *in us* – that is, to say that AP properties exist – would not be to say that there is any necessity (that is, certainty) in the world itself. If this is what Strawson intends, then the difference between Strawson and Wright is not as great as it appears to be at first sight, for there is no disagreement about what, fundamentally, Hume believes in: he believes in AP properties.

There is still a disagreement about the meaning of 'necessity', however: a disagreement about whether or not necessity can be objective. Both authors agree that there is a parallel between Hume's view about real powers and his view about the truths of mathematics: that the necessity that penetration into the essence of numbers delivers is just the same as the necessity that *would* be delivered by the penetration into the essence of objects in the world. But where Strawson sees only subjective necessity in both cases – that is to say, certainty – Wright sees objective necessity.

What is at stake in this remaining disagreement between Wright and Strawson over whether or not necessity can be objective – and who is right? Consideration of the analogy with number might suggest that Strawson has the better view. After all, one might reasonably suppose that the reason we *can* penetrate into the essence of number is that, in some sense, numbers just *are* creatures of the mind: their nature is exhausted by our ideas of them, and so there is no possibility of, as it were, a mismatch between our ideas of numbers and numbers as they are in themselves. This might suggest that the global subjectivism that Strawson attributes to Hume makes more sense, since it is unclear what 'objective' necessity might amount to in the case of reasoning concerning mere relations of *ideas*. In addition – and I suspect that this is part of Strawson's motivation for his subjectivist interpretation – Strawson's subjectivist view also allows the sceptical realist interpretation to fit better with Hume's repeated assertions in the *Treatise* that causal necessity is all in the mind (see §4.4).

On the other hand, Strawson's interpretation requires us to attribute to Hume an element of confusion that is quite absent on Wright's interpretation. For Strawson, Hume is confused when he claims that expressions like 'power' and 'necessity' are 'nearly synonimous'. Granted, Strawson argues that the confusion is understandable given Hume's 'unquestioned belief that Causation has the AP property' (Strawson 1989: 158); but it is still hard to credit Hume with the level of confusion Strawson's interpretation requires, over such a crucial issue. Wright's interpretation, by contrast, imputes no such confusion to Hume: when Hume says that terms like 'power', 'agency', 'efficacy' and 'necessity' are 'nearly synonymous', he means exactly what he says. Still, that point is not intended to be a decisive one. I shall argue in §7.5, however, that there is in fact a decisive reason to think that Hume, *qua* sceptical realist, must believe in objective necessary connection.

While I have so far been trying to show that Wright's and Strawson's views about what Hume's belief in real powers amounts to are very similar – both authors take Hume to think that real powers are AP properties – there is in fact a further difference between them, aside from the disagreement over the subjectivity or objectivity of necessity. The difference is that Strawson clearly takes the most important feature of real powers to be their regularity-guaranteeing nature:

the fact that they are what the 'regular course and succession of objects totally depends' upon (*E* 55). As Strawson puts it, 'Hume never really questions the idea that there is something like causal power in reality, i.e. something in virtue of which reality is regular in the way that it is' (1989: 14). That this is the core of what Strawson takes Hume's belief to amount to is also clear from the general nature of one central strand of Strawson's argument in *The Secret Connexion* (1989). Strawson argues that a regularity theory of causation – the kind of view whose ascription to Hume I discussed in Chapter 5 – is 'utterly implausible in asserting categorically that there is no reason in the nature of things for the regularity of the world' (Strawson 1989: 21).[7] Part of Strawson's ambition in the book is clearly to rescue Hume from having attributed to him what Strawson regards as an absurd view; and Strawson takes the view that there is no more than regularity in the world to be absurd precisely because that view denies that there is a reason *why* the world is regular.

For Strawson, the fact that Hume also takes real powers to be AP properties as well as sources of order seems to be due to no more than Hume's uncritical acceptance of the dominant view of the time.[8] This contrasts sharply with Wright's approach, according to which the *a priori* inference-licensing properties of objects or events appear to be central to Hume's conception of real powers.

The purpose of this section has been to show that there are some significant differences between Buckle's, Wright's and Strawson's interpretations. While they all offer sceptical realist interpretations – they take Hume to hold that our causal talk reaches out to real powers, whose existence Hume takes for granted but whose nature he takes to be beyond our ken – they each take a different notion of real power to be central to Hume's position. For Buckle, the notion of real power is fairly unspecific: it amounts to a belief in mechanism, where 'mechanism' amounts to more than just regularity or the projection of our habits of inference; and Hume's commitment to real powers, thus conceived, is supposed to simply be of a piece with the worldview that had brought, with Newton, such extraordinary scientific advances. Wright appears to get close to Buckle's view on this point (Hume 'clearly accepts the existence of real physical force and believes that science makes progress by postulating such forces *as* physical' (Wright 1983: 147)). Nonetheless, for Wright, the core of Hume's conception of real powers seems to be that real powers are AP properties: a conception that is 'derived from the Cartesians' (*ibid.*). The crucial distinction between how things seem and how they really are, so far as causation is concerned, is that our ideas of causes and effects are distinct, while the causes and effects themselves are not. Finally, for Strawson, Hume's core commitment is to real powers as sources of order: as the reason why the universe is regular in the way that it is.

It is striking that while sceptical realists officially hold that, according to Hume, we can have no 'positively contentful conception' of real powers, they all offer on Hume's behalf quite specific accounts of what they *are*. So which account *should* sceptical realists attribute to Hume? One answer would be that we should simply take Hume to be neutral on this issue; but no actual sceptical realist, so far as I know, has suggested this. In any case, it matters which specific account we attribute to Hume. Buckle, for example, has a broadly scientific conception of Hume's overall project, and his preferred conception of real powers fits well with that scientific conception; but the alternative conceptions of real powers – or neutrality with respect to them – would not fit nearly so well. In particular, it is hard to see why Hume would think that a mechanistic worldview would require, or even suggest, any commitment to AP properties. It is one thing to think that a thing's causal powers flow from its nature or essence; it is quite another to think that that nature or essence is such that grasp of it would license *a priori* inference from causes to effects. Similarly, Strawson's conception of real powers – powers as a source of order – seems to play a role in his story about why Hume believes in them, as we shall see in §7.6; and that story would not do its job if we attributed a different conception, or neutrality on the issue, to Hume.

The point here is not that there is a problem with attributing a view to Hume that can be characterized as *a* sceptical realist view. It is, rather, simply that different sceptical realist interpretations *are* different, and in a way that affects what counts as a general reason to think that Hume *is* (or is not) a sceptical realist. I pursue this point further in §7.5, §7.6 and §7.7.

7.5 Belief in real powers

The viability of a sceptical realist interpretation of Hume on causation requires, *inter alia*, that it explain how, for Hume, belief in real powers comes about, and why he thinks that that belief will not be destroyed by a sceptical attack, both of which he explicitly does in the case of belief in the external world. The key to Hume's explanation of both the genesis and the indestructibility of belief in the external world is the claim that it is a *natural* belief: a belief that is 'due to the ultimate instincts or propensities which constitute human nature' (Kemp Smith 1941: 86) – that is, due to the operation of the imagination. That something is a natural belief already tells us something about its genesis, although of course to say that a belief is due to the operation of the imagination is not yet to say very much about how such beliefs are formed. And the naturalness of a belief explains its indestructibility, since the source of the belief – our 'ultimate instincts or propensities' – is a source that we have no control over, so that the belief will persist even in the face of sceptical attack.

Let's start with indestructibility: with the claim, which sceptical realists need to attribute to Hume, that belief in real powers is psychologically mandatory. Is there a good reason to attribute this view to Hume? There is if we read what he says about the relevant kind of scepticism with a sceptical realist eye. In the *Enquiry*, he starts out by pointing out that the sceptic 'seems to have ample matter of triumph' when keeping 'within his proper sphere':

[The sceptic] justly insists, that all our evidence for any matter of fact, which lies beyond the testimony of sense or memory, is derived entirely from the relation of cause and effect; that we have no other idea of this relation than that of two objects, which have been frequently *conjoined* together; that we have no argument to convince us, that objects, which have, in our experience, been frequently conjoined, will likewise, in other instances, be conjoined in the same manner; and that nothing leads us to this inference but custom or a certain instinct in our nature.

(*E* 159)

He then points out that while the sceptic's argument 'seems, for the time at least, to destroy all assurance and conviction' (*ibid.*), in the end '[n]ature is always too strong for principle' (*E* 160):

[A] Pyrrhonian [sceptic] cannot expect, that his philosophy will have any constant influence on the mind: or if it had, that its influence would be beneficial to society. On the contrary, he must acknowledge, if he will acknowledge anything, that all human life must perish, were his principles universally and steadily to prevail.

(*E* 160)

Of course, it is optional whether we read the first passage just quoted with a sceptical realist eye. We *can* read Hume as raising sceptical doubt about causal *reasoning*, and correspondingly read the second passage as saying merely that scepticism concerning causal reasoning – scepticism, that is, with respect to the outcome of that reasoning, namely the belief that the sun will rise tomorrow, that bread will continue to nourish us, and so on – will not have 'any constant influence on the mind' (and also that giving up our inferential habits would have catastrophic consequences if we *could* give them up). But we can also read the first passage as raising sceptical doubt about belief in real powers. And sceptical realists need to read it in this way, since this is the only place where Hume says anything that can be read as positively claiming that belief in causal powers is psychologically mandatory (and practically indispensable).

If we read Hume in this way, then, we can attribute to him the view that belief in real power is psychologically mandatory. Moreover, what he says in the first passage quoted earlier – read in this way – also tells us where that belief comes from: it comes from 'custom or a certain instinct in our nature', namely the associative mechanism of causation.

The upshot of all this is that *if* we are to take Hume to believe in real powers, then, given that we need to attribute to him the view that such a belief is a natural belief, we must also take him to hold that that belief is a natural and unavoidable consequence of our inferential habits – that is, a natural and unavoidable consequence of the operation of the associative mechanism of causation. I shall argue that while Wright's and Buckle's versions of sceptical realism succeed in explaining how this can be so, Strawson's version does not.

As we saw in §7.4, Wright holds that Hume's belief in real powers is a belief in AP properties. How might Wright's interpretation deliver the required result that, for Hume, belief in AP properties is a natural and unavoidable consequence of the operation of the associative mechanism of causation? Well, as we have already seen, Hume holds that our coming to think of one event as necessarily connected to another just *is* a result of the operation of the associative mechanism. So if, as Wright maintains, to think of two events as necessarily connected is genuinely to believe that the first event has an AP property which guarantees the occurrence of the second, then our believing that really is a natural and unavoidable consequence of the operation of the associative mechanism. As Wright says, 'the supposition of causal necessity is no less "irresistible" than what Hume calls "the customary transition from causes to effects, and from effects to causes" (*T* 225). In fact, both are the results of exactly the same mechanism, and are in themselves not essentially different' (Wright 2000: 95).

One might be inclined to wonder at this point what, on Wright's interpretation, the force of the sections on the idea of necessary connection in the *Treatise* and the *Enquiry* is supposed to be. If Hume believes in AP properties – indeed, regards such a belief as unavoidable – what exactly is he objecting to in the views of his opponents? The answer is that while, on Wright's interpretation, there is no difference between Hume and his opponents over the *metaphysics* of causation – on what causation *is* – the epistemological difference remains intact, and it is with this epistemological difference that Hume is primarily concerned. Wright says:

> Hume suggests that people ordinarily think they perceive a genuine connection (what he calls 'a natural and perceivable connexion' between cause and effect) because they cannot think the one without the other. The objective connection which they ascribe to the familiar operations of nature on the basis of the associational processes of imagination is nothing but the connection which they would perceive if they had a genuine knowledge of causal connection. It is only philosophers who 'abstract from the effects of custom, and compare the ideas of objects' who are able to recognize the vulgar error and affirm that 'there is no known connexion amongst objects'. They recognize that in ordinary life we are quite mistaken in thinking we directly perceive the necessary connection of the objects of the senses. The vulgar mistake an associational connection for a genuinely perceived rational connection.
>
> (Wright 2000: 94–5)

So, on Wright's interpretation, we ordinarily *think* that we perceive AP properties, and we do so because, given an impression of the cause, we inevitably come to expect that the effect will occur. (In fact, if the argument of §4.3 is correct, this is only part of the story: not only can we not think one event without the other; we also *experience* the events as necessarily connected.) Because we think we perceive AP properties, we are also apt to suppose that we really are inferring the second event *a priori* from the first. But all this is a mistake, even though we are not mistaken in our belief that the relevant AP property *exists*. *We* are not inferring the second event from the first *a priori*, because we cannot perceive the AP property that would make such inference possible. On Wright's interpretation, then, Hume's disagreement with the Image of God doctrine concerns only its epistemological upshot, that is, the Insight Ideal: the claim that *a priori* causal knowledge is possible. We naturally *believe* in AP properties, but we cannot *know* a *priori* that they exist, nor can we detect them.

On Wright's interpretation, then, belief in real powers just *is* what we express when we make causal claims as a result of our inferential habits together with the felt determination of the mind that arises from them. When we project the idea of necessary connection on to perceived events, we legitimately come to believe that there is genuine necessary connection there; we are just wrong to think that we have *perceived* it. This marrying of belief in real powers with our inferential practices provides Wright with a plausible reason to suppose that Hume really does think that belief in real powers is a natural belief. As we just saw, Hume unquestionably thinks that our inferential practices are psychologically mandatory. Moreover, we do not have any control over whether or not we have an impression – and hence idea – of necessary connection: for beings like us, that idea always accompanies our everyday inferences from causes to effects. If we agree with Wright that all this automatically generates belief in genuine, objective necessary connections, then that belief in turn will turn out to be psychologically mandatory.[9]

Buckle appears to agree with Wright when he says that '[w]herever our experience is uniform, there we come to expect things to go on in the same way, exceptionlessly; and this exception-denying expectation just *is* the belief that things are necessarily thus and so' (Buckle 2001: 211–12). Indeed, '[e]xperience *proves* the reality of causal powers to us' (Buckle 2001: 212). What does Buckle mean by this? Well, Hume has a notion of 'proof' – not the contemporary notion – according to which one thing is proof of another if the former generates what might be called practical certainty about the latter: proofs are 'such arguments from experience as leave no room for doubt or opposition' (*E* 56n.). Proofs are to be distinguished from merely probable arguments, which do leave room for doubt. So for example, an 'argument from experience' that a heavily biased die will land on six generates probability rather than proof: we do not regard the die's landing on six as practically certain. By contrast, to use Hume's own examples, the arguments from experience that establish that 'all men must die, or that the sun will rise to-morrow' (*ibid.*) are proofs.

The argument from experience here is, of course, causal reasoning: we have no doubt that the sun will rise tomorrow just because we are naturally compelled, by habit, to believe that it will, and cannot bring ourselves to doubt it (or at least not once we escape from the study back into the world of practical action). In effect, Buckle extends the notion of proof to cover not just the belief that the sun *will* rise tomorrow, but also the belief that it *must*; that is, the belief that conditions are such as to *necessitate* the sun's rising tomorrow (see Buckle 2001: 186–9, 211–12). When Hume says that causal reasoning is inference 'by which [causes and effect] become proofs of each other's existence' (*E* 76), Buckle takes him to mean that they become proofs of each other's existence '*as* cause and effect' (2001: 202). And so they will, if causal reasoning inescapably generates the belief *that* causes and effects are necessarily connected, and if causal reasoning is itself 'proof' of existence.

For Wright and Buckle, then, belief in real powers is generated by the associative mechanism of causation itself, and so is indeed a natural belief. However, Buckle's conception of real powers might be thought to face a worry that is not faced by Wright's conception. Recall that Buckle takes Hume's commitment to real powers to be a belief in 'mechanisms': underlying natures of objects in virtue of which they have the causal powers that they have, but whose nature we cannot grasp (and so we cannot grasp the nature of the powers either). And that commitment is supposed to be simply a part of the scientifically successful worldview which Hume took from Newton. But it seems that it would be implausible to suggest that belief in real powers *conceived in that specific way* could count as a natural belief. So one might wonder whether Buckle's Hume really can help himself to the claim that belief in real powers is a natural belief after all.

Buckle himself, just before he reiterates the point that 'Hume's account of the genesis of the idea of necessary connection is a *proof* from experience' (2001: 211) and so concludes that belief in real powers is indeed a natural belief for Hume, says:

> If . . . [Hume] is trying to marry a first-personal analysis of impressions with the best available third-personal story about the nature of the world itself – trying to show that our first-personal experience conforms to a consistently-applied third-personal mechanical conception of the world, then it will not surprise if his language runs up against the difficulties embedded in such an ambitious enterprise. In such circumstances, however, we already recognize that conceptual purity is not the solution when confronted by the difficulties of any such task. Thus we do not ridicule the physicists of a century ago for affirming what is inconceivable, the wave-particle duality of light; nor do we ridicule contemporary physicists who accept the Copenhagen interpretation of quantum mechanics, despite its affront to common sense. We instead accept that the world is, at the microlevel, a very strange place, and that such views, despite their obvious conceptual difficulties, are not *therefore* to be dismissed. An adequate account of the complexities of the world is no easy task, and we should not simply leap on infelicitous claims, and thereby reject investigative projects. My suggestion is that we should treat Hume's project in the same way.
>
> (Buckle 2001: 210–11)

Buckle's point here seems to be that Hume is perfectly entitled to appeal to a mechanical conception of the world – complete with a commitment to real powers – despite the fact that it affirms 'what is inconceivable'. For there can be merit in 'affirming what is inconceivable': it can lead to genuine scientific advances. Hume's project, his science of man, affirms what is inconceivable by presupposing a mechanical conception of the world; indeed it is that very project, underpinned by the mechanical conception of the world, which shows that our *idea* of real powers, our idea of causation, is itself obscure or inadequate. But that consequence does not undermine the project itself or the mechanical conception of the world that underlies it.

The worry, however, is that even if we accept that Hume himself is entitled to his mechanical conception of real powers, just as physicists are entitled to believe that the act of measuring a quantum-mechanical process collapses the wave function – the 'inconceivability' in each case is no grounds for rejecting the project that is being pursued – a gap remains between the claim that *Hume* is entitled to his mechanical conception of real powers and the claim that belief in real powers can count as a natural belief for Hume. Physicists do not have to show, as part of their project, that belief in the power of the act of measurement to collapse the wave function is a natural belief; but Hume *does* have to show, as part of his project, that belief in real powers is a natural belief. Not only that; he apparently needs to show that it is the very belief that he himself has – belief in mechanisms – that is a natural belief. For of course there is, on Hume's own theory of the mind, no other source from which a belief in mechanisms can arise.

Well, I am not sure how much of a problem this really is. Buckle could perhaps respond as follows. When we consider the way in which belief in real powers is generated, and the mistakes that it is apt to give rise to – for example the mistake of thinking we really do perceive properties which license *a priori* inference from causes to effects – we can tell that it is a belief to the effect that objects have hidden natures in virtue of which they have the power to produce the effects they do produce. And that is close enough to a mechanistic conception of the world for there to be no serious tension between Hume's 'third-personal story' about the nature of the world and the natural belief in real powers.

Strawson, however, takes a different tack to both Wright and Buckle, and, I shall argue, it gets him into more serious trouble. He claims that 'one can go further than saying that Hume believes in causal power because such a belief is part of natural belief. He believes in causal power even when suspending natural belief as far as possible for philosophical purposes' (Strawson 1989: 2). Strawson's central concern is to argue that *Hume* believes in real powers. He appears to hold that appealing to the doctrine of natural belief is, as it were, a quick and easy way of showing that *Hume* believes in real powers – if belief in real powers is a natural belief, then of course Hume has it, just like everyone else – and he attempts to argue that Hume believes in real powers on independent grounds.

I take it that Strawson's point is that Hume does not simply believe in real powers because he, like everyone else, cannot help it; he also endorses that belief from a philosophical perspective: he holds that we are entirely correct to believe in them, and not merely that we have no choice. Strawson's view thus contrasts with, for example, Stroud's view. Stroud holds that, for Hume, we *do* genuinely believe in objective necessity, but what we believe in is something that could not really exist. So, for Stroud, Hume's philosophical position compels him to reject, from a philosophical perspective, the natural belief generated by the associative mechanism of causation. But Strawson's view also contrasts, in a sense, with Wright's view. For Wright, it is enough that belief in real powers is a natural belief, because (*pace* Stroud) Hume *can* simply endorse that belief from a philosophical perspective: the idea of necessary connection *can* represent how things really stand in nature, though it can do so only imperfectly. Wright's Hume, I think, simply sees no reason *not* to endorse our natural belief in real powers, while Strawson's Hume thinks there is a positive reason to endorse it.

I assess Strawson's argument for that conclusion in §7.6. My present concern, however, is with the doctrine of natural belief. Suppose that Strawson is right that one can make the case for the thesis that *Hume* believes in real powers without appealing to the doctrine of natural belief. Still, if Strawson's overall interpretation is to credit Hume with a position that is plausible by Hume's own lights, then that position needs to be one that is fully consistent with the claim that belief in real powers is a natural belief, otherwise he will be in the unfortunate position of committing himself to a belief whose origin his own philosophical system cannot account for. In other words, if Hume cannot explain how belief in real powers gets to count as a natural belief, he will be unable to avoid the charge that he himself is engaging in just the sort of speculative metaphysics that ought, by his own lights, to be consigned to the flames.

As I said earlier, if one is to make sense of the claim that belief in real powers is a natural belief for Hume, one needs to show how he accounts for the genesis and inevitability of that belief, and the only way to do that is to argue – as Wright does – that belief in real powers is automatically generated by our inferential practices. Can Strawson help himself to the same strategy? It is not clear that he can.

The problem is that, as we saw in §7.4, Strawson – unlike Wright – takes Hume to be a global subjectivist about necessity. So it seems that what the associative mechanism of causation generates, for Strawson's Hume, is the *false*, or perhaps incoherent, belief that events are objectively necessarily connected. Strawson holds that, nonetheless, our causal talk *refers* to real powers: powers that are not, since they could not be, genuine necessary connections. While I do not claim that this is an incoherent view – perhaps we can successfully refer to things even when we do so by attributing to them properties that they do not have – the worry is it seems that we now need an independent reason to think that Hume takes causal beliefs automatically to refer to real powers. For all that Strawson's Hume has told us, the only relevant *natural* belief here is the false (or incoherent) belief that events are necessarily connected.

Here is another way to put the worry. Strawson says:

> [T]he necessity-we-attribute is not in fact and cannot in fact be in objects, given that the source of our idea of necessity is an impression of reflexion or feeling of determination of the mind. And to say this is obviously not to exclude the possibility that there is some sort of Causation in the objects of which we can have no impression . . . i.e. something about objects in virtue of which they are regular in the way that they are.
>
> (Strawson 1989: 162)

Well, let's grant all of that. What we need, however, if the view Strawson attributes to Hume is to be one that is consistent with Hume's overall position, is not simply the claim that subjectivism about necessity does not *exclude the possibility* that Causation exists. What we need is an account of how actual, natural *belief* in Causation can arise.

Perhaps the clearest way of seeing what the problem is is to spell out the different views that Wright and Strawson offer concerning the semantics of 'cause'. Wright's Hume takes the idea of necessary connection to be an *inadequate* idea of what it represents, namely AP properties. Strawson's Hume, by contrast, does not take the idea of necessary connection to be a representation of anything at all: nothing outwith the mind answers, or could answer, to the idea of necessary connection. In order to explain how we can *refer* to real powers without having any 'positively contentful conception' of their nature, Strawson draws an analogy with natural-kind terms (1989: 124–7).

According to the standard view, natural-kind terms are semantically distinctive in that the reference of natural-kind terms like 'water' and 'gold' – unlike non-natural-kind terms like 'chair' – necessarily goes along with the real essence of the kind, rather than its nominal essence. (Or, to put it another way, members of a natural kind share a real essence, whereas members of a non-natural kind do not.) But we can perfectly successfully deploy a natural-kind term without having any inkling whatsoever of what the real essence of the kind is: we can perfectly legitimately talk about water even if all we have a 'positively contentful conception' of is its nominal essence. Similarly, Strawson suggests, for causation. We have a perfectly good, positively contentful conception of what real powers give rise to, namely regularities; regularities are analogous to the nominal essence of water. But the word 'cause' refers to the *real* essence of causation, namely real powers, just as the word 'water' refers to the real essence of water: its chemical constitution.

Let's grant that this is a perfectly coherent view to have of the semantics for 'cause'. The problem for Strawson is that it is not enough to attribute to Hume a coherent semantics for 'cause' that is *compatible* with sceptical realism; what is needed is a plausible story, attributable to Hume, about how that semantics automatically and unavoidably arises from our inferential habits. Consider the analogy with natural-kind terms. Imagine that we have no idea what the under-lying chemical constitution of water is. We can still ask whether the reference of the term 'water' goes along with superficial qualities – freezing point, taste and so on – or rather with its unknown essence. Our answer to that question will depend on seeing how we would use the term in various counterfactual situations – by considering Twin Earth thought experiments, for example. If we can all agree that it is perfectly possible for something to have all the manifest properties of water and yet not *be* water, then we can conclude that the reference of the term goes along with underlying essence. And what we will thereby have shown is that, perhaps for reasons we do not fully understand, that semantics has somehow or other been forced on us by the role that water plays in our cognitive lives – in our theorizing, in our patterns of inference, or whatever.

If one could somehow show that the semantics offered by Strawson for 'cause' has the same character – that reference to underlying 'essence', that is, to real powers, is somehow forced on us by our inferential practices – then one would thereby show that belief in real powers is mandatory to just the same extent as are those practices: the practices generate causal belief, and causal belief *must* be belief in real powers. But Strawson does not, and Hume himself certainly does not, attempt to make that case. Without a story about how our inferential practices automatically generate reference to real powers, as opposed to the mere claim that our causal talk does in fact refer to real powers, it is hard to see why Hume would be entitled to hold that belief in those powers is unavoidable.

In fact, it seems to me that Strawson faces a second, rather more straightfor-ward problem, arising from the dilemma that is faced by the traditional interpretation discussed in Chapter 5. If the idea of necessary connection has no legitimate application to the world – if 'the necessity-we-attribute is not in fact and cannot in fact be in objects' (Strawson 1989: 162) – then it seems that Hume either needs to be recommending a revised concept of causation, with the trou-blesome idea of necessary connection excised from it, or else he needs to hold that our causal talk – talk which cannot but involve attributing necessity to the world – is irredeemably false. The problem faced by those versions of the tradi-tional interpretation which take Hume to hold that the idea of necessary connection has no legitimate application to the world is that Hume shows no inclination either to recommend conceptual revision or to think of our causal talk as irredeemably false.

Strawson's interpretation faces that problem too; but it faces a further problem. Even if it could be argued that Hume does in fact take one of the paths just identified, he cannot do so and still be a sceptical realist about real powers. For, either way, our ordinary concept of causation – the one that involves the idea of necessary connection – will be the one that determines the content of any natural belief in real powers. If necessity is subjective but our natural belief is a belief in objective necessity, then that belief must, on Strawson's account, be false. And so there is no way for Hume to have the view Strawson needs to ascribe to him: the view that belief in Causation – real powers as sources of order – is a natural belief. The specific belief that Strawson attributes to *Hume* – belief in powers as sources of order – is not one that Hume can, by his own lights, legitimately count as a natural belief.

The point I have been pressing in this section is that the question of whether Hume can plausibly be characterized as holding that belief in real powers is a natural belief is not independent of the question of what he thinks that belief consists in. Wright's interpretation provides answers to all these questions which together form a coherent overall package, though there is some room for doubt about whether Buckle's does. But, more seriously, if one denies, as Strawson does, that real powers are genuine necessary connections, then it is unclear how belief in them can get to count, for Hume, as natural belief.

7.6 The cosmic luck argument

Strawson, as I said in §7.5, attempts to argue that Hume himself believes in real powers – conceived as sources of order – on grounds that are independent of the doctrine of natural belief. He argues both that we should take Hume's references to secret powers as genuine expressions of belief and that Hume can coherently hold that real powers exist even though only a relative idea of them is possible. I argued in §7.2 that Hume's references to secret powers can be interpreted as mere suppositions for the sake of the argument. So appeal to those references, just by itself, does not establish that Hume believes in real powers. And so the question arises: are there any *general* reasons why Hume might or should believe in real powers, conceived as sources of order, given his overall philosophical purposes?

Textual references aside, Strawson's reason for thinking that Hume believes in real powers seems to be that that is what *any* philosophically sensible person ought to think, because the claim that all there is to the world is regularity is 'utterly implausible' (Strawson 1989: 21): 'one of the most baroque metaphysical suggestions ever put forward' (1989: 87). Well, as we saw in §5.2 and §6.1, *qua* regularity theorist or *qua* projectivist Hume need not be taken to hold such a view. He need only be taken to hold the weaker view that there *might* be more to the world than regularity but, if there is, it does not serve as the referent of our causal talk. In fact, Strawson is rather more sympathetic to this view. Still, the claim that there *may* be no more than regularity is, he says, 'magical thinking', and the claim that if there is more it is not the referent of our causal talk is 'wonderfully implausible' (Strawson 1989: 91*n*.). For if there were nothing to keep things regular – if there were no power as a source of order – the ongoing regularity of the world would be 'a complete and continuous fluke' (1989: 21).

Well, it might be that Strawson does not intend the 'magical thinking' complaint to constitute an argument for the existence of real powers, or at least he might not intend it to constitute an argument that Hume might have found compelling. I shall revisit that possibility at the end of this section. Craig, however, explicitly suggests that Hume's belief in real powers is the result of a 'powerful argument' (2000: 115) – an argument from the existence of regularities to the existence of something that keeps them regular:

> The philosopher begins to think about the regularities which he has just conjectured to be the trigger for the everyday business of 'causalizing'. This regularity is wondrously pervasive, and wondrously regular. While he was thinking about our tendency to talk the language of causality, he did not need to worry about whether this language had any real corre-spondent in the world, since the whole purpose of his theory was to account for our addiction to it starting from just our experience of regu-larities. But these regularities themselves he regards as real, and their existence raises the possibility that we need to postulate something or other, just as real as they are themselves, to be whatever it is that keeps them regular. This is at least a *prima facie* option. And we are not now explaining a human practice or mindset; we are trying to get into the real ontology of nature and the real basis of its uniformity.
>
> (Craig 2000: 114–15)

I shall call the argument that is supposed to lead from the existence of regulari-ties to the existence of something that keeps them regular the 'cosmic luck argument'. Of course, it is debatable whether the cosmic luck argument really is a powerful argument at all, as Strawson and Craig think (see Beebee 2006b). But I shall leave that issue aside and focus on the interpretative question: could 'the philosopher' Craig is here describing conceivably be Hume? That is, could Hume have been persuaded by the cosmic luck argument?

An immediate reason to suspect that Hume would not have been persuaded by the argument is simply that he nowhere suggests any such argument: it is Strawson, and not Hume himself, who argues that we need to postulate some-thing to keep the regularities in check. Still, I suppose it could be argued that the cogency of the cosmic luck argument would have seemed more obvious to Hume – obvious enough for him not to feel the need to spell it out – than it does to us. Most of us were taught that Hume held a regularity theory of causation, and it is therefore part of our philosophical education to take seriously the possi-bility that there is nothing lying behind the regularities. But of course Hume's philosophical education would have been rather different.

Nonetheless, another objection can be made to the claim that Hume was persuaded to believe in real powers by the cosmic luck argument, which is that Hume's overall epistemological position is such that he is not in a position to be convinced by that argument in the first place. It seems to me that the urge to believe that there is something keeping things regular – that it *can't* all be a big, happy fluke and that it would be absurd to think otherwise – is an urge whose basis is epistemological rather than straightforwardly metaphysical. As Blackburn puts it:

> We want there to be some secret spring or principle, some ultimate
> cause, 'on which the regular course and succession of objects totally
> depends' (*E* 55). This is whatever it is that ensures the continuation of
> the natural order, that dispels the inductive vertigo that arises when we
> think how natural it might be, how probable even, that the constrained
> and delicate pattern of events might fall apart.
>
> (Blackburn 2000: 103)

Inductive vertigo is an epistemological ailment. Here we are, happily engaged in
causal reasoning, and yet that reasoning might in principle at any moment
completely fail us. We want to be reassured that this will not happen, and so we
postulate something that keeps the causal reasoning in line with the regularities,
so that the 'pre-established harmony between the course of nature and the
succession of our ideas' (*E* 55) is a harmony not merely between our inferential
habits and nature's regularities, but a harmony between the habits and the *source*
of those regularities. But from Hume's perspective, the belief that nature's regularities have an unknown source is no better a guarantee that our inferences will
continue to track the regularities than is the belief that nature is, in fact, regular.
For we have no *better* reason to suppose that objects will not change or lose their
secret natures than we have reason to suppose that they will not stop behaving in
a regular manner: that is exactly Hume's point when he argues that even if we
infer secret powers from observed regularities we cannot *deduce* effects from
causes without assuming the Uniformity Principle – a principle that cannot itself
be established without appealing to causal reasoning (see §3.6).

Admittedly, it could be argued that the argument Craig proposes on Hume's
behalf is not one that is intended to cure an epistemological ailment in the first
place, but is rather intended to provide a straightforwardly metaphysical explanation for the regularity we have already observed, without claiming to somehow
shore up future inferences from causes to effects. But I doubt whether much
sense can be made, from Hume's perspective, of the thought that belief in some-
thing-or-other-that-keeps-things-regular genuinely *explains* the regularity. To
believe that there *is* an explanation for something – an 'explanation' that Hume
must regard as for ever beyond our comprehension – is not the same as to actually explain it.[10] Consider the analogy with belief in the external world: Hume
does not attempt to argue that belief in external objects *explains* the existence and
coherence of our sensory impressions and is therefore justified.

Third, and most seriously, it seems to me that to claim that Hume is
persuaded by a distinctively *philosophical* argument to believe in real powers runs
counter to his overall epistemological position in a more fundamental sense. For
isn't one of the overarching aims of Hume's philosophy to show that philosophical argument will not establish the obtaining of *any* matter of fact? Consider the
case of the external world again: Hume argues that belief in the external world
can arise neither from *a priori* reasoning nor from reasoning from experience. In
particular, it cannot arise through reasoning from effects (our sensory experience)

to causes (external objects), because we lack an adequate idea of external objects when considered 'specifically different' from our impressions. And so he seeks to explain why we *do* believe in the external world (it's because we systematically take impressions to *be* external objects) and why that belief cannot be undermined by sceptical attack (it's because it is a natural belief).

As Craig characterizes him, however, Hume is doing in the case of real powers precisely what he claims cannot be done in the case of the external world: supposing that there can be an *argument* whose conclusion is an existence claim. But such an argument can be neither *a priori*, since the denial of its conclusion is certainly conceivable, nor empirical: we can no more legitimately reason from regularities to something lying behind them than we can argue from the existence of sensory impressions to the existence of something lying behind *them*.

In fact, Craig himself – who, as we have seen, wants to see Hume's belief in real powers as the 'result of a powerful philosophical argument' – raises something close to the objection just made, and admits that he does not know how to answer it; and he ends by asking whether there is a 'clash . . . between [Hume's] realist utterances and his epistemology' (Craig 2000: 121). The answer, I think, has to be no: it is implausible to suppose that, in the case of real powers, Hume could have somehow forgotten that, by his own lights, existence claims cannot be established by philosophical arguments. And that leaves us with a clear choice. Either Hume's apparent realist utterances *are* realist utterances, but there is no clash with his epistemology because he holds that such utterances are no more than a manifestation of natural belief; or his apparent realist utterances do not express a belief in real powers.

The moral of all this is that, given his own account of human nature, not only does Hume need to think of belief in real powers as a natural belief – that is, as a belief produced by the imagination, via the operation of associative mechanism of causation and the resulting idea of necessary connection – but that process must be the only *possible* source of belief in real powers. Hume simply does not have any other possible account of the formation of belief in real powers at his disposal; in particular, he cannot appeal to any philosophical argument to establish their existence.

However, neither the argument of this section nor the argument of §7.5 was supposed to undermine Strawson's conception of real powers as sources of order. I have tried to establish only that, since the only possible source of belief in real powers for Hume is the operation of the associative mechanism of causation, and since Hume clearly takes that belief to involve the idea of necessary connection, Hume cannot be a subjectivist about necessity if he is to be a sceptical realist – at least if we understand subjectivism about necessity to involve the claim that 'the necessity-we-attribute is not in fact and cannot in fact be in objects, given that the source of our idea of necessity is an impression of reflexion or feeling of determination of the mind' (Strawson 1989: 162). On a sceptical realist interpretation, the attribution of 'necessity' to objects, whatever that amounts to, *must* be what we do when we come to believe in real powers, since it is precisely the attribution of necessity that is generated by the associative mechanism. So while Hume, *qua* sceptical realist, may yet hold that real powers are sources of order, he cannot be a subjectivist about necessity.

7.7 Varieties of sceptical realism again

What constraints, if any, does the fact that Hume must take belief in real powers to amount to the attribution of necessity place on the kind of view about the nature of real powers we can reasonably attribute to Hume? It might be thought that it tips the balance in favour of Wright's conception of real powers – in favour of the view that, for Hume, real powers are AP properties, so that causes really are objectively necessarily connected to their effects. But in fact it is not at all clear that this is so. Recall Stroud's conception of what it is we do when we ascribe necessity to the world, described in §5.1. Given that the idea of necessity is a simple idea, Stroud claims that it 'will simply be an idea of whatever it is we ascribe to the relation between two events when we believe them to be causally or necessarily connected' (1977: 86). The idea of necessity is thus no different from the idea of red, in that we 'get our simple idea of red from an impression of red, but if we ask what our idea of red really is an idea of, we can say only that it is an idea of *red*. It is an idea of whatever it is we ascribe to a ripe apple when we believe that it is red' (*ibid.*). Stroud's claim here is that there is simply nothing more to be said about the nature of what it is we believe in when we attribute necessity to the world: we can only point to the idea of necessity and say that it is the content of *that* idea that we attribute.

That seems to be a sensible claim to make on Hume's behalf if he is a sceptical realist, because it captures the thought that the true nature of real powers – of what it is that our causal claims express our belief in – eludes us. And if the claim is right, then the balance does not tip decisively in Wright's favour. Since the idea of necessity reveals nothing about the nature of what it is we believe in, it cannot be said that, since the idea of necessity is the idea of *necessity*, it must be the case that what we *really* believe is that the cause is such that true knowledge of its nature would license *a priori* inference to the effect. For of course we cannot hope to spell out some feature of the *nature* of necessity by saying that the idea of necessity is the idea of *necessity*; Stroud's point is precisely that no such trick can be turned.

Where does all this leave us with respect to the different conceptions of real powers offered by Wright, Buckle and Strawson? It seems that each of them attributes to Hume a view that is rather more specific than, strictly speaking, he is entitled to, given that by his own account we cannot penetrate at all into the nature of those powers. But Hume himself, read as a sceptical realist, seems to oscillate between those different, more specific conceptions – sometimes writing as though real powers are sources of order, sometimes as though they are what is presupposed by a mechanistic worldview, and sometimes as though they are AP

214

properties. So there is a sense in which Hume himself appears to say more about the nature of real powers than he is strictly entitled to.

This point is not intended to be an objection to a sceptical realist interpretation, however. After all, *qua* regularity theorist or projectivist, Hume does something very similar: despite telling us that the most we can legitimately assert is that 'there may be several qualities both in material and immaterial objects, with which we are utterly unacquainted' (*T* 168), he still makes just the same speculative suggestions about 'a kind of attraction', that on which the 'regular course and succession of objects totally depends [*sic*]' (*E* 55), and so on. Adding an implicit 'if they exist' to such comments does not explain away the fact that Hume seems to be offering speculative suggestions about precisely those 'qualities' whose nature is supposed to be utterly beyond our cognitive grip.

On the other hand, I do hope to have shown at least that 'the sceptical realist interpretation' is not one interpretation but several, which agree on a central core – the claim that Hume believes in real powers – but differ on important issues. The disagreement between Strawson and Wright over whether or not necessity is objective is the most obvious one, but there is also the disagreement between Wright, Strawson and Buckle about whether the real powers Hume ultimately believes in are AP properties, sources of order or mechanisms.

That disagreement matters, in part, because it touches on broader questions concerning Hume's conception of his own project. For example, on Buckle's view, Hume's belief in real powers (that is, mechanisms) is central to his whole explanatory project – his account of the workings of the mind: without a commitment to a mechanical conception of the world, that project would not even get off the ground. But it is not at all obvious that real powers as sources of order or as AP properties would be central to Hume's project in anything like that sense. Hume, as a scientist of man, does not *need* to presuppose that AP properties or powers as sources of order exist, even if one consequence of that project is that belief in them is unavoidable.

Another way in which the internal disagreement amongst sceptical realists has broader implications concerns Hume's attitude towards the metaphysical element of the Image of God doctrine, as applied to causation: the claim that the causal structure of the world is such that *in principle* effects can be inferred *a priori* from causes (though of course only for beings that can penetrate into the essences of things). For example, I said in §7.6 that Strawson does not explicitly claim that Hume himself is persuaded by the cosmic luck argument. It might be that Strawson's view is that that argument is something which only needs to be wheeled out when confronted with crazy positivists who apparently sincerely deny what is obvious to everyone else: that the regularity of the universe is not simply a matter of cosmic luck. In that case, Hume himself, who has no such opponents, does not need to feel the force of the cosmic luck argument: the belief in real powers as a source of order can perfectly well count, for him, as a straightforward piece of common sense.[11] But that piece of common sense does not contain within itself any remnants of the metaphysics of the Image of God doctrine: the claim that the world contains not just order but also sources of order does not, or at least not in any obvious way, deliver any possibility of *a priori* knowledge, even in principle. According to Wright's interpretation, by contrast, Hume's view of the metaphysics of causation is precisely the same as that of the upholders of the Image of God doctrine. Of course, Hume's arguments against the epistemology associated with that doctrine still stand: the qualities of objects that *would* license *a priori* inference if only we could apprehend them are completely beyond our cognitive reach, and so our reasoning concerning causes and effects is oblivious to their existence. But their *existence*, according to Wright's interpretation, is not in dispute.

Again, the point here is not that the existence of these kinds of internal disagreements within the sceptical realist camp provides any grounds for suspicion about the adequacy of a sceptical realist interpretation – though I shall be rather less neutral about the matter in §7.8. It is merely that the disagreements are important, and that there are therefore issues that need to be resolved before it can be decided *which* sceptical realist interpretation ultimately makes the best sense of Hume's project, if a sceptical realist interpretation turns out to be preferable to the alternatives.

7.8 Which interpretation is right?

I argued in Chapter 5 that the traditional interpretation, in all its various forms, fails. In a nutshell, its major failing is that it is unable to make sense of the manifest fact that Hume takes the idea of necessary connection to be an essential part of the idea of causation. The traditional interpretation takes it as given that the idea of necessary connection has no legitimate application to the world, and so is forced to attribute to Hume either the view that the idea of causation therefore also has no legitimate application to the world or the view that the idea of causation can somehow be purged of the idea of necessary connection. But Hume says nothing to suggest that he holds either of these views. As a projectivist or a sceptical realist about causation, by contrast, Hume can happily do what he seems to do: to hold that the idea of necessary connection is an essential and ineliminable part of our idea of causation and that it can legitimately be applied to the world.

I hope to have shown, then, that the interpretative choice is between projectivism on the one hand and sceptical realism on the other – but which of these is the right interpretation? Unfortunately, it is unclear to me that that question can be decisively answered. So, rather than give an answer, I shall, first, say something very general about why I do not find the sceptical realist interpretations discussed above compelling and, second, say something about why a decisive answer is so difficult to provide.

The major reason why I do not think a compelling case has been made for a sceptical realist interpretation is simply that the specific issues which divide sceptical realism from the kind of projectivist interpretation developed in Chapter 6 are considerably more subtle than those that divide sceptical realism from its more traditional opponent. Strawson in particular explicitly sets the sceptical realist interpretation up against a version of the traditional interpretation which has Hume believe that there is definitely no more to the world than mere regularity. But the arguments that Strawson brings to bear against that version of the traditional interpretation are mostly ones which do not engage with the projectivist interpretation developed in Chapter 6. Suppose we agree with Strawson – as I think we should – that Hume is no dogmatic defender of the view that there is no more to the world than regularity, and that he maintains a sceptical attitude in the sense that he holds that the fundamental nature of the world lies beyond our cognitive grip, that its nature cannot be known. Agreement on those issues generates no reason to believe that Hume is a sceptical realist rather than a projectivist.

It is true, of course, that the sceptical realist and projectivist interpretations come into conflict over the precise sense in which the ultimate nature of the world is unknown. On a sceptical realist interpretation, Hume holds that we believe in real powers but cannot come to *know* that they exist; nor can we hope to conceive their true nature. On a projectivist interpretation – and indeed on a less dogmatic version of the traditional interpretation than the version Strawson mostly attacks – Hume simply remains agnostic about the existence of real powers: the imagination generates no belief whatever about them. The most we can do is, as Hume puts it, allow 'that there may be several qualities . . . with which we are utterly unacquainted; and if we please to call these *power* or *efficacy*, 'twill be of little consequence to the world' (*T* 168). What the imagination does generate is the projection of the idea of necessary connection, so that we come to think of the world as a world of causes and effects, but in a way that does not amount to a positive belief in real powers. Thus conceived, Hume's position is both sceptical, in that it acknowledges the impossibility of knowledge about those qualities with which we are unacquainted, and also realist, at least in Thomas Nagel's sense: it is 'a form of realism according to which our grasp on the world is limited not only in respect of what we can know, but also in respect of what we can conceive. In a very strong sense, the world extends beyond the reach of our minds' (Nagel 1986: 90).

A second reason why I find the case for the sceptical realist interpretation to be less than compelling connects with the differences between the different versions of that interpretation discussed in §7.7. The question is, why would Hume himself, given his philosophical agenda – in particular, given his antipathy to the Image of God doctrine and his commitment to the experimental method – feel the need to believe in real powers? I argued in §7.6 that Hume cannot seriously be persuaded by Craig's 'powerful philosophical argument': regularities exist, and so there must be a reason *why* they exist, and so real powers, *qua* sources of order, must exist. Since Hume so clearly sees that no such argument is available in the case of the external world – we cannot argue for its existence on the grounds that it explains the orderly nature of our sensory impressions, since no such argument can be delivered on the basis of either *a priori* or causal reasoning – it is unlikely that he would fail to see that the same point applies to powers conceived as sources of order. That seems to leave a sceptical realist interpretation with two options. Either Hume simply takes natural belief in real powers to be the upshot of his theory of the workings of the mind – real powers are just part of our ordinary and unavoidable conception of the world, as are chairs and tables; or he takes a commitment to real powers to be required by the very experimental method he employs in his exploration of the workings of the mind, as Buckle claims. In other words, Hume either takes belief in real powers to be a commitment that is delivered, but not presupposed, by his 'science of man' or he takes it to be a commitment that is *both* delivered and presupposed by his 'science of man'.

Either way, however, the grounds for attributing the relevant commitment to Hume are not overwhelming. Let's start with the second disjunct: the claim that Hume takes a commitment to real powers – that is, to mechanisms – to be required by his own experimental method. According to 'mechanical philosophy', Buckle says,

> [The world] works in the specific way that it does because of the different mechanisms that make each thing what it is. . . . Thus the power of the clock to keep time, or of the pulley to lift weights, is constituted by their different mechanisms. The mechanical model of the world proposes the same type of explanation for the natural powers of objects, whether the power of bread to nourish, or of rhubarb to purge, or of opium to induce sleep: powers are at bottom mechanisms. Since the mechanisms are inaccessible to perceivers like us, the powers of the objects must remain hidden: all that we can observe are their effects in the world, including their effects on us.
>
> (Buckle 2001: 193–4)

As we saw in §7.4, Buckle argues that Hume appropriates the view that the true essences of things must remain hidden from us straight from Newton. As Hume puts Newton's view, in his *The History of England*, '[w]hile Newton seemed to draw off the veil from some of the mysteries of nature, he shewed at the same time the imperfections of the mechanical philosophy; and thereby restored her ultimate secrets to that obscurity, in which they ever did and ever will remain' (Hume 1778: 542; quoted in Buckle 2001: 89). The issue, however, is whether or not Hume takes those 'ultimate secrets' to include mechanisms themselves. Consider, for example, the explanation of the power of bread to nourish. In one clear sense, such an explanation – indeed, a broadly mechanistic explanation – is now available to us, given the scientific advances that have allowed us to understand facts about the chemical composition of bread, the way in which different substances are dealt with by the human digestive system and so on. Such an explanation reveals hidden *causes*, that is, further objects and events which cause observable phenomena, such as the removal of feelings of hunger. For Hume to be a sceptical realist in Buckle's sense would be for him to regard an explanation of this nature – one that reveals hidden causes in the above sense – as one which still fails to reveal the underlying 'mechanism' by which bread has the power to nourish, since it is central to the view Buckle ascribes to Hume that mechanisms are inaccessible in principle to 'perceivers like us'.

My worry here is whether there are very good reasons to think that the 'mechanical model of the world' *requires*, or rather might be thought by Hume obviously to require, the claim that 'the mechanisms are inaccessible to perceivers like us'. For remember that part of Buckle's claim is that Hume's project requires the existence of real powers precisely *because* it appeals to a mechanistic worldview. But why should a mechanistic worldview require a commitment to real powers that are in principle beyond our ken, rather than merely a commitment to the thought that, for example, we should not speculate as to the causes of the nourishing effects of bread if those causes are not, in fact and as things currently stand, available for inspection?

Buckle argues that, on balance, Newton takes the former rather than the latter view, but notes that 'Newton does not always keep strictly to this position. He clearly entertains the hope, at least, that ignorance of ultimate causes is not final, but merely our *present* condition' (Buckle 2001: 87). Indeed, even in the passage quoted from the *Opticks* in §7.4, Newton says that the causes of his laws of motion and principle of gravity are not *yet* discovered. Buckle claims that Newton himself is 'inconsistent' on this issue (2001: 88), but that Hume is not. However, Buckle's central aim here is only to establish that Hume connects 'Newtonianism to the preservation of nature's secrets' (2001: 89); and that is a point over which there need be no dispute between the sceptical realist and projectivist interpretations. That there may be features of reality that we cannot in principle have access to is something that Hume is 'ready to allow'; the question is why Hume should feel the need to think that those features include real powers in order to help himself to the mechanical model of the world.

What about the first alternative of the two I mentioned earlier in this section: the thought that Hume *merely* takes natural belief in real powers to be the upshot of his theory of the workings of the mind, as opposed to also taking a commitment to them to be required by his own 'science of man'? Well, in that case, it seems to me that there is a *prima facie* worry for sceptical realism, at least if we hold Hume to the claim that we have a natural belief in AP properties and hence in objective necessary connections. As we saw in §7.7, to hold Hume to that claim is, in effect, to hold him to the view that the picture of the causal structure of the world that is implied by the Image of God doctrine is a picture that is simply enshrined in our ordinary understanding of the world: we ordinarily suppose that, if we *could* penetrate into the essences of causes, we would be able to infer their effects *a priori*.

The worry here is this: why should Hume have been so happy to accept uncritically this particular metaphysical consequence of the Image of God doctrine? Recall from §1.2 and §6.3 that the metaphysics of causation suggested by the Image of God doctrine is motivated by epistemological considerations. We want our epistemic access to the world to be, at least in principle, of the same nature as God's; and it is for that reason that we want to think of causes in such a way that in principle their nature licenses *a priori* inference from causes to effects, so that the relation between causes and effects is analogous to the relation between successive stages of a mathematical proof, or to the relation between one proposition and another proposition which it entails. But Hume rejects precisely that epistemological picture, and so he has no motivation to think of the world as a world of AP properties. If Hume's target is the Image of God doctrine, then surely he would have seen that, from a philosophical point of view, the belief that the world is a world of AP properties has nothing whatsoever to recommend it.

Of course, Hume does think that reasoning from causes to effects can *seem* like *a priori* inference: in cases where our inferential habits are very well established 'we are apt to imagine that we could discover these effects by the mere operation of our reason without experience' (*E* 28; see also §3.8). But Hume also seems to think that it does not take much to show that that particular mistake *is* a mistake: all that is needed is to point out that we can imagine the cause without the effect, and he does not appear to regard this as something that we find it especially difficult to do.

This is not to say that there is any internal problem with the view Wright ascribes to Hume: there is no incompatibility between believing that c is necessarily connected to e and yet being able to conceive of c without e, since of course the feature of c that *would* make the absence of e inconceivable is unavailable to us. The point is, rather, that it is unclear why, given his target, Hume would want to hold that belief in necessary connections is an unavoidable feature of our ordinary, commonsense understanding of the world. For, first, insofar as the belief in objective necessary connections can be construed as having some *prima facie* plausibility given the phenomenology of inference from causes to effects – it can *seem*, in some cases, that one can infer the effect from the cause without the aid of experience – the Conceivability Principle shows, in a pretty straightforward way, that that phenomenology is misleading. And, second, from a philosophical point of view, the belief in necessary connections is *motivated* by a theistic conception of our epistemic access to the world that Hume rejects. It is hard to see, in other words, why Hume would concede so much to his opponents by holding that, as far as causation is concerned, their metaphysics is in fact a metaphysics that we are naturally compelled to endorse.

It could be argued that Hume's demolition of the Insight Ideal is actually strengthened by the claim that we are naturally compelled to believe in the objective necessary connections that the Insight Ideal requires. For that claim might seem to provide Hume with an explanation for *why* it is that the thought that effects really can be inferred *a priori* from causes – by us, and not just in principle for a rather more God-like being – is so compelling, despite being mistaken. If we naturally believe that causal powers are the kinds of thing whose existence makes *a priori* inference possible in principle, then it is easy to see why we might erroneously believe that such inference is not just possible in principle but is something we actually engage in.

That argument would be mistaken, however, because it clearly puts the cart before the horse. Since the alleged natural belief in objective necessary connections would, for Hume, be a *result* of our natural tendency to suppose that we can infer effects from causes *a priori*, the natural belief in question cannot be used to explain that tendency. It is the tendency that explains the belief – whatever that belief amounts to – and not the other way around.

The moral of all this is that the case for a sceptical realist interpretation of Hume, as opposed to a projectivist interpretation, is not, as things stand, over-whelming. That is not, of course, to say that an overwhelming case cannot be made.

Finally, however, I want to say something about why it seems to me that a decisive resolution to the interpretative issue is so difficult to come by. The major barrier, I think, is the differences between the *Treatise* and the *Enquiry*: differences that have been noted in §4.4 and §7.3. If we look at the relevant differences in piecemeal fashion – by comparing what Hume says about secret powers in his discussion of causal reasoning in the *Treatise* with the corresponding passages in the *Enquiry*, or what he says about occasionalism, and so on, the differences can be made to seem marginal: differences in style rather than substance. But if we read the two works as a whole, separately and with no preconceptions about what Hume's view about causation is, the differences seem – or seem to me at any rate – to be much more marked. Putting it bluntly, the Hume of the *Treatise* seems to me to be a projectivist. But the Hume of the *Enquiry* seems to me to be a sceptical realist, notwithstanding the fact that, as I argued in §7.2 and §7.3, no particular thing he says there (or fails to say) decisively demonstrates that he is.

Strawson feels this tension too, and argues that we should therefore judge Hume's considered view to be the one put forward in the *Enquiry*: 'If you want to know what Hume thought about causation', he says, 'you have to give priority to his first *Enquiry*' (Strawson 2000: 31). And so we should proceed as follows:

> We can read the *Enquiry* back into the *Treatise*, when trying to under-stand his considered view; we cannot go the other way. Everything in the *Treatise* that is or appears incompatible with the *Enquiry* must be discarded. Nothing in the *Treatise* can legitimately be used to throw light on any passage in the *Enquiry* unless two conditions are fulfilled: the passage in the *Enquiry* must be unclear (this is not often the case), and the passage from the *Treatise* must not be incompatible with anything in the *Enquiry* that is not in dispute. Even when a passage from the *Treatise* is called in evidence, its claim to make a contribution to interpretation must be weak when compared with competing claims from passages in the *Enquiry* other than the passage under consideration.
>
> (Strawson 2000: 32)

How seriously should we take Strawson's uncompromising rules? Well, he certainly has some remarks of Hume's on his side. Hume says: 'The philosophical principles are the same in both [the *Treatise* and the *Enquiry*]: but I was carried away by the heat of youth and invention to publish precipitately. . . . I have repented my haste a hundred, and a hundred times' (Hume 1932: 158); and 'I . . . acknowledge . . . a very great mistake in conduct, viz my publishing at all the Treatise of Human Nature. . . . Above all, the positive air, which prevails in that book, and which may be imputed to the ardour of youth, so much displeases me, that I have not patience to review it' (Hume 1932: 187; both quoted in Strawson 2000: 32). And in the 'Advertisement' he says that he is correcting '*some negligences in his former reasoning and more in the expression*' (*E* 2).

The case for adopting Strawson's rules is certainly not overwhelming, however. First, it is not entirely unheard of for a philosopher to change his or her mind over a period of some eight years or so and then claim that their later view is in fact the view they had all along, so that they do not get taken to task over views which they no longer endorse.

Second, if the Hume of the *Treatise* really is a sceptical realist, he there expresses his view incredibly badly. Take the following passage, where Hume is describing his own position on behalf of the opponent who finds his view 'extravagant and ridiculous':

> What! The efficacy of causes lie in the determination of the mind! As if causes did not operate entirely independent of the mind, and wou'd not continue their operation, even tho' there was no mind existent to contemplate them, or reason concerning them. Thought may well depend on causes for its operation, but not causes on thought. This is to reverse the order of nature, and make that secondary, which is really primary.
>
> (*T* 167)

Of course, Hume is putting words into the mouth of his opponent, and is hence providing a very unsympathetic characterization of his own view. But as a sceptical realist, Hume could not seriously put his own view in these terms, for they are terms which, rather than characterize his view unsympathetically, fail to characterize his view at all. *Qua* sceptical realist, Hume denies that the efficacy of causes lies in the determination of the mind, accepts that causes operate entirely independently of the mind and accepts that thought depends on causes: precisely the opposite of what he is here claiming. This is hardly a mere 'negligence' in 'expression'; it is difficult to believe that a writer of Hume's ability could manage to express his view so badly that he ends up clearly asserting claims that he actually intends to deny.

Strawson's own version of sceptical realism might be thought to make better sense of this passage, because, as we saw earlier, Strawson holds Hume to the view that *necessity* is all in the mind, but 'Causation' – that is, real power – is not. But, as I argued in §7.5, Strawson's attempt to hold Hume to a combination of subjectivism about necessity and realism about Causation fails, since it rules out something that a sceptical realist interpretation requires: the claim that belief in real powers is a natural belief.

Unfortunately, attributing a genuine change of view to Hume seems to be rather an unpromising suggestion too. It gets him off the charge of having expressed his (single) view extremely badly in one or other of the *Treatise* or the *Enquiry*. On the other hand, it is hard to see how he could change from being a projectivist about causation to being a sceptical realist and yet manage to mark such a radical change of heart in such a subtle way that the majority of readers simply fail to notice the difference.

Perhaps a more promising approach to the whole issue is to take Hume to simply be insufficiently interested in distinctively semantic and metaphysical issues to actually take a stand on them. This is suggested by Craig, who says:

> I have argued before now . . . that Hume's concentration on the refuta-
> tion of the Image of God Doctrine tended to move ontological issues
> out of the focus of his attention. The fatal weakness of that doctrine,
> as he saw it, lay in its false implications about our epistemic potential.
> So he was primarily concerned with where . . . causal beliefs cannot
> come from, and where they can and do come from; whether they are
> true or not was very much a secondary issue, and one that he thought
> about at a much lower level of intensity. So, I went on, we should not
> be too surprised if he provided material for both the anti-realist and
> the realist interpreters, but never bothered to decide firmly and
> unequivocally where he himself stood; we can just shrug that one off.
>
> (Craig 2000: 120)

Craig abandons this view, however, on the grounds that 'there was no need for him to decide, since the two views [that is, projectivism (or 'anti-realism') on the one hand, and sceptical realism on the other] are not in collision; he can perfectly well hold both of them, and there is plenty of *prima facie* textual evidence that he did, and that he expressed them openly and clearly' (Craig 2000: 121). Craig says this because he argues earlier in the same paper that Hume can be both a projectivist about our causal talk *and* a sceptical realist of Strawsonian stripe, that is, one who is convinced that secret powers exist thanks to a 'powerful philosophical argument'. But I argued in §7.6 – and Craig himself is worried by this objection – that Hume cannot be convinced by any such argument. And, in any case, projectivism and sceptical realism cannot be reconciled in the way Craig suggests because they make claims about the semantics of 'cause' that are incompatible with one another: Hume cannot hold that our causal talk *both* non-descriptively expresses our inferential habits *and* refers to real powers. So perhaps, since Hume's holding *both* a projectivist and a sceptical realist view is not an option, Craig's original thought is right: that Hume 'never bothered to decide firmly and unequivocally where he himself stood' (Craig 2000: 120).

Is this a plausible view? In one sense, of course, projectivism and sceptical realism are radically different positions, since they differ irreconcilably over the metaphysical commitments of our ordinary talk and thought; and this in itself makes it seem unlikely that Hume might not have bothered to decide between them. On the other hand, if we do see Hume's major interest as an interest in genetic and epistemological issues, then all the theses he really cares about can be established without addressing the issues that distinguish projectivism from sceptical realism. Hume has an account of reasoning concerning matters of fact that appeals, at bottom, to brute habit. He also has an account of why we come to think of the world in causal terms that appeals to that same brute habit together with the projection of the idea of necessary connection on to events between which sensation can discern no connection. Either way, as I argued in §6.5, our conceiving of the world as a world of causes and effects plays an important role in our ability to predict and explain the world around us. So if Hume's primary interest is an interest in refuting the Image of God doctrine and replacing it with a conception of our access to the world according to which we are peculiarly clever animals rather than pale imitations of God, there is no particular reason for him to want to decide between – or even seriously wonder about – whether our causal talk represents real powers whose existence we cannot help taking for granted or whether it merely expresses our inferential habits.

Even if all this is right, however, it at best explains why Hume 'provided material for both the anti-realist and the realist interpreters' (Craig 2000: 120); it does not explain why most of the material he provides for the anti-realist interpreter is to be found in the *Treatise* and most of the material for the realist interpreter is to be found in the first *Enquiry*. The best I can offer here is the suggestion that, *if* metaphysical and semantic issues are of only marginal concern to Hume, then perhaps he could have had a change of heart between writing the *Treatise* and writing the *Enquiry* without feeling the need to announce it explicitly. Perhaps the change of heart was even provoked by the criticisms that were directed at the *Treatise*. But, if the change between the *Treatise* and the *Enquiry is* a change of view – especially if it is a change to those aspects of Hume's overall philosophical position which he himself regards as of relatively little importance – then Hume does not, *pace* Strawson, lay 'a clear obligation on us' (Strawson 2000: 32) to follow Strawson's interpretative blueprint by reading the *Enquiry* back into the *Treatise* and discarding everything in the *Treatise* that is incompatible with the *Enquiry*. Indeed, it would be a mistake to do so; though of course it would equally be a mistake to read the *Treatise* into the *Enquiry*.

Well, I don't set any great store by the suggestion just made. What I hope to have done is make the case for the claim that there is a genuine problem concerning how the differences between the *Treatise* and the *Enquiry* are to be explained – a problem to which I can see no decisive solution. What I do want to resist is the claim that Hume, in the *Treatise*, presents – extremely badly – a sceptical realist view of causation, and the corresponding claim that we should actually ignore those parts of it that cannot be made to fit the sceptical realist mould. It is hard to see how that could be fulfilling any obligation to Hume.

NOTES

1 INTRODUCTION

1 In the scholastic and modern literature on causation, causes are often treated *both* as objects or events in the world and as premises in arguments. This traces back to Aristotle's view that causes are 'middle terms' in syllogisms, and gives rise to the corresponding lack of a distinction between the causal relation that obtains between objects or events in the world, on the one hand, and the relation between premises and conclusions of arguments *about* those objects and events, on the other. (See, for example, Clatterbaugh 1999: esp. 11–15 and 53–8.) Of course, given the metaphysical picture just described, such a lack of distinction between causal relations on the one hand and entailment relations on the other is just what one would expect.

2 See Buckle 2001: ch. 2, esp. 30–43.

3 This is an oversimplification: not everyone I shall characterize as a traditional interpreter subscribes to exactly the view just described.

2 *A PRIORI* REASONING AND THE GENESIS OF KNOWLEDGE

1 Use of the term 'mechanism' in this context is not intended to foist any metaphysical commitments on to Hume; it is intended to be consistent with, for example, the thesis that all there is to the 'mechanism' is simply a set of correlations between ideas of different kinds. I use the term 'mechanism' rather than Hume's 'principle' to reinforce the fact that, for Hume, the calling up of one idea thanks to the presence of another does not, or at least need not, proceed by any invoking of a principle that one consciously entertains. A dog's mind, for example, operates according to the associative 'principle' of causation when it comes to expect its owner's appearance on hearing the familiar sound of the key in the front door, despite the fact that dogs (presumably) lack the ability to entertain the thought that one thing causes another (see, for example, *T* 177–8).

2 I am avoiding the expression 'causal *belief*' because Hume himself does; see §6.2. The expression 'causal judgement', which I shall mostly stick to, is supposed to be read in a noncommittal way: all I mean by our 'judging' that c caused e is that we 'call the one object, *Cause*; the other *Effect*' (*E* 75).

3 In fact, while it might seem obvious that causation is a class B relation, and while Hume himself does not bother to provide much argument at this stage for so classifying it, it becomes clear later on that he thinks that taking causation to be a class B relation is controversial and needs to be established by argument (see Chapter 3).

4 See, for example, Bennett 1971: ch. 10; Stove 1973: ch. 2; and Dicker 1998: ch. 2.

5 See Owen 1999: chs 3 and 5.

NOTES

6 Strictly speaking, of course, it is the *contents* of the ideas that stand in relations and not the ideas, *qua* mental objects, themselves: the idea of one million is not itself a million times larger than the idea of one.
7 I am here using 'belief' in its ordinary sense, and not in Hume's sense – about which more in a moment.
8 See Garrett (1997: ch. 3) for an extended discussion of the use to which Hume puts the Separability Principle.
9 Of course we might start out with a belief rather than an impression of memory or sensation – the belief that Caesar was killed on the ides of March, for example. But, Hume argues, the source of *that* belief must eventually trace back, via a causal chain, to some impression: there is a (very long) causal chain running from someone's witnessing the event to my reading about Caesar in a history book. So the basic case, to which all cases of inference from causes to effects ultimately reduce, is the case where what we start with is an impression (see *T* 82–4).

3 CAUSAL REASONING AND THE GENESIS OF BELIEF

1 For example, causation barely gets a mention in David Stove's *Probability and Hume's Inductive Scepticism* (1973) and does not so much as appear in the index of Colin Howson's *Hume's Problem: Induction and the Justification of Belief* (2000).
2 See, for example, Wright 1983: 12–13; Broughton 1983; Garrett 1997: ch. 4; Noonan 1999: 110–31; Owen 1999: ch. 6.
3 See Owen (1999: 132–4) for a brief discussion of, and an objection to, Garrett's interpretation. Owen's account, by contrast with Garrett's (1997), does not attribute to Hume a univocal use of 'reason', since Hume often *does* refer to the inference from causes to effects as 'reasoning', even though that inference is an activity of the imagination rather than the faculty of reason. In this broader sense of 'reason', both relations of ideas and matters of fact are 'objects of reason', even though reasoning concerning matters of fact is not performed by the *faculty* of reason.
4 For example, other things being equal, the speed of a car increases and decreases according to how much pressure is applied to the accelerator. So we should think of the total pressure and total speed in a given case as made up of 'parts' – smaller quantities of pressure and speed – so that each of these smaller quantities of pressure causes one of the smaller quantities of speed.
5 A different translation of the same passage is quoted by Wilson (1983: 665).
6 Wilson here seems to be failing to distinguish (Q2) from (Q3). Hume wants, he says, 'to defend science against superstition' (Wilson 1983: 667); but I take it that there are two distinctions here: one between causal reasoning and superstition (to which (Q2) is addressed) and one between 'vulgar' and sophisticated causal reasoning (Q3).
7 Of course, this is not to say that following the scientific method is *guaranteed* to get us to more of the truth, since there is no *guarantee* that causal reasoning is reliable.

4 THE IDEA OF NECESSARY CONNECTION

1 Don Garrett argues that since Hume holds that the ideas of space and time are abstract ideas he does not need to hold that we have a standalone impression of space and time; 'although there is no *separate* impression of space, every spatially complex impression is *an* impression of space – and of various other things as well' (Garrett 1997: 53). So the idea of space has an impression-source, but that source is not a standalone impression. If Garrett's interpretation is right, the question one might ask is why Hume does not consider the possibility that the idea of causation might also be abstracted from our experience of seeing events-causing-other-events.
2 See Strawson 1989: ch. 11. I shall use the term 'AP property' sometimes to mean a property of an impression (so that if an impression of *c* has the AP property we can

infer *a priori* that *e* will occur) and sometimes to mean a property of *c* itself (so that *were* we to have an impression of that property we would be able to deduce that *e* will occur).

3 'Causation', with a capital 'C', is Strawson's word for causation conceived of as involving something more 'in the objects' than mere regularity.

4 I am here skating over some large interpretative issues. One might hold, for example, that Hume's purpose in uncovering the impression-source of the idea of necessary connection is to show that the idea of necessary connection is in fact illegitimate or incoherent, since the fact that the impression is an impression of reflection shows that we cannot coherently apply the idea of necessary connection to objects and events outwith the mind. I argue that the interpretation just sketched is mistaken in Chapter 5.

5 See §6.1, however, for the claim that Hume is not quite as confused about this as he might appear.

6 Noonan's claim that, according to Hume, there is a 'feeling of helplessness or inevitability' is close to A.H. Basson's claim that, for Hume, 'on experiencing *A*, *we feel compelled* to expect *B*. It is not simply that the expectation always follows, or even that we *are* compelled, but we have a *feeling* of compulsion' (Basson 1958: 77).

7 I am thus agreeing with Simon Blackburn, who says that we fail to engage with Hume 'if we merely insist, as many thinkers do, that we properly describe the *perceived* states of affairs in causal terms – *see* bricks splashing in water, balls breaking windows, things pushing and pulling' (1984: 211–2), and with Peter Kail, who says that, on Hume's view, 'experience has a certain character that fools one into thinking that it is genuinely modal experience' (2001: 45).

8 By 'experience' I just mean how things *seem* or look to us. So to speak of 'causal experience' is simply to talk about how pairs of events which we judge to be causally related seem: do they seem loose and separate or not? Similarly, to speak of 'aesthetic experience' is simply to talk about how objects which we judge to be beautiful, ugly, etc. seem or look to us: do they seem or look beautiful or ugly, or do we merely *think* of them as beautiful or ugly, even though they do not seem or look so? 'Experience' here is thus a weaker notion than 'perception': to *perceive* causation would be for one to have a *sensory* impression of necessary connection which detects a real relation between two events.

9 There are, of course, two obvious differences here: the *Enquiry* version drops the contiguity requirement and also offers us an alternative, counterfactual, version of the definition. But neither difference is relevant to the present issue. I shall not have anything to say about Hume's counterfactual definition; see Buckle (2001: 212–13) for some useful discussion of it.

10 In fact in the *Treatise* Hume also raises the 'foreign to the cause' worry (*T* 170), but only with respect to the first definition; he takes the second definition to remedy this defect. I discuss the significance of this in §7.3.

11 See, for example, Robinson 1962.

12 As we shall see in §5.3 and §5.4, Garrett himself is not neutral on this issue.

13 'Relations' is in scare quotes here because Hume does not, and need not, count entailment amongst the relations: all of his relations are relations between *distinct* ideas, and the ideas 'related' by entailment are not distinct.

14 In §5.5 I argue that there is no evidence that Hume *ever* means 'constant conjunction *simpliciter*' rather than merely 'observed constant conjunction' when he talks about constant conjunction.

15 This is not to commit Hume to a very deep distinction between the normative 'must' and the psychological 'must'. As I argued in Chapter 3, the claim that, for example, differences in events must be due to differences in their causes is itself – like any

empirical claim – established on the basis of causal reasoning; that is, thanks to the operation of the associative mechanism.

5 THE TRADITIONAL INTERPRETATION

1 See Garrett (1997: 41–8) for discussion of this point.
2 Whether or not such mind-independent objects exist and how we come to believe that they do are difficult questions for Hume; nonetheless, he does believe that they exist, and he does think (as he must if he is to have that belief) that our ideas represent them. See §7.1.
3 Kripke 1982: 67; quoted by Strawson 2000: 31. Strawson gives other examples on the same page and in a footnote.
4 Thomas Uebel tells me that this is, in fact, the right way to read Schlick – though doubtless the business of interpreting the positivists is just as fraught with controversy as is interpreting Hume.
5 In fact, Strawson does sometimes note this distinction; but he still regards the claim that 'even if there is something about reality in virtue of which it is regular in the way that it is, this something is no part of what causation is' as 'wonderfully implausible'. For defence of regularity theories against Strawson's assaults, see Beebee (2006b).
6 Stroud himself makes something like this move (1977: 92–3).
7 Berkeley restricts the expression 'abstract idea' to ideas formed by abstraction, and hence denies that there are any abstract ideas (there are only general *words*, which 'indifferently' suggest any one of a number of particular ideas to the mind). Hume, by contrast, is happy to talk about 'general or abstract ideas' (for example at *T* 161), even though he agrees with Berkeley about abstraction, and hence agrees that all ideas are really particular ideas.
8 He does, however, offer a somewhat obscure *a priori* argument for the claim that causes precede their effects at *T* 76.
9 See, for example, Beauchamp and Rosenberg 1981: ch. 5.
10 See also Dicker 1998: 120–5.

6 PROJECTIVISM

1 A version of some of the material in this chapter also appears in Beebee (2006a).
2 As in Chapter 4, all I mean by 'visual experience' here is how things seem to us when we open our eyes and look: in the causal case, events seem causally connected rather than loose and separate.
3 Well, not exactly a relation, strictly speaking, for Hume, since P_1 and P_2 are not distinct; see §2.4.
4 'Compels' is, of course, rather too strong in any case. Hume cannot hold that it is impossible for us to refrain from drawing the inference, for then we would not be able to separate the idea of the cause from the idea of the effect: we could not imagine one without the other.
5 See Fodor (2003: esp. ch. 1) for a robust attack on Stroud's claim that Hume would have been better off without the theory of ideas.

7 SCEPTICAL REALISM

1 Note that 'sceptical' here bears little relation to 'scepticism' in the sense employed in Chapter 3 with regard to inductive scepticism, and which I shall shortly be employing with regard to scepticism about the external world. 'Sceptical' positions in this sense – which Hume certainly does not endorse – claim that a given belief (in the rationality of causal reasoning, or in the external world) should be abandoned because it lacks justification. The 'sceptical' in 'sceptical realism' is a different kind of scepticism: the

nature of real powers cannot be known, but the consequence is not that we should not believe in them or should remain agnostic about their existence. *Qua* sceptical realist, Hume holds that agnosticism with respect to real powers is not an option: we cannot but believe in them.

2 There is a further problem here too. Real powers are supposed to be those features of reality in virtue of which events cause other events. It is unclear whether much sense can be made of the thought that real powers *themselves* are also causes.

3 The passage at *E* 77 to which Winkler is referring is Hume's claim that '[w]e have no idea of this connexion, nor even any distinct notion what it is we desire to know'.

4 See Wright 1983: ch. 4; Buckle 2001: ch. 3.

5 See, for example, Buckle 2001: 47–8, 61–63, 76–7.

6 See Wright 1983: 136–9, 142–5.

7 Of course, as I argued in §5.2, the traditional interpreter need not hold Hume to this position. There are no serious grounds for claiming that Hume positively holds that there is nothing over and above regularity; the most the traditional (or projectivist) interpreter needs to be committed to is the claim that, whatever there may be over and above regularity, our causal talk fails to latch on to it: it may exist, but it plays no role in any positive conception of the nature of the world.

8 See Strawson 1989: 158–9.

9 See Winkler (2000: 64–7) for criticism of Wright's claim that the projection of necessary connection has the mandatory character required for natural belief; and Wright (2000: 92–5) for Wright's response.

10 See Beebee (2006b) for a more detailed elaboration of this worry.

11 This is not, of course, to retract the argument of §7.5: the point that Hume needs to think that the idea of necessary connection picks out the sources of order, since only then can belief in sources of order count as a natural belief, still stands.

BIBLIOGRAPHY

Armstrong, D.M. (1983) *What is a Law of Nature?*, Cambridge: Cambridge University Press.

Baier, A. (1991) *A Progress of Sentiments: Reflections on Hume's Treatise*, Cambridge, Mass.: Harvard University Press.

Basson, A.H. (1958) *David Hume*, Harmondsworth: Penguin.

Beauchamp, T.L. (ed.) (1999) *David Hume: An Enquiry Concerning Human Understanding*, Oxford: Oxford University Press.

Beauchamp, T.L. and A. Rosenberg (1981) *Hume and the Problem of Causation*, New York: Oxford University Press.

Beebee, H. (2006a) 'Hume on causation: the projectivist interpretation', in Huw Price and Richard Corry (eds), *Causation, Physics and the Constitution of Reality: Russell's Republic Revisited*, Oxford: Oxford University Press.

——(2006b) 'Does anything hold the universe together?', *Synthese* 149, 509–33.

Bennett, J. (1971) *Locke, Berkeley, Hume*, Oxford: Clarendon Press.

Berkeley, G. (1710) *A Treatise Concerning the Principles of Human Knowledge*, ed. J. Dancy, Oxford: Oxford University Press 1998.

Blackburn, S. (1984) *Spreading the Word*, Oxford: Oxford University Press.

——(1993a) 'Morals and modals', *Essays in Quasi-Realism*, New York: Oxford University Press, 52–74.

——(1993b) 'How to be an ethical anti-realist', *Essays in Quasi-Realism*, New York: Oxford University Press, 166–81.

——(2000) 'Hume and thick connexions', in R. Read and K. Richman (eds) *The New Hume Debate*, London: Routledge, 100–12.

Broughton, J. (1983) 'Hume's scepticism about causal inferences', *Pacific Philosophical Quarterly* 64, 3–18.

Buckle, S. (2001) *Hume's Enlightenment Tract*, Oxford: Oxford University Press.

Clatterbaugh, K. (1999) *The Causation Debate in Modern Philosophy, 1637–1739*, New York: Routledge.

Craig, E. (1987) *The Mind of God and the Works of Man*, Oxford: Clarendon Press.

——(2000) 'Hume on causality: projectivist *and* realist?', in R. Read and K. Richman (eds) *The New Hume Debate*, London: Routledge, 113–21.

Descartes, R. (1641) *Meditations on First Philosophy*, trans. and ed. J. Cottingham, Cambridge: Cambridge University Press (1996).

Dicker, G. (1998) *Hume's Epistemology and Metaphysics*, London: Routledge.

Ellis, B. (2001) *Scientific Essentialism*, Cambridge: Cambridge University Press.

——(2002) *The Philosophy of Nature*, Chesham: Acumen.

Flage, D. (2000) 'Relative ideas re-viewed', in R. Read and K. Richman (eds) *The New Hume Debate*, London: Routledge, 138–55.

Fodor, J.A. (2003) *Hume Variations*, Oxford: Clarendon Press.

Garrett, D. (1997) *Cognition and Commitment in Hume's Philosophy*, Oxford: Oxford University Press.

Harré, R. and E.M. Madden, (1975) *Causal Powers: A Theory of Natural Necessity*, Oxford: Basil Blackwell.

Heathcote. A. and D.M. Armstrong (1991) 'Causes and laws', *Nous* 25, 63–73.

Hobbes, T. (1656) *Elements of Philosophy*, in *The English Works of Thomas Hobbes*, vol. 1, ed. W. Molesworth, London: Routlege/Thoemmes Press (1997).

Howson, C. (2000) *Hume's Problem: Induction and the Justification of Belief*, Oxford: Clarendon.

Hume, D. (1739–40) (*T*), *A Treatise of Human Nature*, ed. L.A. Selby-Bigge, 2nd edn, rev. and ed. P.H. Nidditch, Oxford: Clarendon Press (1978).

——(1748) (*E*), *Enquiries Concerning Human Understanding and Concerning the Principles of Morals*, ed. L.A. Selby-Bigge, 3rd edn, rev. and ed. P.H. Nidditch, Oxford: Clarendon Press (1975).

——(1757) 'Of the standard of taste', first published in *Four Dissertations*; reprinted in *Essays: Moral, Political and Literary*, ed. E.F. Miller, Indianapolis: Liberty Press (1985), 226–49.

——(1778) *The History of England*, vol. 6, Indianapolis: Liberty Press (1983).

——(1779) *Dialogues Concerning Natural Religion*, ed. N. Kemp Smith, Oxford: Oxford University Press (1935).

——(1932) *The Letters of David Hume*, ed. J.Y.T. Greig, Oxford: Clarendon Press.

Jacobson, A.J. (2000) 'From cognitive science to a post-Cartesian text: what did Hume really say?', in R. Read and K. Richman (eds) *The New Hume Debate*, London: Routledge, 156–66.

Kail, P.J.E. (2001) 'Projection and necessity in Hume', *European Journal of Philosophy* 9, 24–54.

Kemp Smith, N. (1941) *The Philosophy of David Hume*, London: Macmillan.

Kneale, W.C. (1954) 'Natural laws and contrary to fact conditionals', first published in *Analysis* 10 (1950), 121–5; reprinted in M. MacDonald (ed.), *Philosophy and Analysis*, New York: Philosophical Library.

Kripke, S. (1982) *Wittgenstein on Rules and Private Language*, Oxford: Blackwell.

Lewis, D.K. (1986) *Philosophical Papers, Vol. II*, Oxford: Blackwell.

Mackie, J.L. (1962) 'Counterfactuals and causal laws', in R. Butler (ed.), *Analytical Philosophy*, Oxford: Blackwell; reprinted in T.L. Beauchamp (ed.) *Philosophical Problems of Causation*, Encino, Calif.: Dickenson (1974).

——(1974) *The Cement of the Universe*, London: Oxford University Press.

——(1977) *Ethics: Inventing Right and Wrong*, New York: Viking.

——(1980) *Hume's Moral Theory*, London: Routledge.

Martin, C.B. (1993) 'Power for realists', in J. Bacon, K. Campbell and L. Reinhardt (eds), *Ontology, Causality and Mind: Essays in Honour of David M. Armstrong*, Cambridge: Cambridge University Press.

Millican, P. (2002) 'Hume's sceptical doubts concerning induction', *Reading Hume on the Understanding*, Oxford: Clarendon Press, 107–73.

Nagel, T. (1986) *The View from Nowhere*, Oxford: Oxford University Press.

Newton, I. (1730) *Opticks, or a Treatise of the Reflections, Refractions, Inflections, and Colours of Light*, 4th edn, New York: Dover (1979).

Noonan, H. (1999) *Hume on Knowledge*, London: Routledge.

Norton, D.F. and M.J. Norton (eds) (2000) *David Hume: A Treatise of Human Nature*, Oxford: Oxford University Press.

Owen, D. (1999) *Hume's Reason*, Oxford: Oxford University Press.

Price, H. (1998) 'Two paths to pragmatism II', in R. Casati and C. Tappolet (eds), *European Review of Philosophy* 3, 109–47.

Read, R. and K. Richman (eds) (2000) *The New Hume Debate*, London: Routledge.

Robinson, J.A. (1962) 'Hume's two definitions of "cause"', *Philosophical Quarterly* 12, 162–71.

Schlick, M. (1936) 'Meaning and verification', *Philosophical Review* 45, 339–69.

Smith, M. (1993) 'Objectivity and moral realism: on the significance of the phenomenology of moral experience', in J. Haldane and C. Wright (eds), *Reality, Representation, and Projection*, New York: Oxford University Press, 235–55.

Stove, D. (1973) *Probability and Hume's Inductive Scepticism*, London: Oxford University Press.

Strawson, G. (1989) *The Secret Connexion*, Oxford: Oxford University Press.

——(2000) 'David Hume: objects and power', in R. Read and K. Richman (eds) *The New Hume Debate*, London: Routledge, 31–51.

Stroud, B. (1977) *Hume*, London: Routledge.

——(2000) '"Gilding or staining" the world with "sentiments" and "phantasms"', in R. Read and K. Richman (eds) *The New Hume Debate*, London: Routledge, 16–30.

Tandy, V. (2000) 'Something in the Cellar', *Journal of the Society for Psychical Research* 64, 129–40.

Tooley, M. (1977) 'The Nature of Laws', *Canadian Journal of Philosophy* 7, 667–98.

Wilson, F. (1983) 'Hume's defence of causal inference', *Dialogue* XXII, 661–94.

——(1986) 'Hume's defence of science', *Dialogue* XXV, 611–28.

Winkler, K. (2000) 'The new Hume', in R. Read and K. Richman (eds) *The New Hume Debate*, London: Routledge, 52–87.

Wright, J.P. (1983) *The Sceptical Realism of David Hume*, Manchester: Manchester University Press.

——(2000) 'Hume's causal realism', in R. Read and K. Richman (eds) *The New Hume Debate*, London: Routledge, 88–99.

INDEX

234